Current Issues in World Politics

Current Issues in World Politics

Edited by

SARIKA DUBEY

Foreword by

DR. MIYAN JAAN
Director, Higher Education
Allahabad, U.P

ANAMIKA PUBLISHERS & DISTRIBUTORS (P) LTD.
4697/3, 21A, Ansari Road, Daryaganj
New Delhi 110002
Phone: 2328 1655

First Published 2009

ISBN 978-81-7975-278-4

PRINTED IN INDIA

Published by Anamika Publishers & Distributors (P) Ltd., 4697/3, 21A, Ansari Road, Daryaganj, New Delhi 110002. Typeset by Aadil Printographics, Delhi 110092 and Printed at Nagri Printers, Delhi.

To

My Mother

CONTENTS

FOREWORD

Current issues primarily concerns with the entire socio-politico and economic structures at world arena, and also with the human affairs in society. The book deals with the changing world scenario, in respect to the politico-economic setup. It gives a critical appraisal of the political trends developing in new world order, having its own significance. The book discusses, not only the problems and the challenges faced by the world, but also suggest the probable solution. The present work is an excellent compilation of articles, papers, on various aspects of politics, foreign and bilateral relations, globalization, terrorism, environmentalism, democracy etc.

I have read some portions of this book. It attempts to cover the entire scope of the subject and is written in an analytical manner. Through it is not a general text on the subject, yet it provides an insightful introduction to various problems and changes, taking place in world today. All the articles have latest literature on the subject, research studies and journals. This adds relevance and freshness to her exposition. I, congratulate Dr. Sarika Dubey for editing the learned work on Current Issues which would be of interest as well as great use for students, competitors, and scholars of the subject.

I, do believe that Dr. Dubey's present volume will earn wide appreciation and she will have the satisfaction that this scholarly effort of her, has been a satisfying exercise and a rewarding experience.

Dr. Miyan Jaan
Director, Higher Education
Allahabad, U.P.

PREFACE

The twentieth century has witnessed the many changes in world political sphere. This situation has highly affected entire socio-economic and political structure at world arena. In accordance with this, several changes can be seen at state level too. My interest in the international relation and politics made me realize these changes and tempted me to undertake the present study. This is an effort to analyse various political issues and their impact on national and international arena. It attempts to give a critical appraisal of the political trends developing in new world order. The study of current issues in world politics during this period has a significance of its own. It is therefore, an attempt to give analysis of these issues in world politics to sort out the solutions of the challenges, facing the world today. It has become the necessity of our time to know and be aware of all such things, which are affecting not only the human society but the human race too. This volume is a modest effort to put together the perspective of scholars from India on current issues in world politics and international relations. It is an outcome of our serious efforts to paint a picture on international relations and studies to the benefit of scholars on the subjects.

In conceiving and executing the idea of writing this book, I received unstinted cooperation and constant encouragement from Prof. M.P. Dubey, the then Head of the Department, Political Science, University of Allahabad. I express my gratitude to him. I am grateful to Prof. K.K. Misra and his wife Maya Misra for their appreciation and encouragement. I would like to thank Prof. M.P. Lama, Prof. Subrata Mukherjee and Prof. Chandrakala Padia, for their inspiration and good wishes. I am indeed thankful to my colleague Dr. Sanjay Barnwal, Dr. Sabhash Shukla and Dr. H.K. Sharma, who helped me in many ways. I am very much indebted to all contributors of this volume for their chapters. I want to thank them all for their unflagging encouragement. I am also thankful to one of my colleagues Mr. A.K. Singh who always inspired me, and who is no more now. I am grateful to my parents and husband Mr. Arvind Kumar Singh who has always encouraged me to do my best. I am also thankful to my brother Anand and Anurag who helped me a lot. I am especially grateful to Mr. Pankaj Sharma of Anamika Publishers and Distributors (P) Ltd. for publishing this book in a short time. It has been my pleasure to work with him. The views expressed in the papers are those of contributors and not of the editor.

Sarika Dube

CONTRIBUTORS

Dr. Subrata Mukherjee—Professor, Department of Political Science, University of Delhi, South Campus, New Delhi.

Dr. Mahendra P. Lama—Professor and Vice Chancellor, Central University of Sikkim, Gangtok.

Dr. Chandrakala Padia—Professor and Head, Department of Political Science and Director, Centre for Women's Studies and Development, Banaras Hindu University Varanasi.

Mr. Shambhu Nath Chaudhary—Deputy Director Aakashwani, I.A.S. (All), New Delhi.

Dr. K.K. Misra—Professor (Retd.), Department of Political Science, Allahabad University, Allahabad

Dr. Sarika Dubey—Senior Lecturer, Deptt. of Political Science, M.G.P.G. College, Fatehpur.

Dr. H.K. Sharma—Reader, Department of Political Science, Allahabad University, Allahabad.

Dr. Vimla Vyas—Asstt. Director, Academic Staff College, Allahabad University, Allahabad.

Dr. Mohammad Shahid—Reader, Department of Political Science, Allahabad University, Allahabad.

Dr. Sanjay Barnwal—Lecturer, Department of Political Science, Govt. Degree College, Rampur, U.P.

Dr. Subhash Shukla—Asst. Director, UPRTOU, Allahabad, U.P.

Mr. Arvind Kumar Singh—J.R.F., and Research Scholar, Department of Political Science Allahabad University, Allahabad.

ABBREVIATIONS

MNCs	:	Multinational Corporations
TNCs	:	Transnational Corporations
NGOs	:	Non-Governmental Organizations
WTO	:	World Trade Organization
AIDS	:	Acquired Immune Deficiency Syndrome
IMF	:	International Monetary Fund
GDP	:	Gross Domestic Product
UNDP	:	United Nation Development Programme
NIEs	:	Newly Industrialized Economies
EU	:	European Unions
GNP	:	Gross National Product
NAM	:	Non-Aligned Movement
UN	:	United Nation
NIEO	:	New International Economic Order
NDA	:	National Democratic Alliance
UPA	:	United Progressive Alliance.
IAEA	:	International Atomic Energy Agency
NPT	:	Non-Proliferation Treaty
NSG	:	Nuclear Suppliers Group
USA	:	United States of America
USSR	:	Union of Soviet Socialist Republics
ASEAN	:	Association of South East Asian Nations
APEC	:	Asia-Pacific Economic Co-operation
LAC	:	Line of Actual Control
CTBT	:	Comprehensive Test Ban Treaty
LOC	:	Line of Control
WMD	:	Weapons of Mass Destruction

NSSP	:	Next Steps in Strategic Partnership
MTCR	:	Missile Technology control Regime
CBMs	:	Confidence Building Measures
SAARC	:	South Asian Association of Regional Co-operation
SAFTA	:	South Asian Free Trade Area
MFN	:	Most Favored Nation
NATO	:	North Atlantic Treaty Organization
TMNP	:	Temporary Movement of Natural Persons.
GATS	:	General Agreement on Trade in Services.
MSG	:	Mono Sodium Glutamate
GHG's	:	Green House Gases
IPCC	:	Inter-governmental Panel on Climate
WMO	:	World Meteriological Organization
FDI	:	Foreign Direct Investment.

INTRODUCTION

After the disintegration of the Soviet Union in 1991, the post-cold war world has undoubtedly witnessed an advent of a new phase in international relations and world politics. The demise of the Soviet block had a significant impact on the history of capitalism as a world system, as well as, on international politics, since the last decade of the twentieth century. During the era of ideological war Soviet Union had emerged as a large, powerful, multinational, socialist state, which aimed at posing a major ideological challenge to capitalism as a mode of development by espousing socialist ideology. But after the disintegration of the Soviet Union, Communism failed and lost its credibility as a mode of development. Capitalism emerged as a winner of the race between two ideologies, and now it is knon as liberal capitalism. Entire economic set-up of the world system has changed gradually. As a consequence of the fall of the Soviet Union, the socialist countries of the third world, such as Afro Marxist regimes in Africa including Angola, Mozambique and Vietnam, lost their major supporter. In the third world, only Cuba was talking the orthodox communist language. Not only this even China too, has chosen to run on the path of capitalist development by toying with the notion of market socialism. Countries like India have shed their socialist orientation by initiating reforms since 1991. The states belonging to the commonwealth of Independent States, unequivocally embraced the trends of liberalisation and privatisation. In fact, these states opted to become a part and parcel of the world capitalist economy. This was the time when a number of the countries decided to be the part of global economy and globalization, and the process of globalization was facilitated by the establishment of World Trade Organization (W.T.O.) in 1995. Now the 'liberal capitalism' has got the new name of 'globalization'. Actually, capitalism and the process of globalization are inextricably intertwined. For, globalisation involves gradual development of consciousness of the world as whole. This entire process involves free flow of ideas, goods, services, capital, technology, information, values, arms, people and negatively, diseases, terrorism, violence, across the world, and, at this juncture, capitalism as a system is internationally enough to achieve a global reach in the long run. That is why; globalization can well be construed as a phase in the development of capitalism as a world system. In this new form capitalism could function smoothly because of the hegemonic state. The United States has emerged as a lone superpower, and it started to dominate international economy, and relations. The U.S. justified all their doings by espousing a theory, that America is Super-Sovereign state, and pre-eminent power in the world. It has the license, and the responsibility to act as a global policeman, and punish the errant nation-states. President George Bush Sr. declared that the decade of 1990s has begun with the emergence of a New International Order, which in reality meant unipolar world in place of post-world war II situation of bipolarity, where space was occupied by two super-powers, and the two alliances-North Atlantic Treaty Organization and the Warsaw Pact. The last decade of the twentieth century has provided the full space for American hegemony in International politics. The arrogance of power by the sole policeman can be seen through several instances when they did not bother about international institutions, and the voice of peoples. These are-American war on Iraq in 1991, on the pretext of liberating Kuwait from Iraq. The second American war against Iraq in 2003 was launched under the doctrine of 'pre-emptive' strike against the most dangerous enemy of America. President Bush Jr. launched his so-called global war against terrorism in the form of a response to the terrorist attack on World Trade Centre on September 11, 2001. In this connection Americans have changed regimes in Afghanistan and Iraq between 2001 and 2003. Iraq war in 2003 is the example of America's 'Dadagiri' when they showed a contempt for the security council of the United Nations and unilaterally declared pre-emptive war against Saddam Hussain of Iraq. They have not only shown contempt for the United Nations, it has, at its sweet will, refused to be a party to the Kyoto Treaty on Global Warming or international treaty "on Ozone destroying chemicals" (1989).

This was the time when the war for profit and the war for dominance in the world, has become the main doctrine of Americans. To some extent their eagerness to dominate the world has led to the American Imperialism, and for all this they, were using Democracy, Human Rights, Human Security and Anti-Terrorism, as a tool to fulfil their own interest (till the Clinton Period). The states, having strategic importance were the hitting targets for the Americans, for example Iraq for oil, Afghanistan for base to control Asia and to keep an eye on China, and Iran for atomic and cultural confrontation. They exercise their military power in the name of peace and terrorism, to protect their strategic interest in world scenario because new conservative forces believe in power politics (Bush Jr. Period). On the other hand they have used globalization as a tool to exploit the economy of weak nations.

Though it is said that globalization is a key of solutions to all problems, yet it is not true. The gap between rich and poor countries, and the rich and poor people within countries has deepened. Many peoples in African countries are dying of hunger. Food riots in Mexico, warnings of hunger in Jamaica, Nepal, Philippines, and Sub-Saharan Africa are the example of all this. Record world prices for most staple foods have led to 18 per cent food price inflation in China, 13 per cent in Indonesia, and Pakistan, and 10 per cent or more in Latin America and Russia, according to the United Nations Food and Agricultural Organization (FAO). Wheat has doubled in price, maize is nearly 50 per cent higher than a year ago and rice is 20 per cent more expensive, says the U.N.[1] In India many farmers have committed suicide due to bad impact of liberalisation policy. Multinationals and Transnational corporations are gaining strength and accumulating a huge amount of world's wealth.

All such institutions like MNCs, TNCs, WTO, IMF, NGOs and civil societies have emerged as a powerful new actor in the international political scenario. The logic behind proliferation of these organizations and the changing role and status of nation-state can be well understood in the framework of globalization. Many national, regional problems now have become of global importance, and they are not limited to particular boundary, such as non-proliferation, terrorism, child labour, Environment, human rights, labour standards, gender equalities and women rights etc. This is all about the picture of the end of twentieth century, but the dawn of twenty first century is looking quite different in terms of the centres of new power structure. The fall of the Soviet Union and the development of post cold war era has now become the story c past. The first decade of the 21st century has brought the new waves of changes in international relations and politics. Unipolarity is going to change into multipolarity in economic sphere with the emergence of BRICS (Brazil, Russia, India, China, South Africa) are growing as a powerful economy. Many international organizations and reports from pentagon have forecast that China and India are going to become super powers in future. Once again Russian economy is also gaining strength. They have nationalised their oil and gas companies. Russia's suspension of the conventional Forces in Europe (CFE) Treaty signals its resolve to reconfigure the post cold war shift in the balance of power in favour of the U.S. The destiny of Asia in this century will be shaped by the relationship between China, India, Russia, and Japan. 'The strategic footprint' of that rectangle will cover the world. So in this connection, there is a need to analyse international relations, bilateral relations and the major concerns of tomorrow.

The set of papers in the present volume is a modest effort to analyse the various issues, and relations in the context of entire global scenario. They recast international relations in the phase of globalization through diverse perspectives, by highlighting aspects related to economy, security, technology, democracy, religion, finance, civil society etc. They have discussed the current issues at national level and internationally as well. Irrespective, of such diverse perspectives, the contributors uniformly deal with the core actor, i.e., the nation state, and its changing status in the phase of globalization. The essays in this volume deal with wide-ranging issues from integration of national economies within the globalizing world. They not only discuss the issues in the context of present scenario but they also analyse in terms of future perspectives. Indo-centric bilateral relations, foreign policies, and some major concerns in this globalized world are the heart of this volume. We shall proceed to capture the essence of the numerous themes that figure in this volume.

Subrata Mukherjee's paper entails the need for a just universal order in the international arena as a prerequisite for combating the global threat of terrorism, especially after the 9/11 attacks on the United States of America. He traces the historical dialectics of violence and non-violence in the twentieth century, right from the First World War to the Second World War and the cold war that ensued thereafter. He also analyses the effort of the USA and the other western powers, with the help of their Clientalist regimes, to perpetuate their hegemony over the rest of the world. Mukherjee also questions the wisdom of establishing democracy by force in different parts of the world by the western powers. He also analyses the role of the West's policy of establishing Clientalists regimes in different parts of the world in leading to today's problem of terrorism. He concludes by observing that until the larger question of deprivation, discrimination and inequality are addressed uniformly, the fight against terrorism would remain ineffective.

M.P. Lama's paper offers detailed analyses of the scope of the bilateral trade relations between India and Pakistan. He traces the major deterrents between the two neighbouring countries in consolidating their economic linkages. Lama also focuses on the confidence building measures that have been initiated in recent years by the two countries as well as on the factors such as the end of the cold war, access to modern communications technology, greater human mobility, heavy doses of reforms and liberalization etc., that have created an environment conducive for better bilateral relations between the two countries. He also explores the avenues of cooperation in different sectors of trade between the two countries and how they are losing revenue because of non-cooperation between them. Lama makes a detailed study of chances of cooperation between the two countries in different sectors of power. He also makes an assessment of the dividends that both countries would reap from better relations. He tries to show that both countries would benefit mutually if they were able to bridge their differences and create a conducive environment for mutual economic cooperation.

Sarika Dubey has discussed about the opportunities, challenges and the outcome of globalization in present scenario. She defines globalization as growing economic, political, technological and cultural linkage that connects individuals, communities, business and government around the world. In the geographical terms globalization claims, countries having no borders or the boundary less world. Dubey traces the historical development of globalization after the end of the cold war era. She analyses the real picture of globalization in the twentieth century. She reveals the fact that globalization has increased disparity, poverty all over the world; only rich and developed countries are gaining benefits through it. Dubey proves her view through several instances, reports etc. She focuses towards the challenges, that globalization poses in today's world, and also sort out the solutions at domestic and international front as well. She concludes that in the global age, peace, security and prosperity depends upon the co-operation of nations. We should be the partners in prosperity but also in adversity, in respect of the threats the world faces. So, there is a need to establish democratic set up of all international institutions to maintain the equality of all countries.

K.K. Misra's paper examines the need for a new international economic order (NIEO) in the world, which is, based on the principles of economic sovereignty, real interdependence, non-discrimination, equity and justice. Besides tracing the efforts made by the non-aligned countries and the developing countries to establish a new international economic order, he also sets forth the reasons why such a new international economic order is required in the global arena.

Shambhu Chaudhary has discussed the current picture and future of Indo-U.S. Nuke deal. Prime Minister Manmohan Singh and President Bush signed this landmark agreement on July 18, 2005. This was a path breaking agreement because U.S. law, specifically the Atomic Energy Act of 1954 prohibits nuclear commerce with nuclear weapons states that have not signed the Non-proliferation Treaty (NPT) and not accepted International Atomic Energy Agency IAEA monitoring of their nuclear facilities. Chaudhary says that the importance of the deal can be better understood in terms of bilateral relations between the two countries, after the cold war era. Due to strong opposition by the left parties, still it is not finalized. They argued that either bury the deal or face midterm election. Chaudhary highlights the situation during Gujarat election 2007. He says that a number of concerns related to the issue have been raised in India, in which the main concerns are, that India's strategic programme, including nuclear weapons testing, would be compromised; but he further says that Government reaffirms its position in parliament by saying that the deal does not impair either the country's independent foreign policy or the right to conduct a future nuclear test. Actually this assessment is an effort to open closed doors to obtain nuclear fuel, and technology from other countries. This civil nuclear agreement between the two countries would help create a substantial additional power generating capacity in the country. It is also important, because it will end India's nuclear isolation. Chaudhary holds the view that it would be very difficult for the UPA Government to backtrack on it after taking over two-year long negotiations to a final outcome. It will also adversely affect New Delhi's position in the international arena as a responsible nation towards international treaties.

Chandrakala Padia has dealt with the subject of women and her position in the ancient Indian society. She reveals the fact that Indian women had higher place than men in the social and religious value system. Many of us believe that intellectual traditions of India have never thought highly of women, but this is not true. Padia says that ontologically or as human beings, women have all along been given an equal status in the Indian Intellectual Tradition. And in respect of character and contribution to cohesion and welfare of society, they have even been regarded superior to men. She proves women's position through several texts from ancient Indian thought like Rg Veda, The Nasadiya Sukta, the Kathoprisad, and the Manusmriti etc. All these texts of ancient thought speak about gender differentiation but not the same thing as gender discrimination. Padia highlights the fact that in the post Samhita period, woman was regarded as *ardhangini*, that is one half of the very being of man and in no way subordinate to him. In the same way the term *sahadharmini* is used for her that is, a co-participator in discharging the obligations of life and fully capable of taking her own decisions. Lastly, she denied the view of some Western or Indian Scholars who alleged that women occupied a very insignificant place in India's intellectual tradition, and proved it wrong, through several examples.

Sanjay Barnwal has dealt with the issue of environmentalism in world arena. Among the major issues which are at work at world stage, the most alarming one is that of environmentalism which encompasses within its ambit the whole planet, conscious and sub-conscious, all beings included. The issue perturbs the intellectual community all the world over, and hence various theories, related to the subject have emerged. Many global Summits have been held with a view to address the challenges. Even disastrous fallouts have also been articulated, and foreseen in this realm. Barnwal has divided the article into five parts. The introduction, theoretical foundations of the concept, various menaces and consequences, possible solutions and final remarks. He advocates that every human being has the right to life. For the safety of human being, it is necessary to reduce our needs and move towards the sustainable development. He focuses the maxim of "think globally, act locally" needs to be adhered to, by all, because victims may be some, but the sufferers are all.

H.K. Sharma's paper provides perspectives on Indian constitution, which gives shape to the concept of the secular state. Many interpretations that have been given by the state High Courts and Supreme Court, related to the secular nature of the state, are also very important part of his discussion. Secularism is the foundation stone upon which the edifice of Indian democracy rests. The article 'Secularism and the constitutional Framework' tries to examine the concept of secularism as enshrined in our constitution. He examines Indian constitution in terms of the three components. First, Freedom of Religion, Second, citizenship, and third, separation of state and religion. He has also discussed the limitations imposed by Indian Constitution. Sharma Concludes that the nature of state to all religions is neutral, but at the same time, individual can enjoy the freedom, to profess and practice his religion. So the balance can be seen in Indian constitution where secularism is neither a religion, nor an indifference towards any religion, but it stands for equal respect to all religions. He concludes that the concept of secularism as provided by the constitution of India is a mix of the Nehruvian and Gandhian concept of secularism.

Vimla Vyas has dealt with the problems of democracy in the era of globalization, After independence India has enjoyed its 50 years with its multi-ethnic, pluralistic character, and democracy. She clears the picture of early 1991, when India adopted globalization and liberalization policy, "profit" became the slogan for not only business, but the government as well.

The private sector was touted as the only remedy for the ailments of the Indian economy. All the successive governments continued these policies. It was the common slogan of the time, that globalization opens up tremendous potential for growth, and poverty alleviation. This process has changed the entire set-up of liberal democratic state in which the states control the market forces in favour of social cause. Now globalization has reduced the role of state and it supports to create environment of open competitiveness. Vyas focuses that this change has far reaching implications for the future of democracy, particularly in the third world. Vyas defines the relationship between the community, the state and the corporations. She says that the globalization as the expansion of the economic space, controlled by corporations therefore, runs into conflict with the democratic space for citizens, to determine and influence the conditions for their health and well being. It has increased inequality all over the world, and these corporations have become the centres of accumulating huge amount of world's wealth. This is fatal for democracy, because "government by the people" exists, but "government for the people" does not exist in this new era of globalization. Vyas talks about biodiversity rights and says that biodiversity, land and waters are the three vital resources that the majority of our people depend on, for their livelihood and survival, but according to liberalisation policy of free trade agreement, multinationals impose monopoly property rights on indigenous agriculture. Vyas raised an issue of land reforms, and water trading too. By discussing all that she says that which type of control on the natural resources should be needed, corporate control or community control, it's a big question. In this way she highlights the issues, which are negatively affecting the democracy in the era of globalization.

Subhash Shukla has dealt with the changing notions of India's Foreign Policy. The end of the cold war in international relations saw the disintegration of the USSR resulting in the U.S.A. becoming the sole superpower in politico-military sphere. However, in the economic sphere, it saw the emergence of multiplicity with Japan, European Economic Community and China along with U.S.A. emerging as major powers. It also saw the dominance of economic factors over security affairs in international politics. Shukla traces the evolution of foreign policy of India during this time by analysing it under the tenure of the different Prime Ministers. Beginning with the Narsimha Rao Government, he analyses the readjustment of India's relations with the two superpowers and the efforts to normalize its relations with China. He also studies the various aspects of India's economic diplomacy during the tenure of Prime Minister P.V. Narasimha Rao. The Gujral Doctrine during the United Front Government regime has also been referred to in this article. Shukla elaborately discusses the changes in the Indian nuclear policy with the decision of the A.B. Vajpayee Government to openly declare India's nuclear weapons programme. The article also refers to the growing strategic relationship between India and the U.S.A. It also dwells into the reasons behind the Kargil war and its aftermath. He also analyses the developments in Indo-Pak relationship after incident of 11-9-2001. Shukla also analyses the efforts made by the Manmohan Singh Government of further strengthening the Indo-U.S. Strategic partnership, he examines in detail the Indo-U.S. civilian nuclear agreement and covers the steps taken by India and Pakistan, during Prime Minister Singh's era, to ensure peace in the sub-continent. He also traces the efforts made by the Indian Government to maintain the process of normalization of Sino-Indo relations over the last two decades. Shukla's article is an attempt to study the shifts and changes, that have taken place in India's foreign policy as a result of the end of the cold war, and the changes that took place in international relations as its aftermath.

Sarika Dubey has analysed the issue of globalization and its impact on Indian economy. She says, that the concept of globalization is inherent in the Hindu philosophy of 'Vasudhaiv Kutumbkam' but the present phase of globalization is different in terms of certain rules and regulations. Dubey highlights the picture of early nineties, when Indian economy was in deep crisis, and joined the structural adjustment policy of IMF and introduced a series of economic reforms to control its crisis. She examined the results of these reforms both positively and negatively. In terms of increase in data, Indian economy shows the big jump, as achieving the 9 per cent of growth rate, which helped improve India's global position. Strong growth in FDI Inflow-outflow, Increase in foreign exchange reserves, rupee appreciation against dollar, Sensex moved up, growing foreign trade, shows the great achievement in Indian economy. But the other side Indian agriculture sector has been badly affected in the era of globalization. Dubey proceeds to highlight the cause of negative impact of globalization on agriculture, Infrastructure and disparity. Lastly she gives solutions and concludes that globalization is not bad, but it is badly managed. So there is a need to develop human face of globalization.

K.K. Misra has discussed the role of NAM in the changing perspectives on international relations. After the end of Cuban crisis in 1962, super powers have changed their behaviour of making distance towards each other. They realize that co-creativity and co-development is essential for their common interest, and despite all ideological differences they can go together. The situation has now changed with the end of the cold war, and the ushering in of a period of New Detente. The demolition of Berlin wall and the ultimate unification of the two Germanys were the examples of this new detente. There are number of issues in which super powers have joined hands for common goals. In view of these changes some of us believe, that the role of Non Aligned Movement (NAM) has lost its relevance, as it was the product of the cold war era to balance, and control superpowers. But Misra, does not agree with this view, he says that there may be some parameters of NAM during the cold-war period, but it would be wrong to think, that cold war was its sole reference point. Though the new detente has played a good role in international politics, yet the power game is not finished. He says that now we see the war of dominance in modified form, security situation is still, unstable, and threatened by the ongoing arms race. Also the doctrine of nuclear deterrence holds sway. Disparity, poverty, underdevelopment, are the major problems of the world today. Tensions among nations and regional conflict are still going on. Strong and developed economies are exploiting the weaker economies. There is a need to establish democratic set-up of international institutions. Terrorism, and ecological disbalance are the major problems of today's world. Misra says, that NAM can play a very significant role to sort out the solutions of all such problems, so this is very much needed if NAM is to be made a more meaningful movement in the long run.

Mohammad Shahid has tried to reveal the Misconceptions of Islam, and analyse the role of Islam in the era of globalization. He focuses to dispel the myth relating to Islam in view of the growth of religious fundamentalism and extremist Islamic groups in different parts of the world, who have tried to use violent means to achieve their aims, and objectives. This article begins by explaining the chief tenets of Islam. Then it traces the spread and rise of Islam over the last 1400 years of world history. Furthermore, it draws attention to the scientific temper associated with Islam. In the end, it makes a comparison of Islam, and the modern western civilization, and it concludes by emphasizing the humanistic aspect of Islam, which is not getting its due attention, because of the rise of extremist, and fundamentalist Islamic groups in the various parts of world, right now.

The article 'Problem of secularization of Indian Polity and National Integration by Subhash Shukla makes an analysis of the various factors that pose a problem or threat to national integration in India. It examines the role played by different factors such as communalism, regionalism, linguism, class and caste in the Indian polity and how they hamper the process of national integration in this country. It points out to the fact that in a country like India where there is so much diversity in terms of language, religion, castes and regional development the task of national integration is not an easy one.

Arvind Kumar Singh has discussed the changing role of administ-ration and bureaucracy in the era of liberalization. He focuses on bureaucracy from British period to liberalization era. Before independence its main responsibilities were to maintain law and order and collect revenue. But after independence bureaucracy became omnipotent, omnipresent even omniscient because it was the real mechanism of government to implement and execute its policies. Singh says that the adoption of New Economic Policy in 1991 brought tremendous change, and it reduced the role of bureaucracy and state, simultaneously, The new approach has focused on stabilising the economy, and giving the private sector a much greater role in India's development. Now the demand raised is of good governance, means people friendly, result oriented, and competitive. He also focuses on management orientation in public administration. Singh has also discussed the emergence of civil society as a supplementary democratic model. He focuses on recasting the role of the state, and emerging issues in administration. He concludes that there is a need to evolve the concept of a new public service which focuses on serving the citizens and the values such as efficiency and productivity should be placed in the larger context of democracy, community and the public interest.

Note

1. *The Hindu*, 5 Nov. 2007.

1. COMBATING TERRORISM:
NEED FOR A JUST UNIVERSAL ORDER

Subrata Mukherjee

I

Both in theory and practice, the doctrines of violence and non-violence have dominated the entire spectrum of human action in the twentieth century. What distinguished the twentieth century from the previous ones is the astonishing resilience of non violence to counter and overwhelm the challenge of violence to such an extent that violence looked more as an aberration, an anomaly in the normal and orderly social, economic and political process. This was true more after the Second World War. Even the Cold War never became hot and the end of communism was relatively peaceful and quick. However, this institutionalization of peaceful change received a rude shock by the 9/11 attacks on the United States, which the president of the United States described as the 'first war of the twenty first century'. Since then, the terror attack has continued to strike, periodically in different parts of the world. The question that looms large now is whether this outbreak of violence would remain an exception or become endemic and frequent. If the evolution of last one hundred years is any guide, then with proper policies and measures of reconciliation pursued universally rather than selectively, then these acts of violence should be exceptions rather than a rule.

The Dialectics of Violence and Non-Violence

The twentieth century was inaugurated with the promise of

extension of democracy by giving the right to vote to all. The slow incorporation of the working class to the democratic process, which began in the nineteenth century, was completed by the early years of the twentieth. Women also secured the right to vote after centuries of struggle. As a consequence of this new situation, the mass political parties started to become important component in the political process in the Western democracies. The social democratic parties, including the Labour Party in Britain emerged with the larger participation of the working class in the political process and the Christian democratic parties were consolidated with massive support from women. This significant change made the earlier extra-parliamentary militancy obsolete, because of the increase in State power but more importantly because of the capacity of the liberal democracies to respond effectively to the needs and aspirations of the majority of the people. This fact of increased State power and the role of the standing army led Engels to raise serious apprehensions about the possibility of a successful insurrection by the working class itself. On the other hand, the first man who could really comprehend the revolutionary potentiality of democracy and obsolesce of revolutionary violence as a means of achieving a political end was Eduard Bernstein (1850-1932). Lenin realized the truth in Bernstein's assertion but felt that the 'economism' among the workers could be taken care of by creating a vanguard party of professional revolutionaries who would make the revolution and deliver it to the working class. Lenin disagreed with Bernstein and the most strident opposition was on the latter's views of the state.[ii] The Leninist version of communism glorified revolutionary violence but a more monstrous from sanctioning violence emerged with the rise of fascism in Italy and subsequently in Germany.

It is in this context of this rise of fascistic brutality that Einstein's commitment to pacifism and non-violence deserve special mention. A conformist, Einstein rejected any form of violence and war as it represented mechanized brutality hindering both progress and good life. Einsetin, A. (1979)[1] He advocated pacifism after the First World War in order to prevent future wars. His commitment to total opposition to war continued till 1931 but with the growing menace of totalitarian Germany, its anti-Semitism and its war against virtually all facets of human civilization, his attitude changed distinctly. From an uncompromising and perhaps utopian position of the late 1920's by early 1930's he took a more relative and realistic position. In July 1933, on an appeal on behalf of two Belgian conscientious objectors to war, Einstein's reply startled the world and disheartened many pacifists. He asserted that if Belgium was occupied by Germany, the situation would be worse than that of 1914. As such, military service is desirable in a situation when the European civilization was under threat. In such a grave situation, refusal to enlist for military service was not advisable even from a pacifist. He also thought that the scientists had a crucial role to play in promoting the idea of peace. Their field of enquiry transcends the narrow limits of national frontiers and considerations that they are in a position to demolish the myths of senseless nationalism.

At the same time, in colonial India Gandhi initiated his novel method of non-violent *satyagraha,* which according to Orwell was a method of defeating the enemy without preaching hatred. While Gandhi could envisage such a struggle in British India he could, according to Orwell never really gasp the nature of modern totalitarianism. However, in a more difficult situation this strategy is bound to fail. Orwell is right in asserting that Gandhi was operating in India and his actions were conditioned by it. But still the fact remains that non-violent mass action is Gandhian creation and his supreme achievement lies in making it a most potent force, which remains alive even today. One of its remarkably successful uses was in the form of people's power in the Philiippines. Gandhi by his own action convinced the majority of the British at the end of the Second World War that their rule in India was morally untenable. Within a liberal democratic framework Martin Luther King jr. followed Gandhian teachings of non-violent mass action for securing racial equality in the United States. By any reckoning it was a splendid success. Universalisation of democracy is one of the major achievements of the 20th century, which the BBC titled as a the people's century. The Gandhian strategy of non-violent mass action has also secured universal sanction. Judged by the Gandhian standard of civility as the minimum requirement of a modern civilized order, aggressive armed action, even when supported by the most powerful nation, whether in Iraq or Lebanon, is seen as morally untenable.

II

Postwar Competition Between Democratic Capitalism and Collectivistic Communism

With the collapse of fascism after the Second World War, the competition was between democratic capitalism and collectivistic communism. But this competition was defined within the ambit of peaceful co-existence, which led to relative peace for forty years. The cold war never became hot. After the collapse of communism, the transition in Europe was remarkably peaceful. In the context of the recent regime changes, relatively less violence has taken place compared to similar changes earlier. With the end of the cold war and grater agreement about the essential structural arrangement of economics, politics and society, less violence is likely than the earlier epochs. It is a fact that quick technological changes bring mass demonstrations as evidenced in the recent meetings of the heads of G-8 held in the United States, Japan, Italy and Hong Kong reflecting the uncertainty of large section of people who feel vulnerable due to the imperatives of the global economy. But these large scale demonstrators did not call for a violent overthrow of a regime or for a non-democratic order. Few today would agree with Fanon's glorification of violence as a cleansing force and in contrast many would agree with Havel that violence is not radical enough. The worldwide revulsion and condemnation of the terrorist attacks wherever it takes place is a testimony to fact that most people do not approve of use of violence as a method of action. Moreover, in a world order with considerable expansion of the democratic space and its capacity to accommodate dissenters it is likely that these terrorist attacks would be an exception rather than the rule. The response to meet the challenge of terrorism by a determined armed might is more in the nature of Einstein's support of armed action in an extraordinary situation. The ordinary situation is likely to be a process of peaceful and orderly change with primacy of economics over politics.

III

The Threat of Global Terrorism

The September 11th attacks and the subsequent resolve by the United States is a turning point in American foreign policy. A parallel was drawn with the Japanese attack on the Pearl Harbour and just as the latter led to the active involvement of the United States into the Second World War similarly 9/11 saw the declaration of the United States' intent to wage a war against terrorism. The evolution of the United States as a novel kind of politics and society is both unique and startling. Beginning with the migration of the pilgrim fathers this country of essentially a migrant European population in its formative years initiated a nation building process that accepted Lockean concepts of the primacy of the individual, government by consent, security of private property and freedom with constitutional guarantees that are legally supervised by the courts. Jefferson typified the idealism of the early settlers by adding pursuit of happiness to the sanctity of life and liberty perceiving United States to be an island of freedom when the situation in Europe looked gloomy and repressive with little hope of advancing towards a democratic and prosperous order.

The quest for an unparalleled and independent evolution was helped by geography and dissemination of the indigenous people notoriously expressed by the statement that 'a good Indian is a dead Indian'. Subsequently the proclamation of the Monroe Doctrine of 1815 declaring both the Americas for the Americans kept the European powers out of a scramble for Latin America. This exclusion compelled the European colonialists to organize the scramble for power in Africa. The much-proclaimed American isolationism has its basis in this geographical factor and the Monroe Doctrine reinforced by the fact that the Americans also fought for their freedom and in this sense was an ex-colonial state. However, this theoretical plank based on practical considerations was violated by the United States a number of times including the American-Spanish war of 1898 and the belligerent policies of President Theodore Roosevelt. Cuba, a Spanish colony in spite of proclaiming itself to be an independent republic following the victory of the United States in 1898 virtually became a protectorate of the United States. The latter also annexed Puerto Rico another Caribbean Island in 1904. An American army crushed the struggle for independence in the Philippines between 1899 and 1902. Roosevelt in 1904 proclaimed the right of the United States to act as a police officer for the entire central and Latin America as a justification of the Monroe Doctrine. But such actions did not really shake the philosophy of Americans exceptionality, isolationism and relative pacifism based on the advice of Washington and founding fathers.

However, the belated United States involvement in the First World War had an ideological plank "to make the world safe for democracy" and the Second World War was fought for protecting four freedoms—speech and worship, from want and fear, echoed in the Atlantic Charter of 1941. Even the long cold war was fought in the name of freedom and opposition to communist totalitarianism. The logical extension of which was to bring the ex-communist countries under the democratic fold after the end of communism like Poland joining the European Union and many of the former communists reincarnating as social democrats. However, this larger universalistic democratic fervour is missing in the current American war agaisnt terrorism.

For the overwhelming majority of the people in the world, the present conflict is not being perceived as an international civil war for or against extension of human freedom within a framework of constitutional democracy but rather the destruction of international terrorism keeping intact the repressive apparatus of the authoritarian states. This terrible double standard has weakened the Western plank of fighting terrorism in the eyes of the majority of the people of the non-Western world. They rightfully perceive it to be an effort of the American might aided by the other affluent nations and with the support from Clientalist regimes to perpetuate their hegemony over the rest with their patronage and armed support for the repressive regimes of the Third World.

IV

Can There Be Democracy By Force?

Military intervention by one country in another is coercive tactics to compel a policy, which otherwise it would not have followed. This is very different from a peacekeeping mission, which tries to maintain peace in a civil war situation normally at the invitation of both the parties of conflict. This is in sharp contrast to the long tradition established by the 1648 Treaty of Westphalia the doctrine of non-interference in the domestic affairs of another country.

However, now at the suggestion of the United Nations the Security Council can recommend military intervention for maintaining international peace and security. The sudden disappearance of a superpower competition and the phenomenal increase in civil conflicts has led to the US-UN interventions ignoring the sanctity of state sovereignty. The ground reality also reflects a change from 90 per cent countries being authoritarian to a situation when the majority nations are democratic in which promotion of democracy even by force looks legitimate and fair. This is a successor to the theory of containing communism and slowly enlarging geographically free community of market democracies.

This massive effort to introduce democracy is undertaken by a very large number of organizations and the programme includes, strengthening the rule of law, and human rights, putting international electoral observers to monitor free and fair elections, efforts at improving financial management, accountability, decentralization, devise ways and means to establish civilian control of the military and improve electoral systems. It also actively supports efforts to improve the quality of legislatures, political parties, media, education and image of police. This impetus is in line with the national-building exercise, which began after the Second World War with building of democracy in Germany and Japan and non communist but not necessarily democratic regimes like Vietnam and Korea and most of central America. Initially the policy thrust was anti communism and anti soviet and the that led to the support of authoritarian forces and even dictatorships like China, Saudi Arabia and Uganda. The support of the US government to these regimes was not the basis of any reform plank or democratic initiative. But this limited anti-communist role changed to a pro-democratic role in Panama, Somalia, Haiti, Bosnia and Iraq. In these later cases there is a marked effort to have at least a rudimentary form of democratic order. This is in marked contrast to the cold war era when containment of communism was all important. The US defeat in Vietnam further reduced the enthusiasm to expand democracy.

The initial success of the Allied powers to install democracy in Germany and Japan was facilitated by three factors: (1) unconditional surrender of both Germany and Japan, (2) a high level of development in education and highly industrialized societies and (3) a firm commitment to create democracies in these countries (von Hippel 2000).[2] An added factor was the long tradition of political parties which included the SPD in Germany and the practice of the Weimar Constitution of 1919-33 which many consider as the finest ever democratic constitution and the different ideological party formations in Japan before the Second World War. This commitment was a consequence of the common interest of the US, Britain and France to see that these two erstwhile enemies do not re-merge as powerful aggressive nations. A stable democratic Germany and Japan was a vital component of the Allied policy, which was not the case with Panama, Somalia, Haiti and Bosnia. However, it should also be noted that the enormous cleavages, disparities in both education and wealth between the governing elite in these countries and the masses is much more pronounced than in post War Germany and Japan. Still in spite of this in-built advantage both Germany and Japan secured huge assistance from the United States in all the Key areas of security, trade and in political relations, which allowed both of them to enjoy an unprecedented prosperity within a short period of time.

Hippel draws attention to may collapses of the states in the contemporary world, which undermines many democracies. A state collapses when both its repressive and ideological apparatuses disintegrate and the central authority is unable to check rampant corruption, violent ethnic conflicts and large-scale territorial disputes. A partial explanation for such collapses is rooted in colonial rule when territorial lines were drawn between rival colonial powers without any consideration of ethnicity, religion, language and natural geographical boundaries. Apart from the internal factors, international situation and behaviour of major powers add to state collapse with mechanisms of support and withdrawal. In these fault lines rogue regimes capture and continue power, which wins elections but does not initiate the expected political reforms. The fundamentalist groups win elections in many such volatile situations like Algeria in 1991 and Palestine in 2006 nullifying one of the basis presumptions of constitutional democracy that extreme forces in a democracy are forced to operate only on the fringe as democracy inevitably with practice of a politics of compromise inevitably leads to moderation. In such unstable and volatile situations the Western intervention is normally (with the exception of Iraq) taken as a last resort with three broad aims: (1) re-establishing internal security which allows normal human activities, (2) a longer effort to empower the different segments of civil society and (3) to find ways and means to strengthen democracy. Apart from strengthening the formal institutions of democracy, the reform agenda includes reform proposals, which indirectly strengthen democracy like police and judicial reforms. The reform of the police is crucial for ensuring both public safety and for gaining popular support. The image of the police from being a gang of organzied state supported gangsters to a force, which provides security to ordinary people and not to a privileged lot is an essential step. The most important step is the commitment to deal with complex problems deftly and comprehensively as Hippel points out that made possible for the emergence of stable democracies of Germany and Japan. Similar successes will multiply only if that commitment is repeated. Whatever may be the net result of these efforts but one thing looks increasingly certain that the Westphalian state system, which allowed insularity to all the important states is coming to a close due to the emergence of a global capitalistic system and the willingness of the US to intervene decisively with or independent of the UN support in a wide variety of situations ostensibly to promote democracy. This policy of installing democracy by force has a strange parallel with Brezhnev's doctrine of limited sovereignty that was invoked to justify the right of the erstwhile USSR in its satellite states of Eastern Europe with the essential difference that while Brezhnev confined it to what was considered as Soviet sphere of influence, the US seeks to encompass the entire world. This plank of promoting democracy also indicates that in the absence of a competing ideological alternative, democratic expansion with peace dividends will be the likely outcome in the existing fault lines even without intervention.

Huntington's Caution on Democratic Expansion

This policy shift however has met with severe criticisms from some new liberal-conservative commentators like Zakaria (2003).[3] In continuation of the theme propounded by Huntington (1955)[4] on a distinction between order and disorder which is more important than the ideological divide between liberal democracy and communism, Zakaria in the context of today makes a sharp distinction between liberal constitutionalism and democratic disorder. Zakaria is not an opponent of democracy but is concerned with its excesses and points out its 'dark sides'. With a framework that heavily draws from the past he argues that the success of the West is not due to democratization but rather due to consolidation of liberal constitutionalism and capitalism. Tocqueville had taken note of the role played by independent i.e. non-state origin and mushrooming of groups and associations in the American democracy. These developments created a solid foundation for the eventual flowering into liberal democracy and without such an evolution of a larger framework, which is societal for the long-term survival of democracy, is doubtful and its absence leads to illiberal regimes. Though Zakaria begins with the past his major concern is with the 'illiberal democracies' in the contemporary world, which 'mix elections with authoritarianism'. The major reason for this degeneration is the absence of liberal constitutionalism and capitalism. Because of the absence of any such tradition in the middle East the West should not try to invent democracy in a hurried manner in this area.

The centrality of his argument hovers around the presumption that constitutional liberalism has less to do with the exact procedure of selecting government rather than the objectives like protection of individual's autonomy by providing a bulwark against any form of coercion perpetrated by the state, church or society. This is a restatement of J.S. Mill's famous dictum that a liberal society, anchored in the rule of law is a precondition for a liberal state. Even in the democratic US, Zakaria advocates that more and more important decisions should be taken outside the democratic process to insulate them from short sightedness and the politics of manipulation of pressure groups. He also delves into the well-known theory of democratic expansion about the link between prosperity and democracy. He points out that in the contemporary world a per capita income of a minimum of USD 6000 (preferably USD 9000) is the minimum necessity for the long-term survival of democracy. But this wealth has to be earned and not merely due to natural resources as that discourages incentives to grant liberty to its people. These are 'trust-fund states' where the problem is easy wealth and not poverty. Zakaria is convinced that only market capitalism can lead to a successful democracy. However, even in the Western democracies increasing democratization has created a vast army of particular interests in the political space. This is because "by declaring war on elitism, we have produced politics by a hidden elite, unaccountable, unresponsive with any larger public interest" (2003, 198). The solution to this problem of excessive democratization is delegation of power to institutions like the Supreme Court and the Federal Reserve Board.

There is a striking parallel between Zakaria's prescriptions of reform with the classical elitists. The only difference is that the classical elitists thought of elite rule as inevitable whereas Zakaria considers such a rule as desirable. He forgets, as Milband points out that even in Western democracies today the ruling class has a privileged position and as such the proposal for further restriction is unnecessary. What is required, instead, is more expansion to include the under-privileged and the under non-represented. Moreover an elite rule without popular control will become something like the Soviet *nomenklaura* or what Djilas called the 'New Class'. The period that Zakaria glorifies is a period of oligarchy and not of democracy. Even in case of United States exceptionalism it was the rule of a few over the many, which Uncle Tom's cabin exemplifies and about which Thoreau protested. With a pronounced western bias, he ignores the possibilities of consolidation of democracy through other routes like Japan's developmental model which South Korea and India have replicated. Similarly he ignores the fact that even in trust fund societies; democracy is feasible as there is a precedent in Mussadeq's Iran. The confusion in Zakaria arises because what he considers liberal constitutio-nalism is actually democratic constitutionalism, which Jefferson describes as a rule under a constitution and not by the will of a single or a few individuals. Liberal constitutionalism is feasible under different types of market capitalism including where the market is more restriction than what exists in the United States. Zakarian forgets that even within western democracies there is a wide gulf between a more market driven capitalism as in the United States and a more statistic version of capitalism as in Western Europe. It is quite possible that with the universalization of democracy there will be multiple forms of democratic order rather than the one that the United States practices.

V

The West and its Clientalist Politics

The fact that non-democratic regimes survive in certain parts of the world is not either because of a particular religion or relative underdevelopment but because of the fact that democracy was throttled in these regions of the world so that the West could perpetuate an exploitative relationship. The Catholic Latin American fate was not very different even a few decades ago when a democratically elected Allende in Chile was assassinated and replaced by a brutal army rule. The violation of human rights was a common phenomenon in all the Latin American dictatorships, which President Reagan described as the backyard of the United States. Similarly, the flowering of democracy under Mussadeq in Iran was crushed by the West and replaced by a repressive regime that tried to modernize from the top without democratic institutions and popular participation and was eventually dislodged by the khomeni's Islamic Revolution of 1979 from which Iran is still struggling to free itself. From 1947 to 1953, Iran after the departure of the occupation forces reflected a tide of nationalist fervour with a strong desire to end foreign intervention in its internal affairs. Mussadeq sensing this nationalistic upsurge nationalized the Anglo-Persian Oil Company to gain control over its economic and political destiny, which became the main cause for his ouster. Mussadeq, the most popular figure in Iran in modern times was heading a popular government. But the removal of the legitimate government was necessitated by the fact that it was not subservient enough. With his ouster ended his theory of negative equilibrium, which can be termed as a forerunner of non-aligned movement devised to cope in a situation of dependency stipulating a policy, which would not provide special advantages to any major power. But the Shah regime was totally subservient to Western interests allowing a sizeable American presence. By 1978, 60,000 Americans were living in Iran. American military personnel were granted extraterritorial rights. These factors fuelled Islamic fundamentalism. The irony of it is that had Mussadeq been allowed to continue it could have led to the institutionalization of a liberal democratic regime in Iran with a spill over effect on its neighbours as India exerts a moral pressure on all the non-democratic regimes of South Asia. But this the West did not allow in the Middle East when it was busy erecting a liberal democratic regime in West Germany which was ruled by the Nazi dictatorships in the immediate past. For the rise of religious fundamentalist forces in many of the Islamic countries, the Western powers are squarely to be blamed. The void that existed following the throttling of liberal democracy led to the rise of fundamentalism. In Afghanistan the fundamentalist forces were totally supported and armed by the United States to fight the Soviet occupation of the country in 1980s. Both Bin Laden and Saddam Hussein were once the blue-eyed boys of the West.'

It is such blatant partisanship and discrimination that has resulted in such widespread suspicion of the real intentions of the Western powers in dealing and targeting the non-European powers even in an issue like combating terrorism, the effect of which is more severe on the third world countries both materially and in terms of loss of human lives. It is this suspicion that fuelled the spontaneous outburst of anti-Western feelings in most parts of the third world during the Gulf War. It was a demonstration of support not of Iraq but rather a denunciation of the double standard of the West and its continued perpetuation and support of neo-colonialism by maintaining an invisible empire locally manned by repressive regimes. Such distrust gets sustenance by the dilly-dallying of the West in regard to the establishment of the Palestine State, to which the West remains committed for a long time and by ignoring and abetting the expansionist and repressive policies of the state of Israel towards the Palestinians and its periodic invasions of Lebanon. The West approves a transplanted Jewish state of Isreal but not an indigenous state of Palestine for the Palestinians.

Concluding Remarks

This makes the entire moral plank of fighting international terrorism terribly weak. A morally defensible position must be based on certain non-negotiable universally valid precepts, which is missing in the present Western War against terrorism. To be ethically strong the Western plank must be based on the following: (a) an immediate commitment to the creation of an independent Palestinian state at an early date (b) not to make any exception in the charter of human rights any where in the world, (c) to make a firm commitment to constitutional democracy by championing it is non-Christian areas just as it facilitated the democratization of the Catholic countries after the Second World War, (d) a firm commitment to include Turkey which is economically linked to

Southern Europe in the European Union within a time frame to demonstrate that West has really secularized (e) to treat all terrorists alike whether the European based IRA or the Basque separatists with other and (f) to take initiatives to create a new Marshall Plan for the poor ex-colonial democratic countries.

One of the most effective ways of taming terror is the people's revulsion to it by demonstrating that whatever may be the cost of terror, the nation collectively will endure it and ultimately end it. As Machiavelli realized long time ago that the best way to get rid of mercenaries is by creating a people's militia, similarly in an age of democracy it is the collective action of the people that will surely eliminate terror. This can be achieved by creating an order in which the people have full faith and are willing to sacrifice their self-interest for the cause of public good as exemplified by the remarkable British collective response to the London bombing in the early phase of the Second World War.

However, the War also brought to the surface the steep inequities from which the British society suffered and the political leadership responded to it by initiating the Beveridge Report of 1942, which provided the blueprint for the post War welfare state. The impact of this can be measured by the fact that the *London Times* the war news as the lead news but most often the second lead dealt with the various aspects of the Beveridge Report. M.N. Roy understood the sea change in the British psyche during the war years and predicted a victory for the Labour Party after the War. One of the big ironies of history has been that the then Prime Minister Winston Churchill, in spite of his heroism and leadership of the War Cabinet lost the General Elections held in 1945. Similarly, in the post Gulf war scenario President Bush senior with his concerns for security became inconsequential and a relatively unknown Clinton with his social welfare proposals appealed to the Americans and won the Presidential Elections of 1992. The re-election of George W. Bush is seen by many as the victory of the military industrial complex of the United States.

Unless the West moves decisively in positive directions of confidence building measures with a essential commitment to democratic values and human rights, its present sponsored fight against terrorism would continue to evoke suspicion and distrust amongst a large section of the people of the non-Western world. With such large areas of alienation and suspicion strengthened by decades of deceit and exploitation by the West the fight against terrorism will sound hallow and selectively brutal in the absence of a credible strategy of a just order in the under-privileged world. This can be remedied if the West renounces its past policies and undertakes bold initiatives at universal confidence building, extension of democracy and following the rules of equity and justice not selectively and exclusively but universally without any exception.

One ray of hope lies in the recent but belated realization of the British Prime Minister Tony Blair that unless and until the larger question of deprivation, discrimination and inequality are addressed the fight agaisnt terrorism would remain ineffective. If this could be the basis for fighting terrorism then much of the menace of terrorism could be effectively tackled.

Notes and References

1. Einstein, A., *Ideas and Opinions,* New Delhi, Rupa & Co., 1979.
2. Von Hippel, K.., *Democracy by Force: US Military Intervention in the Post Cold War World,* Cambridge, UK, Cambridge University Press, 2000.
3. Zakaria, F., *The Future of Freedom: Illiberal Democracy at Home and Abroad,* New York, Viking, 2003.

i Considering Marx's theoretical model of capitalism outmoded as capitalism had begun to reform itself from within he advocated a non-violent revolution by means of a persistent economic and political struggle to widen the areas of democracy. He was confident of the dynamics of universal suffrage because in the long run it will ensure subordination of the State to popular control. In that situation ideas like dictatorship of the proletariat or justification of centralized absolutism and violence were anachronistic.

ii Lenin argued that the state was a special organization of force and the communist control of the state implies a revolutionary seizure of the state and imposition of the dictatorship of the proletariat.

4. Huntington, S.P., *Political Order in Changing Societies,* New Haven, Yale University Press, 1955.

2. INDIA-PAKISTAN RELATIONS: CREATING STAKEHOLDERS AND CONSTITUENCIES FOR INTERDEPENDENCE*

Mahendra P Lama

India and Pakistan remained an integrated economic system and single market before 1947. The undivided India had increasingly sprawling social and physical infrastructures that facilitated economic exchanges both intra-regional within South Asia and cross-regional with regions of central and west Asia and China. The partition abruptly disrupted not only the economic connections but also the very historico-geographical basis of socio-cultural linkages. Suddenly the market was segregated, economic systems dislocated and politico-social linkages cut off. The geographical space shrunk, physical contacts literally ended and psychological gaps increased. The result is abysmally low economic exchanges, sharp erosion on political confidence, huge deviation from the rational matrices and more seriously a major infliction of damage on the psychology of general mass.

The steady disintegration of this compact economic system and single market has done very serious damages to both sides of the border. The cost of non-cooperation has been irrevocably high in every aspect of human lives. India remained a major trading partner constituting over 40 and 22 per cent of its total global

* [This paper is reprinted from Prakash Nanda (ed), *Rising India : Friends and Foe : Essays in Honour of Prof ML Sondhi*, Lancer, New Delhi, 2007]

exports and imports of Pakistan in 1951-52. Over the years India's share in Pakistan's global exports and imports has steadily gone down to touch a very insignificant figure 2 and 2.6 per cent in 2005.[1] This is despite close physical proximity, cost effectiveness, product complementarities, socio-cultural bonds and availability of basic infrastructure developed during the pre-independence period. Such a low level of trading activities have in fact, defied all economic and business logic.

Though the political imbroglios including three wars and Kargil are considered to be the major factors attributed to this poor interaction, there are several other major detractions and deterrents that preclude India and Pakistan to consolidate their economic linkages.

Firstly, there is a strong presence of both indigenous and multinational companies that drive the economic activities in Pakistan. They have their production bases both within and outside the country for which Pakistan has been a captive market. This varies from tea of which Pakistan is one of the largest importers in the world to cement, rubber, textiles, tyres, pharmaceuticals and machineries. The non-extension of most favoured nation (MFN) treatment to India which is mandatory for a member of the World Trade Organisation, the inclusions of a large number of non-tradable items in the limited freely importable lists from India and several other non-tariff barriers based on misplaced apprehensions are all indicators of pressures built on the Pakistani policy-makers by these powerful non-state actors. These companies have in fact, become a major deterrent to any proposal of liberalizing trade with India. Naturally for them the core competence lies in playing and thrusting Kashmir as the central issue.

Secondly, the complex sources of foreign aid to Pakistan mostly as tied aid have changed the entire directions and compositions of its foreign trade. Of the total foreign economic assistance contracted by Pakistan upto December 1980, 91 per cent was tied to specific projects or commodities. This naturally confined Pakistan to purchase all the aid related materials from the donor countries.

Thirdly, Pakistan shifted its trade focus increasingly to countries offering machinery on suppliers credit basis. Late Mahbub-ul-Haq, a well known Pakistani economist, estimated in 1960s, that the prices of commodities supplied to Pakistan under a number of tied credit agreements had exceeded the lowest quoted price in the international market by upto 170 per cent. This deprived the Pakistani consumers from other competitively priced sources and made Pakistan an artificially high cost economy.

Finally, because of the very nature of political systems and regimes, the private sector remained highly patronized, supervised and regulated in Pakistan thereby crushing any independent decisions making on cross border economic interactions.

All these blocks have gradually metamorphosed into "negative" stakeholders implying that they all work mostly on the line of keeping India-Pakistan tensions and conflicts alive. Many of them continue to thrive on this unsustainable economic rationale. More seriously, there has been a parallel presence and institutionalization of another set of parasitic stakeholders created by the politico-military vested interests. This includes smuggling syndicates, arms purchase lobbies, traders through third countries like Dubai, Hong Kong and Singapore, commission agents and of course, border officials. In other words, higher the possibility of conflict between India and Pakistan, the better and the wider are the opportunities for these parasitic miniscule but heavily patronizing conglomerates to maximise their gains.

So far the confidence building measures (CBMs) between India and Pakistan have exceedingly depended on military and political textual agreements. These political and military CBMs either have not sustained or have remained totally emasculated and ineffective. These CBMs were addressed mostly to those who had serious stakeholding in perpetuating the conflict. Many of these CBMs hit the trough without reaching the peak. The fate of many of these crucial CBMs were dependent upon and determined many times by inept and highly unstable political regimes, pathologically insecure military generals and inward looking bureaucrats. The entire civil society were sidelined to the periphery as observers and analysts of no consequence.

The Context of New Regionalism

Last few years the very context of India-Pakistan relations has shown some significant shift. This shift has been caused by a number of factors including the end of cold war, advancement of and easier accessibility to modern communications technology, greater human mobility, heavy doses of reforms and liberalization, onslaughts of multiplicity of economic players with powerful cross border linkages, emergence of new power centres including China and India and the increasing take over of the public affairs issues by a new generation. All these have the potentiality to change the very nature of regionalism in South Asia which for decades together have been driven by orthodox variables including the national security consideration. The question is to consciously encourage increasing induction of parameters that govern new regionalism process into the otherwise volatile and vulnerable relations between India and Pakistan.

The new regionalism forms part of a global structural transformation in which non-state actors are active and manifest themselves at several levels of the global system. It could not be understood from the point of view of a single region. The new regionalism also pre-supposes the growth of a regional civil society, opting for regional solutions to some local, national and global problems. Under such circumstances not only economic, but also social and cultural networks are developing more quickly than the formal political cooperation at the regional level. The new regionalism enlarges the scope of 'old regionalism' by incorporating in it aspects which where hitherto exclusive to the 'old regionalism'. In other words, there are several drivers or actors from the State, market and civil society as the pushing forces in the new regionalism.

"The new regionalism also proposes the growth of a regional civil society opting for regional solutions to local and national problems. The implications of this are that not only economic, but also social and cultural networks are developing more quickly than the formal political cooperation at the regional level."[2] Unlike the top-down approach adopted by most of the regional groupings based on traditional paradigm, the new regionalism is mainly triggered from below by i) private market and business oriented forms of regionalization. Private economic forces have been reacting faster or at least more effectively than the state actors to the new situation and the more liberalized political economy. And ii) society induced ones. This is seen in growing interdependence and cooperation between a great diversity of civil society organizations and inter-personal transnational networks (e.g. diasporas, ethnic or family networks, religious ties).[3]

Besides the traditional state policy planners a far more extensive set of actors are emerging across India and Pakistan which have started questioning the State's monopoly in determining various matrices of issues of public interests. These include transnational religious organizations , environmental groups, human rights organizations, regional economic cooperatives, local communities, MNCs, diasporas and migrants/refugees.[4] These actors have entered into various forms of cooperation and collaboration. They vary from informal coalitions to global conferences and from non-governmental organizations (NGOs) and non-official national and international institutions and regional organization working in diverse areas. Many of these non-state actors advocate and advance regionalism for varied reasons. They exert a lot of pressure on official institutions at different levels.

A revealing facet of this new phenomenon is the induction of a novel bottom up forms of regionalism initiated by the civil society which are emerging partly in response to the social disruptions , inequalities and insecurities. There are already very close networking and interactions among human right activists[5] , media men[6] , social workers[7] and other professionals working on issues of common critical interests. All these have happened spontaneously without the governments coming into picture. Unlike in the past, the Kargil and another bout of military regime in Pakistan did not deter this process.

This is the time to ponder over the vital question of designing new CBMs. And the two very critical interventions in this regard could be easing and promoting people to people contacts and designing layers of economic exchanges and interactions. In the parlance of international relations this is both track II and III diplomacies. As there are stakeholders in keeping the conflict alive, there are stakeholders for building the peace. We have never addressed ourselves to the latter.

Creating Stakeholders and Constituencies for Interdependence

A major drawback of India's diplomacy in Pakistan has been a consistent failure to create its constituency. Unlike other neighbouring countries where there has been a strong Indian constituency based on traditional goodwill, constant and varied interactions and institutional exchanges, there is none in Pakistan where it is needed most. As a result, the orientation of entire Pakistani civil society and people at grass roots for long remained exclusively state driven. The Pakistan as a nation-state has had clear vested interest in propagating a myopic view of India. The impact has been devastating as there has been no popular domestic pressure on Pakistan to strengthen ties with India. Consequently, the people in Pakistan in general lost objective assessment of India's postures and attitudes. This is what India has to seriously address by injecting a range of programmes to sensitise, involve and engage the Pakistanis in a much more constructive and wider framework.

Across South Asia, the CBMs built by the economic stakeholders have always sustained. This is amply substantiated by India's relations with Nepal, Bhutan, Bangladesh and Sri Lanka. There have been serious political crises these countries have faced vis-à-vis India but they have been remarkably momentary and have showed urgent recovery mainly. This is on account of the large scale economic stakeholding on both sides of the border. The most recent example is that of the fiercely adverse diplomatic and media exchange between India and Nepal after the hijacking of Delhi bound Indian Airlines flight from Kathmandu in December 1999. The role played by the tourism lobbies as positive stakeholders on both sides of the border did the trick. No one had expected normalcy to return so fast. These deeply entrenched stakeholders in tourism with their forward and backward linkages literally forced their respective governments to come to the negotiating table.

There will be a constant and concerted moves to thwart and abort any move towards creating positive stakeholdings as can be seen in the case of trade policies of Pakistan, recent sugar deals, proposed cross border power trade and overland gas pipelines. The globalisation process led economic reforms is likely to be the most critical factor that could inject and consolidate such positive stakeholdings in India-Pakistan relations. Even if the mindset of incrementalism persists in the improvement of relationship, the actors behind have become more diverse and dynamic in character. The instruments and channels of interactions have become more transparent because of internet and televisions.

Unlike the typical military-bureaucracy combine in Pakistan

which remained a formidable fortress for long, there are IMF-World Bank led players, there is China and more importantly varieties of trans-national corporations. For the latter, the strategic intent is corporate gains. And in the attainment of these, transnational bodies are bound to put adequate pressure on the "pull factors" in the domestic circle to open up for a substantive transformation in its dealings with the neighbours. This is what these TNCs have done in many other theatres of bilateral contempt-suspicion.

More interestingly, such kind of structural changes triggered by liberalisation process and globalisation norms are more conspicuously present in India with many cross border common actors and elements. The offshoots are innumerable and varied. And they are driven by common goals of an integrated market. The Indian business and industrial federations like FICCI, CII and PHDCCI have started striking ties with their Pakistani counterparts in a much more professional manner under the aegis of SAARC Chambers of Commerce and Industry. India's Infotech professionals are much in demand.

The changing nature of economic actors and their increasing support base in the civil society will rather force policy designers on both sides of the border to procreate modalities for a substantive and lasting interaction. In creating, designing, building and promoting all these economic stake holdings, India's role comes out to be of pivotal nature both as a driving force and consolidating agent. It is however, a purely relative and positive laden concept based on three elements viz., its relatively advanced level of development, experience and accumulated expertise; existing or potential capacity for sharing that knowledge and its relatively important involvement in the global economy. Therefore, instead of traditionally conceived leadership-followership model, Pakistan should be involved as an equal partner. This means India has to consciously and benevolently show a new vistas of partnership.

If we have to visualize 2020 and beyond, losing a few million rupees in extending free trade regime to Pakistan and similar other open arm concessions should no longer be a inhibiting concern. Naturally, Pakistan will have to go much beyond the most favoured nation treatment by reducing the list of negative items to an inconsequential limit, creating a comprehensive investment regime and congenial environment exclusively for the Indian investors and demolishing the archival barriers of flow of information-ideas and most importantly, exchange of people and interaction among the institutions.

Trade Sector Cooperation

The recent announcement by Pakistan to enhance the number of freely importable products from India to over 1000 items has much politico-commercial significance. The inclusion of items like dyes and chemicals, industrial machineries and raw materials indicates an increasing internal pressure on Pakistan to liberalise trade with India. These pressures are in four fronts. Firstly, a large number of MNCs and other Chinese triggered ventures that are operating in Pakistan are eying to access the Indian market in a durable manner. Secondly, there is a bourgeoning constituency including media, consumer groups and development think tanks that favour a normal trading relations with India. Thirdly, a new generation of reforms shabby bureaucrats is now taking over the crucial commercial desks and redefining Pakistan's external economic relations. And finally the massive price gains and diverse product choices that have accrued to India's other neighbouring free trade partners like Sri Lanka, Nepal and Bhutan have increasingly donned on the Pakistani consumers about the futility and high cost of maintaining artificial restrictions. As a result of free trade agreement, Sri Lanka's exports to India recorded a 9 fold increase from Sri Lankan Rs 4.3 billion in 2000 to SL Rs 39.62 in 2004 and the imports recorded a 3 fold increase from SL Rs 45.47 billion to 145.65 billion.[8]

There are strident efforts even by the Pakistani central bank to drive home as to how its consumers are subject to high cost imports from other countries which could otherwise be substantially eased if normal trade relations are established with India. Unlike the earlier studies commissioned by the Benazir Bhutto's government which were kept as 'confidential documents', the very recent study by State Bank of Pakistan is a public document. It has estimated that the potential of Pakistan-India trade is in the range of $1 billion to $5.2 billion per annum as against the officially reported flow of $ 500 million bilateral trade. Against the backdrop of the bilateral trade composition of 2004, it found that there are 1,181 items worth $3.9 billion common between Pakistan's exports and Indian imports. Similarly, against 2,646 common items of Pakistan's imports worth $7 billion in the year

2004, India had exports worth over $15 billion. This study found that in case of over 50 per cent of these items, the unit values for Pakistan's imports are more than the unit values of Indian exports hinting at the possibility of far cheaper cost of imports from the latter. This study further mentions that Pakistan will on an average have national saving in foreign exchange between $400 million to $900 million provided Pakistan government expands its positive list of importable items from India. [9]

Another study conducted by Export Promotion Board of Pakistan compared India's imports of each item from the world, with exports of the same item by Pakistan to the world (reflecting Pakistan's capacity to export that item) and the export of the same item to India. It revealed a high potential for Pakistani exports to India in a number of items including textiles and garments sector.

There are also studies that show how Pakistan annually loses millions of dollars because of irrational policies. It alone loses almost $ 25-40 million annually by not importing tea from India. This is despite the fact that tea has since long remained on top of the 'positive list' of Pakistan vis-à-vis India.[10] Besides the creation of a parallel supra-economy, capitalization of these informal trade routes by criminals, drug traffickers and terrorists are the other dimensions. The State Bank of Pakistan report mentioned normal trade relations will "benefit consumers particularly in Pakistan, increase custom revenue and push out smugglers and trade mafias involved in what is being called circular trade through Dubai, Singapore and Afghanistan".

"Kashmir first" attitude of Pakistan has had plethora of far reaching negative consequences on Pakistan, its economy and more importantly its people. Pakistan's exclusive decision to continue bilateral trade with India through a positive list approach even after the implementation of South Asian Free Trade Area (SAFTA) in July 2006 is the most recent example of how sound economic rationale falls prey to constricted political thinking. Pakistan maintains that it "would not grant the most favoured nation (MFN) status to India until there was a tandem move in other bilateral issues, particularly Kashmir.... there were some provisions in the WTO that allowed the member countries a cushion of not granting an MFN status to any country for some peculiar reasons. When Pakistan did not give the MFN status to India under the

WTO, then how it would be possible to give the same under a regional agreement?"

For three years, Pakistan participated in all the SAFTA negotiations without any reservations on its operational aspects. This unexpected Pakistan's action has undermined the already beleaguered SAARC process and has opened scope for dividing the SAARC members on purely bilateral issues. Though India has now referred the case to Council of Commerce Ministers, it could retaliate by using this same tool to exclude Pakistan from its other SAARC activities.

Pakistan should realise the fact that SAFTA brings new hopes, builds confidence and generates a chain of opportunities for the South Asian countries to look beyond the SAARC region. A free trade regime triggers and mobilises a total reorientation of the existing systems and legal regimes and attracts a massive intervention in terms of infrastructures and institutional reforms. Like in other regional blocks this could detach the economic imperatives from the narrow politics and turn the present shallow regionalism to a robust openness. A critical aspect of this new horizon is the possibility of cross border infrastructural linkages including establishing the power grids, gas pipelines, land bridge and railway line that connect to East, North, West and Central Asian countries. These are key to the success of regionalism in this sub-continent. In fact, the very attraction and taste of free access to these wide varieties of regional products would widen and sustain the process of SAFTA and other regional integration techniques. The issue is to set free the market access and let the consumers gain the maximum utility. Pakistan should therefore, engage India more and more on positive areas that bring sustainability to its recently achieved and widely acclaimed growth rate of over 8 per cent. If China could do so why not Pakistan ?[11]

Pakistan has raised other apprehensions. Despite steady liberalizations, India continues to nurture a host of barriers that prevent the free flow of goods and other economic ties. There is a constant fear that it is India which will gain maximum out of any trade liberalisation efforts in the region. This is substantiated by the fact that during the period 1995-2000, India alone constituted over 70 per cent of the exports made within the region. This means only 30 per cent of the intra-regional exports were shared by the remaining six SAARC member countries. India has for long given

Pakistan the MFN status. Yet India's imports from Pakistan have been very meagre. Pakistan sees it as a de facto ban on its exports.

There is no restriction on the Indian investors in Pakistan and vice versa, yet there is literally no investment in each other's countries. Investors do attribute this to adverse macro political climate. However, there are several examples where investors have made headway into politically adverse situations and helped in improving the political economy of bilateral relations. A conscious integration of trade and investment activities is the way forward. This can be done at a fairly local level initially between two Punjabs. The resumption of cargo service between Indian and Pakistani Punjab and on the Sindh-

Rajasthan sector and exchanging branches of banks are efforts in the right direction.

Energy Sector Cooperation: Key Sector

Interdependence among nations is the best guarantee of peace and regional stability. It helps create multi-dimensional relationship and deepens a sense of empathy and understanding of other partners. However, India and Pakistan have selected distant partners and oriented themselves toward other regions and markets. The overriding issue is therefore to replace primacy of politics with primacy of economics. Perhaps, latent interdependence through starting economic transactions with politically harmless and untangled areas could be an effective instrument to do so. Electricity trade is one of them. There are initial inhibitions on this though as compared to other areas of trade it carries greater potential of stability, consistency, and interdependence scope.[12]

Once the agreement is signed and the infrastructures are put in place and trading operation get started, the cost of withdrawing from an arrangement will be immense for both the parties. For instance, a problem over the division of Indus basin's waters had been lingering since partition. It was amicably settled with the signing of Indus Waters Treaty in September 1960 with the active mediation of the World Bank. For the past forty-six years, both the countries have honoured the Treaty. A permanent Indus Basin Commission comprising of one member from each country was created to resolve any issue, and if it fails the question can be referred for arbitration.[13] It is an impressive record by any standard.

The interdependence theory therefore, revolves round the fact that the costs of disengagement become so high that the parties tend to isolate issue of conflict from economic cooperation, and resort to peaceful means. Once mutual vulnerabilities are well established through power trade between India and Pakistan, the logic of interdependence would prevail, bring about positive change in bilateral relations, and significantly reduce the risk of confrontation.

The other significant point in understanding the effects of electricity trade on latent interdependence is that it will create stakeholders, promote constituencies of interest in both the countries that will serve as a restraint against the historical trend toward confrontation as well as influence governments' policies toward more trade and openness.[14] At the moment the stakeholders are few and the constituencies of common interest are weak. The industrialists, the commercial class, the workers and the common consumers of electricity in India would have a natural interest in peaceful relations with Pakistan. Similarly, the state in Pakistan itself earning a big chunk of revenues from electricity trade, the IPPs and others directly and indirectly connected with this trade will have to weigh the costs and benefits of confrontation with India.

Economic rationality is one of the key assumptions in developing this analysis, and also that those who run the Indian and Pakistan states are rational players. Economic rationality dictates that withdrawal of cooperation or severing of relations, hurts interests in their totality and therefore, it becomes an obsolete option. Disputes do take place over how rewards or benefits are to be distributed as trade and commercial relations multiply, or even occur quite frequently as states change their economic policies, but they require altogether different policy tools, such as, negotiations, bargaining and establishment of institutions to help resolve issues in peaceful manner. It is rational to expect that kind of change to take place as and when India and Pakistan begin trade in electricity and it becomes a catalyst for trade in other areas increasing the density of trade and commercial ties between the two.

Both India and Pakistan have undertaken a series of reform measures to restructure their power sector to make it commercially viable and financially self-sustaining. The reform process has been initiated in a phased manner over the past decade. However, significant developments have taken place in the past few years that promise to introduce competition in the sector and improve general efficiency of the sector. Massive changes have been introduced in their policies on private sector participation in the power sector.

The vertically integrated power utilities in both the countries had a very diffused corporate structure and poor work culture. Lack of corporate governance, absence of commercial independence, inefficient cost structure, and extremely high system losses (including pilferage, theft of power and low collection efficiency and improper billing), coupled with non-remunerative tariffs characterized their subsistence. The end result was, operationally inefficient and financially sick/insolvent power utilities in both the countries. This has led to a sharp fall in public investment in these utilities.

The investments in energy supply require large inputs of scarce physical, human and financial resources for which there are competing demands from other sectors. Both India and Pakistan are capital scarce. The restructuring of power sector has therefore, been necessary. The analysis of demand-supply gap in the power sector in these two countries is very crucial in reaching at any conclusion on the possibility and potentiality of cross border power trade. Both India and Pakistan are largely energy importers and have faced a protracted power shortfall because of the excess industrial and residential demand over their power-generating capacities. Though the demand for power has recorded a much higher growth rate, supply side has recorded both smaller and erratic growth pattern. This has increasingly led to power cuts and rationing. A major chunk of demand comes from the rural areas. The overwhelming rural population in the region is gradually demanding more and more power. The seasonality factor in both generation and demand is noticeable in these two countries. In India, there exists clear seasonality in power generation. It particularly becomes clear in the hydel power generation. The peak months for hydropower generation are August-September while the lean period is from January to June. The thermal plants generation has been mostly designed to match and balance the trough months created by the hydel plants in winter and the pre-monsoon season. This has been the case in Pakistan also.[15]

As long as the demand for electricity in India is not perfectly positively correlated with the demand pattern in Pakistan, trade will benefit both sides. It will not only create a conduit for excess electricity, it can also help in stabilizing the grid. On the other hand, in Bhutan and Nepal, the peak demand is usually during Dec/Jan. This is the period when generation from the hydropower plants is low. Though, Feb-April is the driest period, the demand in these months is relatively lower. In Nepal, power demand (MW), is maximum during the month of December (391 MW) and is minimum during the month of August (344 MW). The supply capacity in turn is maximum during the wet months and minimum during the dry months of February/March (322/324 MW). There is capacity (MW) surplus during wet months and capacity deficit during dry months (maximum during January which amounts to 57 MW). This situation in Bhutan also is somewhat similar. The surplus power from these countries as well can be traded within the region if transmission inter-connections linking their power grids are established. This could consolidate in practical sense the process of regional cooperation in South Asia.

There are quite revealing variations in the installed capacities of power utilities in India and Pakistan. These variations also reflect the potentialities as based on their natural endowments. Thermal power has gradually dominated the installed capacities in India (72 % mainly steam based) and Pakistan (71 %). Share of hydro sources has gone down very steadily in both India and Pakistan.[16] (Tables 2.1)

As per WAPDA estimates, Pakistan has a total hydropower potential of about 41,721 MW. Of which only 9,137 MW has been tapped thus far. This leaves Pakistan with an untapped potential of about 32,584 MW (Table 2.2). Large hydro projects take a long time to build and can have significant environmental impacts as well. But interestingly Pakistan has a significant potential for hydel generation through small projects as well, which could be tapped by the private sector too. The larger projects, like the Kalabagh Dam and Bhasha Dam are also on the cards currently, and the government has announced that one of these dams could be started by next year.

Pakistan's informal offer to India in 1998 of selling surplus power that was available from the IPP units was primarily based on two very compulsive domestic realities. Firstly, Pakistan was

Table 2.1

INDIA AND PAKISTAN: INSTALLED GENERATING CAPACITIES IN POWER UTILITIES (MW)

	India	*Pakistan*
Thermal	**75931**	**13786**
% Share	(72.3)	(71.58)
Nuclear	2700	462
% Share	(2.57)	(2.39)
Hydro	26329	5010
% Share	(25.1)	(26.01)
Total	**104960#**	**19258**

Notes: # In addition to this the installed capacities in the non-utilities is over 16000 MW.

Sources: Government of India, *Economic Survey 2002-2003,* Ministry of Finance; Hilal Raza et al, Pakistan Country Report 2003, CPD, Dhaka.

Table 2.2

INSTALLED CAPACITY AND POTENTIALS OF HYDRO POWER

	Hydroelectric Total Potential [MW] (a)	*% Installed Capacity [MW] (b)*	*Harnessed of the Total (b) as % of (a)*
India	75400	25407	33.70
Pakistan	40000	5010	12.52
Total (South Asia)	231245	32588	14.09

(*) *Power System Master Plan (PSMP), 1995.*

(**) Wangchuk, LK, Bhutan's Minister of Trade and Industry in an interview with *EnergySouth Asia,* New Delhi, January/February 2002, p 14.

under obligation to buy power being produced by the IPPs, which it could not sell in its own market, as the projected industrialization and economic growth did not materialize to absorb the installed capacity. This amounted to making the already sick WAPDA more insolvent. And secondly, the international financial institutions which had either extended loans or the guarantees to the power sector investors in Pakistan wanted to have an uninterrupted repayment of debts which was possible only through power sale to a stable market like that of India.[17]

In India, the northern and the western regions are the potential markets. These regions are the largest electricity consuming industrial areas. At the same time Punjab province in Pakistan, which is mostly adjacent to the Punjab state of India has been the highest power consumer in the country constituting over 60 per cent of the total electricity consumption in Pakistan. Besides being a major source of agricultural production many of the commercial and industrial units are located in this province. This province has recorded a growth rate of almost 4 per cent as against that of Sindh and NWFP. This indicates that this province could be a major destination of any power supplied from India and other South Asian countries.

The possibility of power purchase has opened new vistas of cooperation. Cross border power trade will lead to: (i) effective utilization of natural resources; (ii) increase in reliability of power supply; (iii) economy in operation and mutual support during contingencies; (iv) bring about large scale transformation in the sectors contributing to economic growth; and (v) will act as the single most effective confidence building measure through the participation of stakeholders.

However, the key issues to be settled before the cross border flow is concretized are the cost of transmission line and its sharing mechanism; the determination of power tariff; the payment mechanism and most importantly the power supply sustainability and its geo-political immunization. It is very crucial to maintain a fair balance in the energy security equation in order to avert the risk of 'trade and fade'. There are discussions going on between the organizations like Power Grid Corporation of India Limited (PGCIL) and various independent power producers (IPPs) in Pakistan for import of electricity for the states of Rajasthan, Punjab and Gujarat. Tariff came up as a major stumbling block in the entire negotiation process that was conducted during the second half of 1998 and first half of 1999. The WAPDA offered a price of US 7.2 cents/KWH while the Indian side offered a price of 2.25 cents.[18] It is mainly on this ground the negotiations broke off.

As a reaction to his power purchase proposal, the then Water and Power Minister Raja Nadir Pervaiz said, "GOP is considering a proposal to allow the IPP to export 200 MW of surplus power to India. Pakistan has got a study conducted and found it viable that surplus power could be exported to India through multinationals. MNCs would be asked to lay transmission lines and export electricity to India." The IPPs including Japan Power, Fauji Kabairwala Power and Liberty Power have completed their plants. They could be in a position to sell power to India through MNCs.

WAPDA and KESC have a substantial grid station and transmission line networks across the country. With 45,157 km of lines across Pakistan and 657 grid stations, most of the country is covered. The only exception, are border areas in Balochistan, where supply is provided by the grid stations in Iran. The grid map for Pakistan is attached as appendix. It clearly identifies the grid stations where one could interconnect the Pakistani and Indian grids at minimal cost. The two places could be the Grid stations in Lahore and/or the grid station in Jamshoro. There is another grid planned for Thar. This could bring the Pakistani grid to even closer to the Indian grid. Thar coal is a large project that is under implementation, with technical help from the Chinese, and could be a significant source of power export to India. Pakistan has 500 KV primary transmission system extending from Jamshoro in the south to Tarbela and Peshawar in the north.[19] All these lines run very much near to the adjoining borders of India and may not require complex transmission extensions to the Indian borders. This can be seen from the power transmission map of Punjab in India as given below. "There is a complete network on our side and of course, on the Indian side as well. What is needed, are the connections, which would take only a couple of weeks".[20]

It is stated that each country will construct and maintain a double circuit twin-bundled 220 KV transmission system from the designated substations viz., Dinanath in Pakistan and Patti in India. Power Grid Corporation of India can play an active role in concretizing the Indian side of the transmission of the power purchased from Pakistan. There is a complete network of transmission lines and grids on the Pakistani side along the northwestern border of Indian Punjab.[21]

Will energy trade help improve relations between India and Pakistan? The answer is unequivocally yes. Trading creates constituencies among business communities, industrial sectors, and service providing groups that support peaceful and stable relations otherwise their interests would get hurt. Trade in one area of economic activity spills over into other areas expanding the volume and categories of goods that can be traded, as gains accumulate and their value for national economy becomes well established.

Looking at the dismal volume and highly limited trading basket between India and Pakistan, energy could be a major tradable item, which would increase interdependence and correspondingly reduce vulnerabilities. And the positive gains to these economies will make policy makers both in India and Pakistan sensitive to the needs of each other, help improve political situation and work towards protecting the interests of each other. Energy trade will build confidence and break the old mindset that India and Pakistan are born to be enemies.

In comparison to the social sectors of economy, the defence spending of India and Pakistan is quite large. India spends approximately 2.7 per cent of its Gross Domestic Product on defence. In monetary terms it translates into $16.2 billion annually. Pakistan's defence burden is around 3.9 per cent of the GDP, which is roughly 60 per cent more than that of India.[22] In comparison, the defence burden of the NATO and non-NATO countries of Europe is 2.6 per cent and 1.6 per cent respectively. The positive aspects of military spending including modernization and supply of technological innovations to civilian industries are far offset by the debilitating impact on general human welfare. The energy trading between the two countries will create the necessary trust for rethinking on defence spending.

Peace Dividends[23]

There are several studies that have estimated peace dividends emanating from better relations between India and Pakistan. If adequate confidence is built between these two countries mainly triggered by a deeper and wider economic exchange, people to people contacts and other institutional linkages, there is an increasing possibility that the defence spending in real terms may finally see a downward trend. "*Human Development in South Asia 1997*" provides three different scenarios of either freezing or cutting down in defence spending by these two countries. The cumulative peace dividends of these three scenarios viz., a freeze in real terms, a 2 per cent annual cut and a 5 per cent annual cut would provide a hopping amount of $ 80 billion, $ 100 billion and $ 125 billion respectively over the period 1997-2010. These funds so released as peace dividends could finance a range on social and development projects in both these countries.

There are two scenarios wherein Pakistan can sell power to India and can make handsome differences to the health and education programme at the domestic level. Under Scenario I, roughly estimating that by selling 3,000 MW of power to India, Pakistan will not only earn a net profit of $ 160 million per annum after deducting fixed and running costs but would also gain through the subsequent decrease in defence expenditure (reduction of 10 per cent) to the extent of $ 300 million. In this case, Pakistan's power could be sold to power intensive industries across the border which require qualitative power and is willing to pay a high tariff of 10.97 cents per kwh (Rs 4.82 paise) as the landed cost price in India. This captive power purchase includes 5.7 cents kwh (Rs 2.48) as cost of production in Pakistan and 5.27 cents (Rs 2.32) as other costs including wheeling and profit margin on the Indian side.

Even if Pakistan spends 50 per cent of this total generated revenues of $ 460 million (through both power sale and defence expenditure reduction) on education, it will have radical impact on the current situation in the country. By assuming that an additional amount of $ 230 million will be spent on primary education we estimate that 27, 600 new schools will be built, each school costing around $ 8,330. At the rate of 200 students in each school, 5.52 million more children can be enrolled. In the above calculations, it has been assumed that it would cost $ 6,000 as running cost for each school. With more educational institutions employment opportunities will also increase significantly. Assigning 5 teachers to each school, 138,000 new teachers can be employed.

Under scenario II , this power can be bought on the Indian side on a long term contract basis with the payment of evening peak (1700-2300 hrs) of 7.33 cents (Rs 3.20) per kwh at the busbar. Given the cost of production of 5.7 cents kwh (Rs 2.48) in Pakistan, the sale of 3000 mw would fetch Pakistan a margin of 1.63 cents (Rs.0.72) per kwh i.e. a total revenue of $ 48.49 million. This along with the gains to the extent of $ 300 million arising out of the subsequent decrease in defence expenditure (reduction of 10 per cent) could make a major difference to the education and health programmes. For instance, even if a little over 50 per cent of $ 348.49 million on education, it will have radical impact on the current situation in the country. By assuming that an additional amount of $ 175 million will be spent on primary education, we estimate that 21,008 new schools will be built, each school costing around $ 8,330. At the rate of 200 students in each school, 4.20 million more children can be enrolled. In the above calculations it has been assumed that it would cost $ 6,000 as running cost for each school. With more educational institutions employment opportunities will also increase significantly. Assigning 5 teachers to each school, 105040 new teachers can be employed.

These are very conservative estimates by the current costs in Pakistan. Construction of new buildings will employ thousands of skilled and unskilled workers from economically depressed rural communities. Investment in education, a sector that has long been neglected due to paucity of funds will have positive impact in number of areas including, general literacy, birth control, skills of workers for new stage of industrialization, absorption of new technologies in agriculture and social mobility.

In the financial year 2003-04, the Higher Education Commission, formerly the University Grants Commission was allocated $ 220 million to finance 47 public sector universities and 8 degree awarding institutes. This amount included scholarships for students, salaries of teachers and other employees, maintenance and addition of new buildings. This amount excluded universities and institutes' own income, donations and students fees. If half of the additional amount of $ 230 million generated above is allocated to higher education, Pakistan could double the current spending on higher education. That will give it flexibility to expand higher education activity in some fields, attract more qualified teachers by offering better working conditions, provide better learning facilities, and improve the quality and standard of education.

The confidence built by exchange of electricity even through relatively smaller volume and limited arrangement could be gradually extended to larger ventures like gas pipelines for which both countries have been discussing and deliberating on. Besides electricity, the four areas which can be identified for cooperation in the oil and gas sector in South Asia region are: i) trans-boundary natural gas trade, ii) trade in refined petroleum products and iii) cooperation in oil and gas exploration.

Movement of Natural Persons

For both India and Pakistan remittances from abroad are very crucial in its balance of payment and foreign exchange management. More than this, the real integration with the world economy of this region will only be possible if there is free flow of goods, services, capital and the people to other countries. It is estimated that there are 4-5 million overseas Indian workers who send remittances to the extent of $ 12-15 billion annually.[24] More latest estimate shows that India received total remittances also known as private transfers to the extent of $ 21.7 billion in 2004 which constituted 10 per cent of the total global remittances.[25] This made India the highest remittance receiving country in the world followed by China (US$ 21.3 billion), Mexico (US$18.1 billion), France (US$ 12.7 billion) and Philippines(US$ 11.6 billion).[26]

The International Monetary Fund (IMF) published a list of 20 developing countries with the volume of remittances and its percentage share of GDP. A majority of the South Asian countries figured in this wherein India with US $ 11 billion ranked as number one in terms of the volume of remittances. This was almost 2.6 per cent of its GDP.[27] It is assessed that a major proportion of this is contributed by the increasing number of unskilled and semi-skilled Indian workers employed in the Gulf countries, Malaysia and Singapore. The United Arab Emirates, Saudi Arabia and Kuwait are the top destination countries and Kerala, Tamil Nadu and Andhra Pradesh are the top sourcing States.[28] Today the overseas Indians are estimated at over 25 million spread across 110 countries.[29] There are 1.68 million Indians in US alone which is the single largest destination of Indian migrants.[30]

International Monetary Fund published a list of 20 developing countries with the volume of remittances and its percentage share of GDP. (Table 2.3) A majority of the South Asian countries figured in this wherein India ranked as number one in terms of the volume of remittances with US $ 11 billion and that contributed 2.6 per cent of the GDP. For all these countries the US is a vital source. In Pakistan's US $ 4.16 billion workers' remittances, over 31 per cent comes from the US and 17 per cent from the United Arab Emirates. Over 1.47 Pakistanis proceeded abroad during 1995-2001.[31]

Table 2.3

SOUTH ASIAN COUNTRIES : REMITTANCES FROM ABROAD

Rank	*Country*	*Remittances (US $ Million)*	*% of GDP*
1	India	11097	2.6
7	Bangladesh	1803	4.1
8	Pakistan	1707	2.7
18	Sri Lanka	1056*	6.9

International Monetary Fund, *Balance of Payment Statistics,* Washington, 2000.

* 61.7 from Middle East countries, and 7.3 per cent is from North America, 13.6 per cent form European Union.

Therefore, at least the demand in general by the developing countries about Temporary Movement of Natural Persons (TMNP-Mode 4) is vital in the ongoing trade negotiation process.[32] As of today, the TMNP accounts for less that 2 per cent of global services trade. A study done by Walmsley and Alan Winters in 2002 indicates that through increasing developed countries' quotas on inward labour movements by 3 per cent of their labour, world welfare would rise by $ 156 billion[33].

In the past responses of most of developed countries including the US to this demand of the developing countries have been marred by a large number of questions and resistance.[34] This includes :

(i) extreme political sensitivity to the very question of TMNP as reflected in various laws and other legal regimes including the immigration provisions.

(ii) consciously equating the temporary mobility with larger issue of migration both legal and illegal and forced and voluntary

(iii) advocacy by some sections about the cost of social commitment, economic burden and displacement of indigenous workers and

(iv) linking even the limited movement of natural persons under TMNP (mode 4) with the extension of provisions like that of national treatment of the foreign investors in the developing countries
(v) consistently ignoring the movement of natural persons as barrier to exports and therefore, essentially a trade matter rather than a migration issues and
(vi) failing to recognize advantages of liberalisation

This is in sharp contrast to the market demand situation since the developed countries where demand for skilled work forces have increased as against the backdrop of fast ageing population. The existing skilled workers in the developed countries cater mostly to the upper echelons of job market thereby leaving a major supply gap in the lower echelons of job market. The developed countries would like to have restricted or regional arrangements for recruiting specific service providers. They fear that labour mobility under the General Agreement on Trade in Services (GATS) could serve as a tool to establish permanent residence and thus conflict with immigration policies is increasingly used by the developed countries to restrict access to even the skilled and qualified people from the developing countries.

The other side of the story is that despite no commitments under the GATS, the health workers from India and Pakistan have been going to the developed countries. But Mode 4 of the GATS makes an argument that such commitments would benefit the sending countries by providing a more predictable and transparent framework that is based on non-discrimination. This will encourage the flow. Secondly, this makes the inflow more secure and employers will have both continuity and certainty and could provide better adjustment in the direction towards comparative advantage. The mode 4 could also be used as tool to overcome the bias in favour of highly qualified labour.

Both India and Pakistan are facing more or less similar the problems vis-à-vis accessing the global labour marketing But, there has not emerged any meaningful dialogue and effective cross border cooperation between these two countries to highlight these issues related to migrants. To a certain extent this move has been so far thwarted by the competitive nature of labour migration. However, frequent consultation may help in ultimately generating a conscious check on restricting the movement of labour migrants and also creating a consortium of migrants based on an analysis of skills and supply capabilities.

There are serious problems of irregular-illegal migrants also. By their very nature the migrants from South Asia tend to flock together across the world for purposes of convenient passages and transits, cultural and social similarities, food habits, community services and modes of sending the money. In terms of any difficulties also they tend to be guided by the South Asian diaspora, each other's embassies and other agencies. For instance, in the recent evacuation of South Asians from Lebanon during the Israeli bombings, it was the Indian Embassy which evacuated maximum South Asians to their respective home countries. What is needed is an overarching regional convention on migration and its operationalisation by various governmental and non-governmental sources spread globally. This will ensure protection of migrants from India and Pakistan under single umbrella and generate tremendous amount of goodwill back home on a cross-border basis.

Notes and References

1. Pakistan's total global exports and imports in 2005 were US$ 14391.1 million and US$ 20598 million respectively. State Bank of Pakistan, *Annual Report 2004-2005, Reviews of the Economy,* Vol. I, Karachi, pp. 108-109.
2. Hettne, Bjorn, "The New Regionalism: Implications for Development of Peace" in Bjorn Hettne and Andras Inotai (ed), *Comparing Regionalism: Implications for Global Development and International Security,* A UNU/WIDER Study, Helsinki, 1994.
3. Michael Schultz et al., in Bjorn Hettne and Andras Inotai (ed), *Comparing Regionalism: Implications for Global Development and International Security,* A UNU/WIDER Study, Helsinki, 1994, pp 254-255.
4. Latham, R, "Thinking about Security after the Cold War", *International Studies Notes,* Vol. 20, No 3, 1995, p. 13.
5. Asma Jahangir and IA Rehman of Pakistan are the two icons that have brought together the South Asian community to a common platform to discuss human rights violation issues.
6. The South Asian Free Media Association brings together the most eminent and influential media people in one forum.
7. The Neemrana Initiative started in 1991 that brings together

former diplomats, military personnel and academics of India and Pakistan and Pakistan-India People's Forum for Peace and Democracy initiated in 1994 consisting of activists, trade unionists, artists and intellectuals have been playing major role in pressurising both these governments to take steps towards improving mutual relations.

8. Lama, Mahendra P, "Markets can bolster Indo-Pak Ties", *Indian Express,* New Delhi, 1 December 2006.
9. Rashid, Tariq, et al., *Implications of Liberalizing Trade & Investment With India*, State Bank of Pakistan, Karachi, 2006, (Draft For Comments)
10. Lama, Mahendra P, "Integrating the Tea Sector in South Asia: New Opportunities in the Global Market". *South Asian Survey,* Delhi, January-June 2001.
11. Lama, Mahendra P., *SAFTA—Benefits to Business Community,* Keynote Paper presented at the SAARC Business Leaders Conference organized by FICCI, New Delhi, 13 March 2006.
12. See a regional study done by Mahendra P Lama (Jawaharlal Nehru University, New Delhi), Rasul Baksh Rais (Quaid-e-Azam University, Islamabad)) and Faisal Bari (Lahore University of Management Sciences) on "India Pakistan Power Exchange: Assessment of Economic and Social Benefits", NEXANT /USAID / SARIE, New Delhi, May 2004.
13. We have taken information on this section from S. M. Burke and Lawrence Ziring, *Pakistan's Foreign Policy: An Historical Analysis,* 2nd edition (Karachi: Oxford University Press, 1990). pp. 10-11, 230-234.
14. Lama, Mahendra P and Rasul Baksh Rais, *Pipelines and Powergrids for Peace* (Kings College, London and International Centre for Peace Initiatives, Mumbai: 2001, p. 12.
15. Lama, Mahendra P & AR Kemal, *Cross Border Power Trade between India and Pakistan*, Jawaharlal Nehru University (JNU), New Delhi and Pakistan Institute of Development Economics (PIDE), Islamabad, sponsored by World Bank under South Asia Network for Economic Research Institutes (SANEI), 2002-2003.
16. For example in India, hydro sources constituted as high as 43 per cent of the total installed capacity in 1970-71 which steadily went down to present level of 25 per cent. This is despite the fact that the installed capacity of hydel power recorded a 44 fold increase from a mere 575 MW in 1951 to almost 25407 MW today. In Pakistan also the share of hydel power in the total installed capacity has gone down from 44 per cent in 1980-81 to 30 per cent in 1999. In Pakistan, the earlier installed capacity of 15996 in 1997 was shared by WAPDA (72% including

Kot Addu), private producers (17%), KESC (9.5%) and Karachi Nuclear Power Plant (0.85%). Government of Pakistan, *Economic Survey 1997-98*, p. 113 and *Statistical Abstract India, 1997*, Central Statistical Organisation, Department of Statistics, Ministry of Planning and Programme Implementation, New Delhi, p 176.

17. Lama, Mahendra P, Mohan Man Sainju & QK Ahmad, "Reforms and Power Sector in South Asia: Scope and Challenges for Cross Border Trade" in Mohsin S Khan (ed) *Economic Development In South Asia*, Tata McGRaw Hill, New Delhi, 2005.
18. Masood, Malik, "A Note on Pakistan Power Sector/WAPDA Restructuring and Privatisation and other Issues of Interest for South Asian Energy Forum", *South Asia Regional Energy Forum Proceedings*, USAID, Kathmandu, 1999.
19. The 500-KV transmission lines currently under construction in the public sector in Pakistan are estimated to be 1726 km long. An additional 1727 km of 500-KV transmissions lines are planned to be constructed by the private sector.
20. Statement by the Power Minister of Pakistan Gohar Ayub Khan, *Hindustan Times*, January 16, 1999. Also see Lama, Mahendra P, "Economic Reforms and Cross Border Power Trade in South Asia", *South Asian Survey*, New Delhi, September–December, 2000
21. On the south-western border, there are relatively few lines on the Pakistani side of Punjab. The only weak possibility of transmission appears to be in the areas of Fort Abbas and Faqir Wali grids (with relatively low KV) in Pakistani Punjab to the Indian lines near Anupgarh.
22. *The Military Balance*, Vol. 103, Issue, 2002-2004. The figure for Indian defence expenditure is for year 2003, and for Pakistan 2002.
23. See a regional study done by Mahendra P Lama (Jawaharlal Nehru University, New Delhi), Rasul Baksh Rais (Quais-e-Azam University, Islamabad)) and Faisal Bari (Lahore University of Management Sciences) on "India Pakistan Power Exchange: Assessment of Economic and Social Benefits", NEXANT /USAID / SARIE, New Delhi, May 2004.
24. Ministry of Overseas Indian Affairs, *Annual Report 2005-06*, Government of India, 2006, p 17.
25. World Bank, "Global Economic Prospects 2006," as quoted in *Economic Survey 2005-2006*, Ministry of Finance, Government of India, New Delhi, p 105.
26. Ibid. p. 105
27. International Monetary Fund, *Balance of Payment Statistics*, Washington, 2000.
28. Ministry of Overseas Indian Affairs, *Annual Report 2005-06*,

Government of India, 2006, p 17.

29. Ibid. p 4.
30. Ministry of External Affairs 2001, as quoted by ESCAP, *Dynamics of International Migration from India: Its Economic and Social Implications,* August 2003.
31. SAARC Regional Poverty Profile 2005, SAARC Secretariat, Kathmandu, 2006, p 134.
32. The General Agreement on Trade in Services (GATS) covers four different modes of supply :
    Mode 1 : Cross border supply of services (mode1)
    Mode 2 : Consumption abroad
    Mode 3 : Establishment of a commercial presence
    Mode 4 : Movement of persons providing the service.
33. Presentation by Manab Majumdar, WTO Division, FICCI, New Delhi, 2003.
34. UNDP, *Making Global Trade Work for People,* New York, 2003.

3. GLOBALIZATION :
THE TWENTIETH CENTURY OUTCOME

Sarika Dubey

Globalization has not just been a recent phenomenon some analysts have argued, that the world economy was just as globalized 100 years ago, as it is today. Basically Its a historical process, the result of human achievement, technological, and economic progress. It refers to the increasing integration of economies around the world, particularly, through trade, and financial flows. It has some distinctive features such as shrinking time, and disappearing borders. This results in mixing of culture, people, rituals and traditions. In the broader sense it is the reversible process of give and take. The term, sometimes also refers to the movement of people (labour), and knowledge (technology) across international borders, So Its a process interpreting not just the economy, but culture technology and governance. So It is a 'death of distance' and the essence is integrated world, with single order.

It describes the growing economic, political, technological, and cultural linkages, that connect individuals, communities, businesses, and government around the world. Globalization is the result of advances in communication, transportation, and Information technologies. It also involves the growth of multinational corporations (MNCs), and transnational corporations (TNCs). The International Institutions, that oversee world trade and finance, play very important role in this era of globalization.

Globalization has become the new buzzword that has come to dominate the world since the nineties of the last century with the end of the cold war and the break-up of the former Soviet

Union, which signaled the official "death" of state socialism, and the subsequent, demolition of Berlin wall; the "Asian Crisis", are some major examples in this regard which facilitated the "rejuvenation" of globalization at the fag end of the 20th century. This, actually re-established the accidental influence upon the world in all senses which resulted into a variety of phenomena-formation of new global market network; gradual decay of government sectors and rapid uprising of private sectors; mushrooming of MNCs, and NGOs, formation of WTO etc. as power centers; rise of G-7, G-10, G-22, OECD et. al., as regional blocks and policy co-ordination groups; invention of latest communication techniques (internet , cellular Phone, fax etc); germination of value based human rights; the scourge of AIDS on the human civilization-each possessing its own importance in respective domains.

The Globalization has brought in new opportunities to developing countries. Greater access to developed country markets and technology transfer hold out promise improved productivity and higher living standard. But globalization has also thrown up new challenges like growing inequality across and within nations, volatility in financial market and environmental deteriorations. Another negative aspect of globalization is that a great majority of developing countries remain removed from the Process.

Meaning and Definitions

The process of globalization is not new, it has long past. International trade relations among nations are also not new, but the pattern, the rules, and norms have changed in recent days. The Term global is an indicator of change. In the 1960s this came to be used to mean "belonging to the world" or "World wide" Marshal Mcluhan (1964)[1] uses the term "the global village" defining a property of the modern culture and believed that global communication and reception of far-off lights, and voices have changed the very concept, and content of culture according to him reason of transforming local life is the world wide network of communication.

The European Commission defines globalization as the process by which markets, and productions in different countries are becoming increasingly interdependent due to the dynamics of trade in goods, and services and flows of capital and technology. This indicates a new type of capitalism known as " flexible accumulation". (Harvey, D. 1989)[2]

Contemporary social scientists discuss globalization as a process by which the world is becoming increasingly interconnected, and unified, subject to homogenous, and uniform processes of cultural, technological and economic unification. This process replaces the concept of modernization, which mainly depends on the dualistic interpretation like " centre-periphery," "North – South" Developed—"Third World" distinctions, etc, (Dasgupta Samir, 2000)[3]

Theoretically, the concept of globalization may be viewed as the expansion of the world system, accompaniment of modernity, creation of a single world market, and a resultant of modernity. Of course, Beck (1993)[4] refers to it as a "Second modernity".

Stephen Gill: defines globalization as "the reduction of transaction cost of transborder movements of capital and goods thus of factors of production and goods."

Guy Brain Bant: Says that the process of globalization not only includes opening up of world trade, development of advanced means of communication, internationalization of financial markets, growing importance of MNC's, population, migrations, and more generally increased mobility of persons, goods, capital, data and ideas, but also infections, diseases, and pollution.

Jagdish Bhagwati states economic globalization means "the integration of national economics into the international economy through trade, direct foreign investment (by corporations and multinationals), short term capital flows, international flows of workers, generally, and as flows of technology". (Jadgish Bhagwati, 2004)[5]

In present scenario of globalization as we see it is a collection of processes in which economic, political, cultural, and other ties are made between different countries. This growing interdependence among nations is forming a new pattern, which have changed the life of people, Internet, fax machines, cellular phones, media networks are the new tools of globalization which are connecting people worldwide, increasing job availability, cross border monetary transaction, and spread of ideas etc. In this way a new type of relationship has emerged, where, boundaries, languages and cultural factors, are not creating hindrance in connecting peoples. Today globalization indicates a phenomenon identified interchangeably as a process, an historical event or the end result of shifting "ethno-techno, media-finance, and ideo-spaces" (Appadurai Arjun 1996)[6]

Simply we can say, globalization means.

(i) The fast movement of people, which results in greater interaction.
(ii) Because of IT revolution people can be in touch with each other in any part of the world.
(iii) The trade and economy of each country is open in non intrusive way so that varieties are available to consumer of his choice .
(iv) Means that the mankind has achieved emancipation to a level, where we can say, it means a social economic and political globalization.

International trade among nations is old phenomenon, statistics show that "Capital flows from the world economic core to the periphery, only $ 150 billion a year in the 1990s, have been less than 15 per cent of their investment and less than 5 per cent of the saving in the developed capitalist economies. These shares are much smaller than comparable figure before 1914, when they were both close to 50 per cent". In terms of internationalization of financial capital and trade, therefore, today's globalization does not seem that new compared to 1914. This was the case of 100 years ago. Now the question arises, what makes the current process of globalization new?

- This is different in terms of foreign direct investment (FDI)
- Increasing trade of services.
- Emergence of multinational corporations (MNCs) and transnational Corporations (TNCs). The U.N. reports that 350 transnationals produced and moved 30 per cent the total world output. This is bigger than the output of all the developing countries combined."
- The emergence of supra-national institutions, with full strength that regulate and enforce economic linkages at a world wide level is another new feature of today's globalization.

Historical Aspect and Development

The inner socio-economic and political spirit of globalization could be traced in the old, classical principle of the 'laissez faire' Policy which claims least government intervention and most freedom to the people in their activities. During the nineteenth century, the enthusiasm for the free- trade policy vanished, thanks to the increased degree of exploitation, that came along with the increased role of capitalism. But the end of the twentieth century shows the major political changes in international scenario, decline of the socialist empire in the world, and politically the world has come under a unipolar system, under the umbrella of the united states. The collapse of communism, and the demise of the Soviet Union in 1991, signaled a radical change in the global strategic framework. This post cold –war world has undoubtedly witnessed an advent of a new phase in international relations. This phase in better term often being described as the phase of globalization.

In the mid-1980s when one pole in the bipolar world collapsed, and went out of the reckoning. The United States emerged as the unrivalled centre of Power – the lone super power. The American economy enjoyed prosperity for an unprecedented decade or more. Despite the signs of downward trend, the U.S. economy is simply the largest in human history, and is the veritable dynamo, that projects the global economy. All the countries in the world have no choice but to accept the lone superpower. This period of transition to a future multipolar world can be called the "**Unipolar movement**" This international political ideological scenario has changed the strategic situation in the world, with the collapse of communism, the centrally planned command economies lost their credibility as models of development in much of the world. Marketisation of economies, and globalization of markets are the reigning doctrines in the post cold war world. Since communism failed, Capitalism is the presumed winner-a clear case of rushing to judgment. In this way during 1990s the world has witnessed the triumph of market-led capitalism of the advanced western capitalist countries, and every other nation-state has to come to terms with the demands of the capitalist dominated New World Order. Such a radical shift to the right in the political and the ideological context of the world has a significant impact on the ethos and strategies of development in

Asia, Africa and elsewhere (Babu 1996)[7] This is referred to as the new face *of liberal capitalism*.

This phenomenon further activated the process of the search for new markets in the developing countries in order to increase the profit and capital accumulation.

By the early 1980s, a large number of developing countries were having trouble, financing their foreign debts. Many third world countries including India faced a political and economic instability during this period International economic institutions like the IMF and the World Bank got directly involved in these countries by imposing certain conditions for loans and, require what are called *"structural adjustment programmes"* from borrowers. These programmes amount to detailed instructions on what countries have to do to bring their economies under control. The programmes are based on a strategy called *"neoliberalism"* also known as *Washington Consensus* (Harshe Rajan),[8] because both the IMF and the World Bank are headquartered in Washington D.C. The strategy is geared toward promoting free markets, including *Privatization* (The selling off of government enterprises) *Deregulation* (Removing rules that restrict companies); and *Trade liberalization* (Opening local markets to foreign goods by removing barriers to exports and imports). Finally, the strategy also calls for dismantling public sector, and downsizing governments around the world.

Three key institutions helped shape the current era of globalization: The International Monetary fund (IMF) , the World Bank, and the world Trade organization (W.T.O.), All three institutions trace their origins to the end of world war II (1939-1945) when the United States, and United Kingdom decided to set-up new institutions, and rules for the global economy. At the *Bretton Woods conference* in New Hampshire in 1944. These and other countries, created the IMF to help stabilize currency markets. Uruguay Round agreement brought the WTO into existence WTO agreements appear to be based on the hypothesis that liberalization is the Panacea for all ills in the economy, trade and commerce for the society.

Every member of the WTO has to accept "in its entirety a common set of rules, and disciplines covering goods, services, and intellectual property" (Richard Blackhurst)[9]

The Uruguay round agreement not only reduced trade barriers- by an average of 40 per cent—but also laid down rules for what kinds of policies governments can make on matters such as intellectual property and investment, making its impact more complex, more expensive to employment and more difficult to predict.

While world Bank, IMF and WTO are expected to work together, many other international organizations and agencies operate to regulate global political economy on the basis of agreements made by the nation-state. They are (Bhambhari, C.P., 2005)[10]

1. World Intellectual property organization;
2. International Organization for standardization;
3. Codex Alimentarious Commission;
4. International office of epizootics; and
5. International plant protection office.

All above organizations have to work in a particular global context, Ann e.o. Krueger says, that the World Bank, the IMF, and the WTO are expected to work in a coherent manner for dealing with global economy. She observes:

"The World Bank, IMF and WTO are instructed by their governments to achieve "Cohercnce" in economic policies between trade, financial, and development issues and the WTO has a mandate in this direction." (Anne O. Kruegger, 1999)[11]

Opportunities

Globalization, is ushering far-reaching changes in the political, economic, social, and cultural spheres across the world. It's multiplicity of linkages and interconnections between the states and societies has brought tremendous opportunities to the people world-wide. Due to removal of trade barriers, and its inter connectivity at all levels as economical, political, and technological, each person of national community have become the part of world society. This was the major change that came through globalization. In principle, globalization could offer the following opportunities:

1. Appropriately acquired, and correctly channelled, it could provide badly needed investment capital, that could enhance productive capacity.
2. Enhance easy flow of technology transfer.

3. Open markets for domestic products.
4. Makes a domestic economy more competitive by imposing work ethics, discipline, and overall productive efficiency.
5. Strengthen international division of labour based on comparable advantage.
6. It increases the choices for consumer; and
7. Generating employment

The Reality of Globalization: 20th Century Outcome

It was the common belief throughout the world, that globalization would bring prosperity for all human beings in each, and every part of the world, but reality is totally different. Recently there has been increasing disillusionment among policy-makers in several parts of the world and some fundamental questions are asked. These are: Why is globalization necessary? Who want globalization? What is the result of this? Do people want globalization? It is said, although the issue of globalization is receiving considerable attention yet there are no expected outcomes. It has increased poverty, inequality, unemployment, and tensions. The 20th century saw unparalleled economic growth, with global per capita **GDP** increasing almost five-fold. But this growth was not steady- the strongest expansion came during the second half of the century, a period of rapid trade expansion accompanied by trade and typically somewhat later, financial—liberalization. In the inter-war era, the world turned its back on internationalism-or globalization as we now call it and countries retreated into closed economies, Protectionism, and pervasive capital controls. This was a major factor in the devastation of this period, when per capita income growth fell to less than 1 per cent during 1913-1950. For the rest of the century, even though population grew at an unprecedented pace, per capita income growth was over 2 per cent. The fastest pace of all coming during the post-world war boom in the industrial countries. Though the century shows average income growth, it is also quite obvious that the progress was not evenly dispersed. The gap between rich and poor countries, and rich and poor people within countries have grown. UNDP informs as that,—"between 1960 and 1991 the share of the richest 20 per cent rose from 70 per cent of global income to 85 per cent while of the poorest declined from 2.3 per cent to 1.47per cent." And by

1999 the poor "more than 85 per cent of the world's population received only 15 per cent of its income" and "the net worth of 358 richest people, the dollar billionaires, is equal to the combined income of the poorest 45 per cent of the world population 2.3 billion people". (UNDP, Report)[12]

Globalization means that world trade, and financial markets are becoming more integrated. But just how far have developing countries been involved in this integration? A larger number of developing countries have made only slow progress or have lost ground. Pearson commission had attracted the attention of developed countries by pointing out that "the widening gap between the developed, and the developing countries has become the central problem of our times" and this gap has been further widened because of the concentration of finance capital in a "few capitalist countries" (Pearson Commission)[13].

Now we consider some aspects of globalization—

Trade—Though developing countries as a whole have increased their share of world trade, from 19 per cent in 1971 to 29 per cent in 1999, it has great variation among the major regions. For instance, the newly industrialized economies (NIE)s of Asia have done well, while Africa as a whole has fared poorly. Another feature is also very important related to country's exports. The share of primary commodities in world exports – Such as food, and raw materials— that are often produced by the poorest countries has declined.

Movement of People—Workers move from one country to another, partly to find better employment opportunities. The numbers involved are still quite small, but in the period 1965-90, the proportion of labour forces round the world, that was foreign born increased by about one- half. Most migration occurs between developing countries. But the flow of migrants to advanced economies is likely to provide a means through which global wages converge. There is also the potential for skills to be transferred back to the developing countries, and for wages in those countries to rise. But unfortunately in the present boundryless world some countries making rules to prohibit migration for their vested interest. The Hindu Reports—astonishing news that " No English no entry into U.K." thousands of immigrants will be affected by the British government's plans to make it compulsory for skilled migrants from outside the European Union (E.U.) to be able to speak, write and understand English before they are allowed to enter Britain"[14] Thousands of immigrants from the South-Asia Region (including developing countries) will be badly hit from the proposed rule. Actually the issue climbs on top of the domestic agenda of British Government to control migration to maintain racial character of the country. This is the dual character of western developed countries *who often claim to developing countries to* open their market under free trade policy of globalization. Actually this is the injustice of globalization. Though the policy of globalization recommends the best use of resources, because to provide cheap products to the people, but here is a paradox that the high tech. professionals like Engineers, Doctors, Scientists are the part of that resources, while the *unskilled labour* was not the part of that resources, So these *Brilliant brains* are invited by the western developed countries, but the unskilled labourers are prohibited to take benefit of this opportunity.

Spread of Knowledge (and technology:) is the other important aspect of discussion. Information exchange is an integral, often overlooked, aspect of globalization. For instance, direct foreign investment brings not only an expansion of the physical capital stock, but also technical innovation. More generally, knowledge about production methods, management techniques, export markets, and economic policies is available at very low cost, and it represents a highly valuable resource for the developing countries.

Inspite of all this a world bank study finds that the poorest 40 per cent of people in developing countries have seen their incomes fall since liberalization began. This powerful evidence discredits the claim of western government ministers that trade liberalization lessens poverty. The New Times (1983) reports that in the third world there are: starving—over 500 million; life expectancy under 60-1.7: billions; lacking medical care—1.5 billion; living in extreme poverty—over 1 billion; unemployed and underemployed—more than 500 million, annual per capita income under $ 150-800 million; illiterate adults—814 million ; children having no access to school education and unable to attend school—over 200 billion.[15]

J. Tinbergen (1976) notes, "we have a situation where, in the third world, millions of people toil under a broiling sun from morning till dusk for miserable rewards, and premature death without even discovering the reasons why." (Tinbergen, Jan, 1976)[16]

The statistics reveal that since the 1960s, (When globalization starting gaining strength) income disparity among countries had increased worldwide. It is evident from the various World Development Reports, that the wealthy countries have experienced a steady growth in their share of the world GNP, while the poorest countries have experienced with a tragic decline in their share of world GNP. Between 1960 and 1991, the richest fifth of all nations had its share of world income rise from 70 per cent to 85 per cent, while the poorest fifth of all nations had its share fall from 2.3 per cent to 1.4 per cent (UNDP, 1994)[17]

In reality globalization increased disparity among nations. Debt burdens have increased the ever growing gap between the developed, and the third world countries. According to the world Bank, the debt of developing countries rose by 8 per cent to just over $ 2 trillion in 1995. The third world debt has grown from $ 9 billion in 1955 to $ 572 billion in 1980, and 2177 billion in 1996. Its debt service –including interest and principal-is close to $ 245 billion in 1998—(Gelinas, 1998).[18] Debt is increasing in percentage of GNP as well the overall third world debt to GNP ratio reached 27 per cent in 1980 and 38 per cent in 1994. In this way the debt burden in the third world countries has reached 2 trillion dollars. All these countries have been destabilized as a consequence of the collapse of national currencies often resulting in the outbreak of social strife, ethnic conflicts, and civil war[19]

There may be some benefits of globalization but presently they are not in the reach of common people. Recent economic development shows the fact that in 1970 the total number of Transnational corporations (TNCs) was about 700, but grew by 1998 to at least 53,607. The six largest corporation in the world (Exxon, General Motors, Ford Mitsu, Daimler-Chrysler and Mitsubishi) have combined revenues larger than the combined budgets of 64 nations that include 58 per cent of the world's population (including India, Indonesia , Brazil, Russia, Pakistan, Bangladesh, Nigeria, And Mexico), (David, Dollar, 2001).[20] Only seven nations have budgets larger than Ford, Exxon. or General motors: namely France, the United Kingdom, Italy China, Japan, Germany and the United States. So the concentration of money is the biggest problem of globalization. The forces of global integration, and technological advance, can and must be harnessed to serve the interests of poor people. In 2000, of the world's 6 billion people, 2.8 billion live on less than $ 2 a day and 1.2 billion on less than $ 1 a day. Six infants of every 100 do not see their first birthday, and 8 do not survive to their fifth. Of those who do reach school age, 9 boys in 100 and 14 girls do not go to primary school. This is the reality of extraordinary disparity and inequality.

The world development report (2000-2001) accepts the view of poverty as encompassing not only low income and consumption, but also low achievement in education, health, nutrition, and other area of human development.

Challenges that Globalization Poses

If proper policies are not in place, especially in the transition period, globalization may be hazardous to our economic health. Some of these economic-health risks include-

1. There is threat to many of the world's small scale industries protected through national governments, due to the open market competitive trade policy.
2. Weakening or destroying whatever little productive capacity there is, particularly in the manufacturing sector due to world competition.
3. Complete vulnerability of the domestic economy to external shocks, particularly when the "freaky character" called speculative capital is involved as was recently witnessed in some Asian countries.
4. Increasing interference of international organizations such as WTO, IMF, or World Bank, on national governments of developing countries to put constraint and to pursue the policy of these organizations
5. Loss of sovereignty of governments.

Now the question arises, how to face such challenges? And what are the optimal policy options available to mitigate its ills and seize the opportunities? In principle each country has an option to either join the process of globalization or opt out of it completely. But as far as i think it would not be the right path to isolate from this, but there is need to make collective effort at domestic level or at the same time at international level.

At the Domestic front

1. Countries should develop their infrastructure first,
2. Identify and strengthen the strategic sectors, which they believe have a comparative advantage in, and invest in such sectors (as India in the computer industry, and Turkey in the textile industry seem to have done in recent years);
3. To establish some necessary institutions which would help the private sector in its drive to be competitive, and the government in designing its policies, such a co-ordination between the private and the public sectors seems to be in fashion in the developed countries in the age of a diminished direct role of the government on the economy.
4. To set-up an efficient bureaucracy that would facilitate smooth operations of the economy;
5. Design an economic policy that takes into account the forward and backward linkages, and links both short-term, and long-term growth of the economy;
6. Focus on skill development, that could easily adapt to modern technology, and negotiate skilfully in dealing with international (bilateral and multilateral) bodies.
7. To promote work culture in public institutions.

At the International front

(i) The very important thing is to maintain harmonious relations between developed, or developing countries so that, the western rich countries could understand the problems of third world.

(ii) Human development should be the core issue, not the economic development.

(iii) In place of profit oriented market economy, we should think about the human face of globalization.

(iv) International monetary organizations (WTO, IMF, W.B. etc.) should not impose their policies against poor, and in favour of western developed countries.

(v) The democratic set-up should be established in all the international institutions.

(vi) Request, that international institutions make funds

available to help countries develop their infrastructure, and human capital to be able to compete on an equal footing. This will include debt relief and other capacity enhancing measures.

(vii) Demand that, they be exempted, from maximum applicability of the stringent rules proposed by WTO—rules such as minimum labour standards, competition and investment policies and rules of environmental protection, at least during the transition period.

Lastly all the analysis shows that the still major part of the world is not the part of the benefits of globalization. Many of them are fighting for their survival. Actually the problem is not with globalization, the process of integrating people is not bad, but the problem is how to manage it? According to Joseph Stieglitz "Globalization today is not working. It is not working for many of the world's poor. It is not working for much of the environment. It is not working for the stability of the global economy————. The problem is not with globalization, but with how it has been managed. (Stieglitz, Joseph,, 2002)[21]. International Policy makers should think about this seriously. It is also seen that the western developed countries played major role in affecting policy issues in favour of their vested interest. So the role of these countries should be diminished in International rule making organizations, such as WTO, World Bank, IMF etc, and the democratic set-up should be established to maintain the equal status of all countries. Only then, we would be able to enjoy global happiness, global prosperity and the real globalization. It has been aptly said—-

"ये कैसी चली है, हवाएं तरक्की,
दिये तो दिये दिल, बुझे जा रहे हैं।"

References

1. McLuhan, Marshall, *Understanding Media,* London, Rutledge, 1964.
2. Harvey, D., *The Condition of Post Modernity*, Oxford, Blackwell, 1989.
3. Dasgupta, Samir, *The Changing Phase of Globalization* (ed) Sage Publications, New Delhi, Thousand Oaks, London, 2000.
4. Beck Ulrich, *Die Erfindeing des Politischen. Frankfurt: Suhrkamp,* as cited in Schuurman, Frans J. (ed) 2001. Globalization and

Development Studies, Vistar Publication, New Delhi, 1993.

5. Jagdish Bhagwati, *In Defence of Globalization*, London, Oxford University Press, 2004.
6. Appadurai, Arjun, 1996. *Modernity at large: Cultural Dimensions of Globalization*. Mannoapolis: University of Minnesota Press.
7. Babu, B. Ramesh (ed.), *Changing Global Political Ideological Context and Afro-Asia: Strategies for Development,* South Asian Publishers, New Delhi, 1996.
8. Harshe. Rajan (ed.), *Interpreting Globalisation : Perspectives in International Relations*, Rawat Publications, Jaipur and New Delhi.
9. Richard Blackhurst, *The Capacity of the WTO to fulfill its mandate* in Kruger (ed), N. 2, p. 33.
10. Bhambhari. C.P., *Globalization: India Nation State Democracy,* Shipra Publications, Delhi, 2005.
11. Anne O. Kruegger (ed.) "Introduction": in the WTO as an international Organization, Oxford University Press, Delhi, p. 14, 1999.
12. United Nations Development Programmes, Human development Report, 1996, New York. Also see David Harvey, " The Geography of class power", *The Communist Manifesto*, in Leo Panitch and Collin, Leys (eds.) Socialist Register 1998, Calcutta, K.P. Bagchi. 06, 1998, p. 66.
13. Pearson commission (commission on international development), Partners in Development, Praeger, New York, 1965.
14. *The Hindu* 10 Sep. 2007.
15. *The New Times* 1983.
16. Tinbergen, Reshaping the International Order. (A Report to the Club of Rome). New York: E.P. Dutton & Co., Inc., Jan. 1976,
17. UNDP (United Nations Development Programme). 1994. Human Development Report. New York. United Nations.
18. Gelinas, Jacques, B., *Freedom From Debt,* Dhaka: The University Press Limited, 1998.
19. World debt table in World Bank 1994.
20. David, Dollar, Globalization, Inequality and Poverty since 1980, (Washington D.C. World Bank), Mimeo, 2001.
21. Stieglitz, Joseph, *Globalization and its Discontents*, Allen Lone, Penguin Press, 2002.

4. INTERNATIONAL DEVELOPMENT AND NEW INTERNATIONAL ECONOMIC ORDER

As early as Oct. 1964, at the second non-aligned summit at Cairo, the leaders of 40 Non-aligned countries had declared that it is the duty of all countries to contribute to the rapid evolution of a new and just economic order under which all nations can live without fear or want or despair, and rise to their full stature in the family of nations. As a consequence of this appeal ten years later in May 1974, the U.N. General Assembly adopted the declaration on the establishment of a new international Economic order and a programme of action for its implementation. It has been more than three decades since the adoption of the declaration, but practical action has been lacking. Speaking before the Economic and Social Council on July 8, 1977, the British ambassador to the U.N. Mr. Ivor Richard said, "We are therefore prepared to support radical proposals for change, provided they are based on thorough analysis of the shortcomings of the present system, and provided they offer the prospect of improved performance."[1] It is to be noted that half of the human race is living below the level at which it is not possible to satisfy their basic needs in food, clothing, shelter, health and education. A quarter of humanity is living in actual poverty. There are about 350 million unemployed and some 700 million illiterate persons in the world.

It has been argued by the Developed countries that there was no point in being emotional, and using moral arguments regarding the questions of economic relations among countries.

But we should not forget that economic relations pertain to living people and are directly related to human misery. It is indeed morally wrong that people in the developed world waste as much energy daily as all the peoples in the developing countries use for productive purposes.

The demand for new international economic order (NIEO) is very much a political action. The third world countries who are championing the new order have neither the military nor economic power to match the dominant forces in the present world. Their strength lies in a consistent political programme which enunciates a set of principles, and demands policy approaches. The political programme has to be translated into a comprehensive coherent and consistent network of economic mechanisms and instruments. New institutional approaches are needed to direct the working of economic forces.[2]

A workable economic order wrote Keynes in his 'essays in Persuation one must combine economic efficiency with social justice and individual freedom. It could be argued that the existing world system has stood the test of economic efficiency. There have been overall increases in production. But this economic growth has not been translated via the mechanism of social justice into greater welfare for all. It has also not brought about greater individual freedom.

Equality is the keynote of the programme for the new international Economic order. The emphasis is on a more equitable distribution. The general political objective of equality should be translated into economic and political terms. Social and economic principles should become the prime motives of the new system. The right to work is one of the elementary human rights, full employment is however, an economic imperative. The right of everyone to a standard of living adequate for the health and well-being of himself and of his family, including food, clothing and housing, is another basic human right proclaimed in articles 25 of the Universal Declaration of Human Rights; the satisfaction of the basic needs is the economic imperative. The right to development has been accepted as an inalienable collective human right; the international development strategy is its economic counterpart. Thus the need today is to translate and transform general political objectives and principles into legal obligations and economic Schemes.

The political forces which are demanding the establishment of the New International economic Order (NIEO) set forth the principles of economic sovereignty real inter-dependence, non-discrimination, equity and justice as the basic pillars of the new order. Expressed in terms of economic instruments, these principles do not only mean a right to nationalization, but also a right to form international producer's association. They should signify the adoption of the whole international institutional framework so that it will implicitly favour the weaker members of the international community.

The question of economic development continues to be one of the fundamental problems facing the third world countries which are mostly non-aligned. The economic aspect of non-alignment is as important as the political dimension, and it is widely felt that the political independence of the third world countries is in many senses linked to this problem.

Secondly, the existing economic order works to the detriment of the non-aligned countries, and other developing nations. Stress is to be laid on the importance of co-operation and self-reliance among the members of the Third world community. This is indeed an essential prerequisite for a new economic order, and there is the need for South-South dialogue. Economic self-reliance does not however, mean the adoption of an isolationist posture. The need to control their own resources is essential for economic liberation.

Thirdly, there is also the urgent need of establishing regional economic co-operation within the third world nations. This is necessary in order to alleviate the problems facing the third world countries. It is suggested that emphasis should be laid on the need for collective economic policies by third world countries towards the Developed world for strengthening their own collective position, and through this, international economic co-operation. In particular co-ordination of manufactured products is to be emphasised. The developed countries are bound to create divisions within the third world community by giving preference to one group of non-aligned countries as against another. The third world should be on constant guard against this.

Fourthly, in future the third world countries should not only arrange development assistance among themselves, but also exchange experience and skills. In this regard the transfer of technology among third world countries offers precious opportunities for strengthening their economy.

Fifthly, the unfavorable consequences of depending too heavily on foreign aid should not be ignored. It may be difficult for the third world countries under present circumstances to forego all foreign aid from nations outside the third world community. However, alternative methods of financing development should be explored. In this connection it is suggested that bilateral schemes of development assistance involving all third world nations be established. It is also suggested that oil producers should recycle some of their surplus to those members of the third world community in need. It may also be suggested that dual pricing system or some other suitable compensatory mechanism beneficial to the members of the community be adopted.

Sixthly, since some third world countries are also importers of raw materials, it is suggested that associations of raw material producers should keep this in mind while fixing their prices. Negligence of this aspect might weaken the unity of this movement.

Seventhly, the need to consider what third world countries should do with respect to transnational corporation is also to be stressed. It is also to be noted that transnationals dominate the transfer of technology and capital in the third world. It is suggested that the members of the third world community should exhibit a greater degree of cooperation for setting up a common code of conduct to supervise the activities and behaviour of transnationals.

References

1. Janez Stanovnik: Towards the new international economic order, Yugoslavia, p. 13.
2. Ibid, p. 14.

5. INDO-US NUKE DEAL—A CHESSBOARD POLITICS

Shambhu Nath Chaudhary

Despite the media indulgence of writing epitaphs over the Indo-US Civil Nuclear Cooperation, the final word has not yet come from the government side that the deal is off. On the contrary the Prime Minister and several of his cabinet colleagues suggest at different public forums the benefits of nuclear energy for India. Even the winter session of Parliament witnessed intense debate over the issue, where the External Affairs Minister Mr. Pranab Mukherji gave a spirited reply to the doubts raised by CPI(M) and the opposition NDA. But the Left and the BJP were not fully convinced by the Government explanation and wanted that sense of Parliament must be taken, before further proceeding on the deal. In the meantime a fresh warning was issued by the Left to bury the deal or face mid-term elections. The CPM on Sunday served a warning to the Centre to "end talks with IAEA before December-end or face Lok Sabha mid-term elections". Party general secretary Prakash Karat made it clear that the only reservation the Left parties had was that the UPA government should not fall before the Gujarat elections lest the BJP would benefit. "We don't want the BJP to win the polls. We have to defeat the Modi government so we don't want to disturb the situation now," Karat said while addressing a meeting of the Delhi state CPM unit in the second week of December. But just on the eve of the second phase of poll in Gujarat Mr. Karat, has ruled out any immediate threat to UPA government and dismissed snap poll reports appearing in a section of media. In a press release, Karat clarified that he had never said that all parties should be ready for 'election any time' and questioned the timing of such reports on the eve of Assembly elections in Himachal Pradesh and Gujarat. He alleged that such reports were aimed at creating an atmosphere of insecurity about the central government and damage the UPA and left ties. So, the flip-flop on the deal continues. But it was on November 13 that the CPM threw a surprise and relaxed its tough stand on the deal, saying that the government can go ahead with the IAEA talks with the condition that no agreement will be signed without the approval of the UPA-Left committee on the deal. I will come to the issue of deadline threat or the prospect of mid-term poll at the end of story, but let me focus now on the sense of the latest debate in Parliament.

Government reaffirms its position in Parliament

Reaffirming its position on the Indo-US nuclear deal, the Government said the deal does not impact either the country's independent foreign policy or the right to conduct a future nuclear test. Maintaining there was a certain distance for the deal to travel, the Government said a final judgement on the deal should be passed only after it fructifies. Replying to the debate in the Rajya Sabha in the first week of December, External Affairs Minister Pranab Mukherjee reiterated that India's foreign policy remained independent. He asserted that India would be bound only by the 123 Agreement and not by the Hyde Act, which has certain "prescriptive and extraneous" elements. On the right to test - a point raised by the BJP - Mr Mukherjee said: "If we feel the test is necessary, we will do it. In the 123 Agreement, it has not been banned." He pointed out that if such a step is taken by New Delhi, "consequences will also follow" as in 1974 and 1998. At the same time, he noted that India was not in for "massive" weaponisation and favoured comprehensive universal disarmament. Mr Mukherjee said a judgement on the deal should be passed only after it is fructified. He said, in the past also the opposition questioned the Congress wisdom on important policy matters, be it on WTO or in the IT or Pharmaceutical sectors, but they had been proved wrong. Mr Mukherji asked the parties opposing the deal to give it a chance. He asked the BJP not to change its policy simply because it had changed seats (in Parliament) after going out of power. "Please give it a try". On concerns that nuclear power would be expensive, he said, "It appears too costly today, it won't be so tomorrow and gave the example of mobile telephony which with progress of technology became a cheap option. The Government, he said, was ready to take a sense of Parliament on the deal after completion of the process of implementing the agreement. "We have never said we will not take the sense of the House, let the process (of operationalisation of the agreement) be completed. We have begun the process and it is not complete yet," he said. Not satisfied with the over hour-long reply, the Left parties joined the BJP and UNPA in staging a walkout, insisting that the sense of the House be taken.

Prime Minister still Hopeful

Acknowledging that the Nuclear Deal with the united states was facing difficulties as some parties are opposed to it, Prime Minister Manmohan Singh said he was hopeful it will go through. Talking to reporters during election campaign in Gujarat, he said, there are difficulties as some political parties are opposed to it. To a question on the status of the deal, he said, "We have miles to cross as we have to go to international atomic energy commission and then nuclear suppliers group. It is an honourable agreement which will open new vistas of opportunities for our country with respect to energy security situation." "I have full faith in the people. Once more and more people become aware about the merits of the deal, they will come to a positive conclusion on it," the Prime Minister said.

A Brief Background of the Deal

The antecedents of the Indo-U.S. civilian nuclear agreement go back to the landmark agreement that was signed on July 18, 2005 by Prime Minister Manmohan Singh and President Bush. The terms of this agreement committed President Bush to seeking an adjustment of U.S. laws and international treaties to allow full civil nuclear cooperation with India. This was a path-breaking agreement because U.S. law specifically the Atomic Energy Act of 1954 prohibits nuclear commerce with nuclear weapons states that have not signed the Non-Proliferation Treaty (NPT) and accepted International Atomic Energy Agency (IAEA) monitoring of their nuclear facilities. India conducted nuclear tests in 1974 and 1998 and became a declared nuclear weapons state in the wake of the second series of tests. The U.S. and some other states reacted by imposing sanctions. The nuclear industry in India remained alive but entered a period of uncertainty with the possibility of eventually reaching a state of crisis. As a declared nuclear weapons state and a non-signatory to the Non-Proliferation treaty (NPT), India lacked access to the international atomic energy trade and was straitened for fuel supplies for its nuclear energy plants. In the absence of the agreement with the United States it would have been necessary to close down nuclear reactors and by extension the nuclear program. The agreement on civilian nuclear cooperation was received with considerable euphoria in many quarters in India precisely because it offered the prospect of release from India's nuclear isolation. But as it is said that the devil lies in the details. The more the negotiations became protracted, the more the media started raising doubts about the final outcome. Gradually the political parties mainly the Left brought the Nuclear Debate to the fore of the UPA agenda. In fact politbureau and central committee of the CPI(M) and its junior partner CPI became wary of the India's growing strategic ties with the US and started targeting the nuke deal to pin down the government to sell its own anti-American agenda. The tough stance of the government and the Left on the issue, even fuelled media speculations of mid-term polls. BJP led NDA and later the Third Front saw an opportunity to force a snap-poll and joined the Left bandwagon in opposing the deal and some sort of stalemate over the issue still persists.

US Reactions to the Civil Nuclear Cooperation with India

Having said so much about the Indian reactions on the nuclear cooperation with America, the readers in India were educated less on the US position on the deal. Initial reactions in the U.S. Congress to the Manmohan Singh-Bush agreement fell short of the euphoric. The leaders of the House International Relations Committee and Senate Foreign Relations Committee were unappreciative of the secrecy attendant on the negotiations that had preceded the nuclear agreement and the fact that Congress had not been consulted. There were concerns in Congress and among political analysts, nuclear scientists and arms control experts over the impact of the civilian nuclear agreement on U.S. non-proliferation objectives and the implications of according special treatment to India. As one analyst put it, the Bush Administration was in effect rewarding India for bad behaviour and proclaiming that having the bomb was OK provided the state in question was a U.S. ally. Then there was the issue of India's relationship with Iran. When hearings were held in the House International Relations Committee in early September 2005 on the civilian nuclear agreement, a number of legislators voiced reservations over the friendship and growing economic ties between India and Iran. At corresponding hearings that were held in early November in the Senate Foreign Relations Committee, Chairperson Richard Lugar expressed reservations on India's non-proliferation record. In view of less than positive responses in both Congressional panels, it seemed that Indian negotiators would be wise to maintain sober expectations as to the future of the Manmohan Singh-Bush agreement.

Despite initial reactions, an almost diametrically opposite scenario emerges from fast forwarding this account to summer 2006. On June 27, the House International Relations Committee voted 37-5 in favour of a resolution that would enable civilian nuclear cooperation with India. Two days later, the Senate Foreign Relations Committee awarded the corresponding resolution a 16-2 vote after a debate lasting only ninety minutes. Subsequently on July 27, the full House of Representatives voted overwhelmingly in favour of the Indo-U.S. agreement, handsomely defeating three proposed amendments two of which were viewed as potential deal breakers. In his introductory remarks, Tom Lantos (D-California) co-author of the legislation spoke of the agreement as a tidal shift in ties between the U.S. and India and of being positioned at the hinge of history, building a fundamentally new relationship with India. Less flowery but not less momentous words were used by Senator Richard Lugar (R-Indiana), Chairman of the Senate Foreign Relations Committee, at the June 29 debate on the bill in the Senate Committee when he referred to the nuclear agreement as the most important strategic diplomatic initiative undertaken by President Bush. Meanwhile, the enactment of the Hyde Act changed the political discourse in India and vehement opposition to it made Mr Hyde a household name in India, without being aware of what it entails in terms of pursuing of an independent foreign policy. Mr Hyde died recently, but his name continues to haunt the deal-makers and deal-breakers on Indian side.

What is Hyde Act ?

In view of continuing debate on the implications of the Hyde Act on the Agreement, it is necessary to decipher the true meaning of it and its implications for Indian security and foreign policy. Article 2.1 is being interpreted by American policy analysts that the 123 agreement is subject to all the present internal laws of the U.S. government, right from the U.S. Atomic Energy Act 1954 to the Hyde Act 2006. They further add it will be subject to amendments to these present laws and to any new law that may be enacted in the future. The fact is that the 123 Agreement will be implemented, as has been emphasised by Nicholas Burns, the U.S. Under-Secretary for Political Affairs and a key member of the U.S. negotiating team, in a manner fully consistent with the Hyde Act. India made it clear on a number of occasions that the Act is not binding on the 123 agreement. Some analysts say, what is important to understand about the Hyde Act is that it is divided into binding and non-binding parts. The non-binding parts are fluff, designed to keep congressman happy. They are not enforced and are not acted upon when the bill becomes law. Almost all the parts the Left and Right have objected to are in the non-binding sections. And the evidence of their irrelevance lies in the fact that not one clause of the non-binding parts is present in the 123 Agreement, the only document India has to act upon. The few clauses in the binding parts that some have objected to require nothing of India. The segments of the Hyde Act that are causing all the flurry. All of them are non-binding and, therefore irrelevant:

Bush Allays Concerns on the Hyde Act

Seeking to allay concerns in India over the Nuclear deal, President Bush has assured Prime Minister Manmohan Singh that what India sees as prescriptive provisions will not be American foreign policy. "Extraneous and prescriptive provisions of the Hyde Act are only advisory and will not be my foreign policy," he said.

In a statement issued shortly after signing the Henry J Hyde US-India Peaceful Atomic Energy Cooperation Act on Monday, Bush indicated that he did not agree with provisions like Section 103 and Section 104(d)(2) in the legislation. Section 103 of the Act contains provisions on India's co-operation in containing Iran's nuclear programme, India halting fissile material production and appears to dilute fuel supply assurances.

It also suggests that the US would oppose development of a capability to produce nuclear weapons by any non-nuclear weapon state within or outside the Nuclear Non-Proliferation Treaty (NPT) regime. Section 103 of the Act purports to establish US policy with respect to various international affairs. My approval of the Act does not constitute my adoption of the statements of policy as US foreign policy. Given the Constitution's commitment to the presidency of the authority to conduct the nation's foreign affairs, the executive branch shall construe such policy statements as advisory," Bush said. The section also says that the US would work with Nuclear Suppliers Group (NSG) members to further restrict transfers of equipment and technologies related to uranium enrichment, reproccssing of spent nuclear fuel and production of heavy water to all countries, including India. However, Bush said that it would not be binding on his government thereby opening up the doors for transfer to India of items not approved by the NSG. These aspects in the Bill are being seen with concern in India, leading to demands there that the agreement be terminated. The statement said section 104(d)(2) of the Act was 'construed to prohibit the executive branch from transferring or approving the transfer of an item to India contrary to NSG transfer guidelines that may be in effect at the time of such a transfer, a serious question would exist as to whether the provision unconstitutionally delegated legislative power to an international body'." In order to avoid this constitutional question, the executive branch shall construe section 104(d)(2) as advisory. The executive branch will give sections 103 and 104(d)(2) the due weight that comity between the legislative and executive branches should require, to the extent consistent with US foreign policy," Bush said. The executive branch shall construe provisions of the Act that mandate, regulate, or prohibit submission of information to the Congress, an international organisation, or the public, such as sections 104, 109, 261, 271, 272, 273, 274, and 275, in a manner consistent with the President's constitutional authority to protect and control information that could impair foreign relations, national security, the deliberative processes of the Executive, or the performance of the Executive's constitutional duties," the President added.

Why the Deal a must for India ?

Citing the heritage of Nehru, Indira and Rajiv Gandhi, the PM told the daylong AICC meeting last month that India was too big a country to be bent by another nation in any direction. He raised the nuclear deal to clear the air and take the party cadres along. The delegates applauded when Singh asserted that the deal was a must for the country's development. Explaining the rationale behind the pact, he said it would open new avenues for supply of nuclear fuel and technology. If the country has to progress, it's imperative to look for alternative sources of power. The existing reliance on coal and hydro-power will not fulfill the energy needs, he said. "The civil nuclear agreement is an effort to open closed doors to obtain nuclear fuel and technology from other countries. You need to understand this reality and explain it to the people," he exhorted the Congressmen. Comparing the Congress-led UPA government's three-and-a-half years' rule with that of the NDA regime, Singh said the country is experiencing all-round growth as against the misplaced India Shining slogan of the previous government. The civil nuclear agreement between India and the US would help create a substantial additional power generating capacity in the country. As per the government estimates, the Integrated Energy Policy-2006, which sets a target of 20,000 MW of nuclear power generation by 2020, could double with international cooperation. Regarding the financial gains the country would have from the nuclear accord, it thinks that energy from this non-conventional source will contribute in the growth of vital sectors, including industry and agriculture. It is also critical that India's current GDP growth rate of 8 to 10 per cent per annum is maintained in order to achieve the objective of eradication of poverty. Government says, it is necessary to explore and exploit all sources of energy, and the inclusion of nuclear energy will help in meeting India's energy targets and contribute to growth in vital sectors, including industry and agriculture. At present share of nuclear power in India is a low 2 per cent while in some of the larger economies such as France, this share is 78 per cent, or for that matter US, Switzerland it is 20 per cent. For a country like India, this share has to go up. Experts also say that nuclear energy is important keeping in mind the high global fuel prices as well as for tackling climate change issues.

Deal will end India's Nuclear Isolation

Highlighting the importance of ending India's isolation from the nuclear community, International Atomic Energy Agency (IAEA) chief Mohammad ElBaradei said that this would not only benefit India as it would give it access to fuel and technology, but getting India into the nuclear "mainstream" was important for the global efforts towards eliminating all nuclear weapons. Speaking at the HT Leadership Summit in October, ElBaradei said that Indo-US nuclear deal would just be a "trigger" to "liberate (India) from the restrictions of the 45 (Nuclear Suppliers Group) countries". While ElBaradei stayed away from commenting on the current political stalemate on the nuclear deal, he said that he was concerned about the "end" and not the "means" by which India comes out of the isolation it faces from the NSG. When asked about the importance attached to nuclear energy, ElBaradei said India needs access to all forms of energy, including nuclear energy, failing which it "cannot sustain 9 per cent growth". In fact, later in a press conference ElBaradei said: "It is just about time when India is free from restrictions imposed since 1974 to be able to interact freely in nuclear technology market both as a recipient and a supplier in the nuclear field". In his interpretation, India is a nuclear weapons state. "It doesn't make much difference whether this was de facto or de jure. ElBaradei, while outlining on what the entire process entails said that this was "standard procedure" involving "standard documents" that just need to be "tailored to make them India-specific".

The Concerns of the Left on the Deal

Ever since the details of the 123 agreement were made public, the Left parties had demanded that the deal should not be operationalised while the government maintained that there was no going back on the issue. The Left concerns are about "certain aspects of the agreement, the implications of the Hyde Act on the 123 agreement and self-reliance in the nuclear sector, the implications of the nuclear agreement on the foreign policy and security cooperation. The UPA-Left panel after its half a dozen rounds of meeting failed to break the impasse. Even after the government clarified that 123 agreement is not bound by Hyde Act, that New Delhi is free to conduct an atomic test when the need arises, that the agreement will allow the perpetuity of fuel supply with a strategic reserve and it does not compromise country's strategic program, the Left leaders are not convinced. Though some of these issues are under negotiation process, the Left has issued a fresh ultimatum on the deal. Government has also made it clear that 123 agreement is only a passport and that it will conduct nuclear commerce with 45 member NSG on cost-benefit manner, but there are no takers for this argument in the Left bloc. As far as the BJP is concerned, their opposition to the deal seems to be more influenced by the political considerations rather than on the foreign and security related matters, as under the NDA, there was a similar attempt to seal a similar agreement.

Deal or Election

The moot point is now, whether the government will go ahead with the deal even sacrificing the government at the centre. My guess is that it would be very difficult for the UPA to backtrack on it after taking over two-year long protracted negotiations to a final outcome. Moreover, it will also adversely affect New Delhi's position in the international arena, as it was sold to most of the powerful countries dealing in nuclear trade. But much will depend on the outcome of the Gujarat elections. It is certain that the opposition of the Left is not so much to the deal per se, but more to the growing strategic cooperation between India and the United States. This is all the more bewildering when the government made it quite clear that it has strategic relationship with ten important countries of the world including with the tried and tested old friend Russia. The fourth additional Koodankulum reactors could not fructify during the Prime Minister's recent visit to Moscow, as the Indo-US deal is not yet complete. Unless an India-Specific safeguards agreement with the IAEA is complete and New Delhi gets a clean NSG waiver, it cannot enter into nuclear trade with any country. This is the point, the government must drive home that there is continuity in foreign policy-government may come and go, but policy remains and until the deal is sealed, India's 30 year old nuclear isolation also remains. So, it may happen that deal and election both will reach to their logical conclusion, but the role of parties depending on minority votes will be important, as the left is hell bent to prove its anti-American policy linking with its opposition to the deal. The question remains, Will the government be ready to take this calculated risk?

6. THE ISSUES OF ENVIRONMENTALISM IN WORLD ARENA

Sanjay Barnwal

The present paper is an attempt 'to deal with the issue at length, not only for the purposes of academic pursuit but also with a personal enthusiasm to ensure the issue discussed and adhered properly. The paper is divided into five parts- the first one is concerned with the introduction of the issue, followed by the theoretical foundations of the concept in the second part, the third part introduces the various menaces and consequences in this respect, part four focuses on possible solutions and the last one is a few words in the form of final remarks.

Introduction

Today, environmental problems are approaching us alarmingly. The menace needs to be handled with utmost care and sensitivity if human extinction has to be avoided in coming centuries keeping in view the gravity of the issue in 2007 the noble peace prize has been awarded to the U.N. body on climate-. Intergovernmental panel on climate change (headed by Mr. Rajendra Pachauri) and to the former U.S. Vice-President Mr. AI-Gore, who too is championing this cause for years.

With the disintegration of USSR and dismantling of communist regimes in East Europe in 90's, the victory of liberalism has been proclaimed with great fanfare but "liberalism" itself is facing challenges from four quarters for the last few decades: '

(i) Post Modernism

(ii) Communitarianism
(iii) Feminism
(iv) Environmentalism"[1]

In this connection, U.N. under-Secretary General Shashi Tharoor has come forward with a new nation of "problems without passport" which means - problems which cross all frontiers uninvited, problems of proliferation of WMD, of degradation of our common environment, of chronic starvation and human rights, of mass illiteracy, and massive displacement."[2] Such problems require solution that cross all frontiers because no single country or group of countries can solve them alone, which is why the issue of environmentalism emerged at world arena and also incorporated into academic pursuit.

Theoretical Foundation of the Concept

Environmentalism deals with the matters of ecology by placing nature at the focus of study. To it, 'man' is one of the many species who exist in 'nature'. This disagrees with the 18th century view that science and technology will help us to control and harness nature. They discard the notion of using nature only as a resource base, as a means to human ends, rather they adore the concept of sustainable development.

The literal meaning of the term environment is \- "surrounding of an object in nature". Derived from French world "environ" or "environner", meaning around, round about, or surround in English usage the term refers to the totality of things or circumstances around an organism."[3] The term broadly indicates the surrounding of an individual-organism ranging upto the entire biosphere (the zone of earth that is able to sustain life). By surround is meant all the non-living and living materials that play any role in the organism's- existence- from soil and air to what an organism feeds on and the organisms that may feed on it. Other factors like heat light and gravitation acting on an organism, also constitutes its environment.

The biological existence of all organisms depends on the harmonious relationship naturally maintained with eco-system. A living and non living organism present in the atmosphere are the part and parcel of the environment. If there is balanced 'harmony' among them it is called environment, if the 'balance' is disturbed, it is pollution. In simple terms pollution can be defined as "introduction of harmful toxic substances in the air, water and land."[4]

Even ecology is different from environment, because the former is the scientific study of inter relation of plants, animals and environment, it studies interactions between organisms of same kind and its environment.

Moreover, the, theory of environmentalism attempts to do two things:

(i) it is critical of conventional ways of thinking about human beings and their proper place in natural world.

(ii) It is constructive, for, it aims to point out the institution of a society that values the natural world, practises sustainability and discusses the long term implications of present policies and strategies.

Global-Menaces

As regards menaces, these are manifold and big in magnitude. A UNESCO report elaborates the environmental crisis in following words: "Imperfect understanding of the natural systems and mechanisms which make possible the' maintenance of life on earth, disregard of the unintentional efforts of technology, in particular the various forms of pollution, poor management of soil, forests and water, unbridled consumption of fossil fuels, uncontrolled urbanization, the relegation of rural population to a marginal position, and crushing of traditional cultures- these are the obvious and most frequent disadvantages of the changes, that are taking place in the relation between man and his environment."[5] Thus population blast, lust for luxurious life and consumerism, illiteracy and poverty, mechanization, industrialization etc, are the main threats to environmentalism.

In fact, with the advent of industrial revolution, in the West, the need for exploitation of nature and natural resources became inevitable, caused disastrous effects on the whole biosphere and its existences. The adverse effects are: Ozone depletion, pollution of air, water, and noise, deforestation and desertification, droughts, flood havocs, acid rain, rise in sea level (due to global warming), soil and marine pollution." By 1950 half of the world's forest cover was wiped out. Every year about 146 lakh hectare forests are cleared which, in turn, is causing desertification, some 800 species of plants and animals have disappeared, and 11000 are at the verge of extinction, due to the destruction of their home, 1/4th of the earth has been converted into deserts, 80 per cent of European and 70 per cent of the Asian sea coasts are lamenting marine pollution."[6] 70 per cent of the earth's mass is covered with water but only 2.5 per cent of it, is potable.

According to an estimate, by 2025, 66 per cent of the world's population would not be able to avail even safe drinking water. "Pure oxygen, the very life line of living beings is rapidly decreasing while CO_2 is at rise. Dust particles are multiplying in the air due to the increasing number of vehicles. These dust particles, named aerosol are ruining the greenery of plants."[7] "The waste of under power plants, now deposited under the sea, are not only causing contamination to fish and other marine fauna but in addition to it there is much greater danger of the contamination of air and water due to the modern agricultural technology. The use of uranium, for obtaining energy, produces waste also which is radioactive for 1000 years. These radioactive particles persist in the soil and contaminate subsequent generation of plants and animals and the people who eat them."[8]

The various expedition missions to Antarctica, are also causing concern among scientists, as the remnants left there, are signalling disturbing trends. Moreover, environmental scientists have measured "a significant slowing in Atlantic currents that :carry warm water towards northern Europe. If the trend persists, the weather there could cool considerably. "[9]

In mid March 2007, the World-Wide Fund for Nature (W.W.F.) made an assessment of the world's 10 magnificent rivers. It warned that time may be running out for rivers. Deeply divisive conflicts, casting their shadow over river water agreements, are all too familiar to us. In addition pollution, dam building, excessive extraction of water, climate change and over fishing are affecting the health of rivers. The WWF projection denotes that annual renewable Ganga's flow could slip into a situation of scarcity by 2025, though present supply is ample. Climate change may also affect the Himalayan glaciers which provide an·estimated 30-40 per cent of present flow to Ganga.[10]

Global warming could change the face of our planet within the life time of our children and grand children. Global warming means- that the temperature of the earth is rising due to the massive emission of poisonous green-house-gases (GHG)- carbon-di-oxide, Nitrogen Oxide, Methane, Carbon mono Oxide, Sulphur Di-Oxide- in the atmosphere. These gases cover the earth, consequently the heat emitted on the earth, does not cross its atmosphere because of the cover of GHG's"[11]

According to a U.N. report "in 2000, some 1,50,000 people died unnaturally due to the ill-effects of global warming."[12] Inter governmental panel on climate change (IPCC) released its 4th report in Feb. 07, under U.N. auspices. According to it, climate change is a reality. Global temperature may rise by 1.8 to 6.4 degree celsius by end of the 21st century. In its previous report 6 years back, climate scientists made assertions by 66-90 per cent certainty only. Now the confidence level has crossed 90 per cent mark. The report warms that existing gas levels (GHG's) in the atmosphere can continue the warming process for centuries. Even agro production might decrease, resulting in famine and acute scarcity of drinking water and an increase in vector- borne diseases. "IPCC chairman Prof. Rajendra Pachauri has strongly" emphasized that if no action was taken on reducing emission of GHG's this would melt glaciers. Research about Gangotri, India's largest glaciers, has found that the rate for retreat has almost doubled to 34 meters a year compared to what it was in 1971."[13] This will bring grave catastrophe for hundreds of millions of people living in low lying coastal areas from Bangladesh to Newyork, China to Nether-lands".[14] Apprehension is that due to rise in sea levels, some island states may sink into the sea. Moreover, massive floods, droughts, storms, heat waves, competition for natural resources could threaten the life of countless millions. Hurricane Wilma which hit Florida in Oct. 2005, was confirmed as the strongest one ever recorded. IPCC report further predicted South Asia" to be the worst affected region due to the climate change. The U.N. Environment Programme included India among the 27 countries that are most vulnerable to sea level rise. About a quarter of India's population lives within 50 (km.) of coast line which might face massive displacement in the event of rise in sea-level. An increase in sea level could also lead to salt water entering the ground water acquifers on which *people* depend for drinking water, and to irrigate their fields. Another study reveals that "an area with multi-story buildings is warmer in comparison to the other having lesser numbers of multi-story buildings, because bricks trap the heat of the sun and then release it in the atmosphere adding to the rise in temperature."[15] Due to the excessive extraction of natural resources, the existence and availability of global commons is at stake.

Moreover, the burning of fossil fuels is causing great amount of GHG's which in turn is absorbed by the people through breathing. According to report, top 10 polluting states are as following:

"1.	U.S.A.	-	20.6%	6.	Germany	-	2.9%
2.	China	-	14.8%	7.	Brazil	-	2.5%
3.	Russia	-	5.7%	8.	Canada	-	2.1%
4.	India	-	5.5%	9.	Britain	-	2%
5.	Japan	-	4%	10.	Italy	-	1.6%"[16]

Thus U.S.A. is the biggest polluter while India stands at 4th place. Nearly 37.5 per cent pollution is caused by just 7 states of North.

Rising temperature draws special attention because last 10 years have been the warmest years on record, barring 1996, with 1998 being the warmest so far, 2005 was the second warmest year on record."[17] Further global warming could melt almost all of the top layer of Arctic perrnofrost by end of the century." The thaw would release vast stocks of carbon-di-oxide into the atmosphere, threaten ocean currents and wreck roads and buildings across Canada, Alaska and Russia. Permafrost (defined as soil that remains below freezing for at least two years) would react to the earth's changing climate.[18]

Like global warming, the theory of global collapse has been put forward by Lord Mayo, David King, and Jared Diamond. These environmental scientists warn that, climate change, resource depletion and population imbalances are interrelated dangers and that "it is necessary tackle them all at once if we are to have any chance of avoiding global collapse. To Mayo- society in Mexico collapsed due to the depletion of resources like trees. Climate change makes some areas less hospitable, resulting in strain in the international financial system".[19] Today when, one part of the world gets into trouble, it can be quickly exported to the other parts. If modern civilization collapses, it will do so everywhere. Everyone now falls or stands together. Global collapse does not mean the end of the world.

The collapse of modern civilization would entail the deaths of billions of people but not the end of the human race. Some would survive, the end of industrial age by reverting to pre-industrial life style.

Like global-collapse, another major concern of the scientists is "globaldimming", which means- the sun rays which fall upon the earth are now getting dim day by day, thus giving birth to the possibility of darkness on this planet. Thus the very existence of light itself is apprehended. The reason for this is happenings on the earth itself. "This research was first conducted in 1985 in Swiss Federal Institute of Technology and was later on ratified by researches in Japan, the then U.S.S.R., and Ireland."[20]

This is why noted environmental scientist Stephen Hawking asked to explore possibility of life on another planet because, the planet earth is not worth living.

Thus altogether environment related problems are two fold:

1. Preservation of environment
2. Development of environment.

Solutions

In order to address the challenge genuinely efforts need to be adopted at three levels

(i) at the global level
(ii) at the state level
(iii) at the individual level

Beginning with the Lake Sakes summit in 1949 various efforts have been made to face the environmental challenges. These included-Stockholm Summit 1972 and consequent foundation of UN Environment Programme, the U.N. General Assembly resolution on Nature 1982, World Commission on Environment and Development 1986; Earth Summit at Rio in 1992, UN Earth Summit at Newyork 1997, World Summit on Environment and Green House at Kyoto (Japan) 1997, Earth Summit at Johanesberg in Aug.-Sept. 2002. Among these, the World Commission on Environment and Development was significant where from arose the concept of sustainable development. The commission published a report in 1987 titled "Our Common Future" in 'which environment and development were not seen as paradoxical rather as complementaries because both are equally necessary for onward march of human society. It defined sustainable development as.- "the development that meets the need of present without compromising the ability of the future generations to meet their own needs."[21] The definition involves 3 "E"'s (i) "Environment" = development should be environment friendly. (H) "Economic Efficiency" = it should be economically sound (H) "Equity" = needs of poor have been accepted. Later in 1992 Human Development Report clarified the notion as, "Sustainable development does not mean only environment protection. It implies a new concept of economic' growth, one which provides fairness and equal opportunity for all, not the privileged few, without destroying the world's finite natural resources."[22] Further in 1992;, from 3-14 June under the U.N. auspices at Rio in Brazil representatives from 172 states and 2000 NGO's gathered in the most significant Earth Summit, which was organized at the occasion of 20th anniversary of Stockholm Summit of 1972. The final resolution passed, called for inter dependence of environment and development and regarded "Earth" as the home of mankind. Besides, the resolution provided for agreement on biodiversity, sustainable development, commission and aid to the developing countries. It also demanded cut in emission of CO_2. It adopted Agenda-21 which is a comprehensive document containing ways to protect and development of environment, ocean, temperature and bio diversity.

Here at this juncture, differences between North and South came to the fore. The South believed that the North has caused environmental problems by squeezing the nature, therefore they should bear the cost of cleaning the environment but South itself does not adhere to the principles related to the environment. Moreover, the U.S.A. did not agree to the agreement on biodiversity but the treaty of biodiversity which originated with Earth summit 1992, came into force in Dec. 1993, even with the exclusion of U.S.A.

In Dec. 1997, at Kyoto World Environment Conference or Green House Conference was held, with a view to cut emission of GHG's. After hectic deliberations, Kyoto- Protocol was signed and accordingly states were required to cut GHG's emission at different levels:

— Between 2008-2012 it will be 7 per cent for the U.S.A.
— Between 2008-2012 it will be 8 per cent for the E.U.
— Between 2008-2012 it will be 6 per cent for the Japan
— Between 2008-2012 it will be 5.2 for other 21 industrial States from the level of 1990.

In the first phase China and India were exempted from emission. On 16th Feb 2005, this treaty came into being when 156 states ratified it with the exclusion of U.S.A., Australia and Canada but with the inclusion of E.U. and Russia. Altogether, Kyoto Protocol, only sets target for reduction in emissions of G.H.G.'s. It did not envisage a phasing out or substitution of fossil fuels.

In August last and September first week, 2002, at Johannesburg (South Africa) World summit on sustainable development was held, hosted by the U.N. commission on sustainable development at the 10th anniversary of Earth Summit of 1992. This was 'well attended by 106 Prime Ministers and Presidents and some 6000 delegates. One major goal of the summit was to put the sustainable development again on global agenda. The most important provisions agreed upon, was reducing the two billion world population which lacks access to water and proper sanitation by half, by 2015, reducing the loss of bio diversity by 2010 and promoting good governance. However, dead lock persisted on phasing out farm subsidies by the North. Key points passed in the resolution were: "All states to ratify Kyoto Protocol in timely manner to reduce loss of species by 2015, to phase out agricultural and other trade distorting subsidies, emphasis on need to fight corruption and promote democracy but not as a condition to receive aid."[23]

Thus growing concern for the environmental cause brought nation states to the negotiation table whereby they are required to part away a meagre quantum of their external sovereignty for the greater cause of humanity. Today, due to the ecological inter-dependence there is a transition of the international society from a mere community of states to a larger canvas encompassing individuals, groups and corporate.

"The dangers are real, therefore, three below mentioned principles should guide US".[24]

(i) Be aware and prepare. As 2005 showed us, no state is

immune from the effects of extreme disasters. So one dollar invested in disaster reduction today can save upto 7 dollars tomorrow in relief and rehabilitation cost. Even IPCC report of Feb. 2007 says—if 3 per cent of the global G.D.P. is spent on checking global warming, 3 degree Celsius temperature can be reduced by 2030. There is a special responsibility on the part of the advanced industrialized countries, accountable for massive GHG's in atmosphere yet they seek commitments from developing states, who also want good life standards of living for their nationals. In fact, "industrial countries should render financial and technical support to the developing economics in reducing emissions simultaneously, the former also must make some sacrifices on their own part, then only sustainable development can be achieved."[25]

(ii) We need to strengthen our resilience to disasters. Disasters can erase gains of decades overnight. Towards this end, the U.N. has formed a new global partnership for risk reduction, that harness support from governments, the world Bank, N.G.O.'s and civic groups.

(iii) We need to go back to the basics. Disaster risk reduction is fundamentally a matter of education and communication well prepared evacuation plans, better land usages, and environmental policies, public awareness campaigns, these and more steps can be taken to help to mitigate tomorrow's threats.

In this connection, some light deserves to be thrown on footing of individual state. The U.S.A., biggest contributor of G.H.G.'s, refuses to accept Kyoto Protocol, citing high cost as reason. However many Americans have privately become deeply worried about global warming. "As a result north- eastern American states have announced that they are about to launch their own carbon system and several U.S. companies including General-Electric- have begun to cut emissions from their plants."[26] California the most populous state of the U.S., is the first to put up a cap on G.H.G.'s emission for utilities, refineries, and manufacturing plants. In America, in the end of Dec. 2006, the U.S. fish and wild life service was considering to add polar bear to its list of threatened species. Thus, at least debate and deliberations are going on in the U.S.A.

also. Moreover, when IPCC report appeared in Feb. 2007 two legislators in California proposed to ban iconic invention incandescent light bulbs in favour of much more energy efficient compact fluorescent bulbs. "Every C.F.L. bulb would reduce 1300 pounds CO_2 being pumped into atmosphere by power plants."[27] A similar culture of efficiency in power generation, industrial manufacturing and automotive sectors can cut Giga-tonnes of emissions. These actions give us hope that the U.S.' government will soon show more sensitivity to this cause.

As regards Europe, in February '07 at Brussels, a meeting of environment ministers of Europe was held which agreed to cut over all CO_2 emission 20 per cent by 2020 and were ready to go to 30 per cent if other industrialized would match European efforts to curb global warming. European Union (E.U.) also sought CO_2 cut from emerging economies like China, Brazil, Mexico, South Africa and India. Further "people of Sydney showed their concern by observing one-hour black-out."[28]

In fact, meaningful cut in G.H.G.'s will require industrialised as well as rapidly industrialising countries to act in unison. After a recent meet in Washington D.C. in Feb. 07, Lawmakers from G-8 and China, India, South Africa, Mexico, Brazil (G-8+5) issued a landmark statement asking their governments to sign 'upto a measurable long term goal to stabilise G.H.G. concentration in the atmosphere. The G-8+5 account for 2/3 of the global emissions.

India and China are exempted from Kyoto protocol even though they are pumping massive amount of CO_2. They risk becoming heavily dependent on carbons for decades if they invest a new in power generation facilities based on fossil fuels. In fact China and India's emissions have increased by 67 per cent and 88 per cent respectively since 1990 and their share is projected to grow steadily in the decades to come. A meaningful solution, thus, demands active participation of China and India also.

Former chief economist of the World Bank Sir Nicholas Stern presented a report to the British government in November 2006, and accordingly, "there would be a loss of 1per cent of global G.D.P. caused by extreme weather. Such a loss will affect everyone including India and China. In 1992, when the problem was first addressed there was an agreement that poorer countries should not be penalised for a problem that has been largely created by industrialised countries and their burning of fossil fuels to power their economics. Thus the old logic that 'China and India were not responsible for the problem so they should not be bound to slow down the pattern of growth: should be re-examined.'

Of late, in March '07, Chinese Premier Wen Jiabao, while addressing Chinese legislature, remarked that China must avoid a strategy of seeking only faster" growth and focus instead on efforts to create more equity, save energy and cut pollution. To quote him—"excessive energy consumption and serious environmental pollution, along with a more balanced growth of economy were the pressing, challenges facing the country."[29] Moreover, in Beijing. University, a national work plan has been prepared which will be executed by the end of 2007. Through it emission of G.H.G.'s in factories, power plants, and vehicles, will be checked.

In India also, in March 2007, Ministry of Environment and Forest proposed the Environment Tribunal Bill which provides to set up "green courts" to deal with environmental disputes. Besides, local environmental groups played an important role in bringing in "coastal regulation zone" rules. Similarly, campaigns by civil society groups, led to changes in antiquated forest laws. On specific issues, monitoring groups were set up to check if a particular project conformed to the environmental laws. For instance "at Dahanu, north of Mumbai along the western coast, Dahanu Taluka Environment protection Authority was set up, following a long battle by local farmers and environmentalists against 500 MW coal fired power plant located in the area. Though the plant is running today yet it was compelled to take measures to limit polluting impacts. Likewise, Mahabaleswar Panchagani Monitoring Committee played a crucial role in protecting the popular hill stations from being destroyed by unchecked construction."[30] In November 2007 East-Asia summit (A two years old grouping, comprising the states of ASEAN and China, Japan, South Korea, India Australiya & New Zealand) issued a declaration on climate change energy and environment. Here Japan came forward with the idea of "sustainable East Asia." East Asia Summit offered to place a cap on per person green house gas emissions at a level equivalent only to a 'cap' that the developed block might be willing to agree upon.

In Australia in recently held elections in Nov. 2007, Labour Party under the leadership of Mr. Kevin Rudd, has won elections. Mr. Kevin Rudd, has decided to support not only the Kyoto protocol but also the cause of climate change and environment in the long run. In Britain new leadership of Gorden Brown has proposed new proposal to cut the carbon emissions by 60 per cent by 2050 the recent changes emerging in Australia, Britain, Japan and China are welcome sign for the cause of environment. At Bali Indonesia, a 15 days conclave of around 10,000 delegates from over 190 states is deliberating as to how to save the planet. Earth from the dangers of climate change. The significance of the summit is that U.S.A. is also participating in it. Even the U.S. Senate now agrees to enact laws to reduce that the summit will be concluded by mid Dec. 2007 with positive results for the planet earth.

In 1992 at Rio, the concept of "common but differentiated responsibility was accepted. Under it, industrial states were supposed to extend financial and technological support to the developing states to decarbonise their energy system and switch over to cleaner technologies but it could not make much headway. In this background, in the early days of November 2006, a meeting on global-warming ended inconclusively at Nairobi (Kenya) where delegates from 165 states met to deliberate reduction of use of fossil fuels with view to contain G.H.G.'s emission. All that was agreed upon was to meet again in 2008. Of late in May 2007 at Bangkok' a meet of 120 states was held where lack of "will-power" was identified as the main stumbling-block in the fight against global warming. The final resolution read that by development of non conventional sources of energy, cut in use of fossil fuels, giving priority to agro-sector, the disaster of global warming can be faced. At the global level, efforts are on for the last six decades, to combat the challenge.

Even in the era of liberalization, privatization and globalisation, when there is emphasis on "selective intervention by the state", "state" being a political society and not a private profit making company, its welfare role can not be entirely discarded. Today, states need to perform environment related functions also because the most important fundamental right-right to life, itself is at stake. The state has to hinder the hindrances of good life in the new scenario. Under Art. 48A of the Indian Constitution—state is supposed to protect and improve the environment and save the forest and wildlife of the country. In 1995 India's Supreme Court in Virender Gaur vs. State of Haryana case ruled that—"Sanitation and hygienic environment~

is fundamental right of the citizens and corresponding constitutional duty of the municipalities. "[31]

Hence, states, at their own level, need to take some steps. Other viable sources of energy needs to be explored. Wind energy has emerged as a good option which is being adopted in India and some European states. Other states can follow the same track.

States need to spend more on environment related research and development with a view to explore new avenues like' "geo-engineering"— rearranging the earth's environment on a large scale to suit human needs and promote habitability. Under it a plan has been out-lived to put into orbit small lenses that would bend sunlight away from earth"[32] "In England experiment with bio-fuel is made out of fermented Brazilian sugarcane. The use of plant material as a substitute for fossil fuels; could help the environment and halt the global warming."[33] Therefore the option of clean coal technologies must be detected at earliest. Energy efficiency in manufacturing process; offices and houses can be adopted, better irrigation pumps can be used. Thus, 25 per cent electricity consumption can be reduced. Mass transportation system needs to be revamped. State must heavily invest in railways so that goods could be transported with the least consumption fossil fuels.

State should also encourage private .sector participation in research and development. State should use policy tools like taxation to enhance market signals which provides incentives for long term investment in those technological, innovation. Non conventional sources of energy and renewable sources of energy needs to be popularized widely by inculcating public awareness.

State should also encourage organic-farming which does not use any kind of fertilizers or other agro-chemicals and is dependent entirely on organic sources for crop nutrition and crop husbandry. "It is a system in which maintenance of soil fertility and control of pest and disasters are achieved through the enhancement of biological process and ecological interaction."[34]

State should encourage water conservation with the help of civil-society groups and for the purpose, maintenance of tanks, introduction of modem irrigation practices (sprinkle and drip system), diversification of cropping pattern, promotion of scheme for artificial re-charge of ground-water, conservation of rain water, etc. should be propagated. The task ahead is to make more economical use of water for farming and other purposes. For this

"Save water campaigns" must be popularized and practised.

In election manifestoes political parties must address the issue genuinely. For the green-cause political parties were formed in Sweden in 1983, and New Zealand in 1972. Efforts towards poverty alleviation should be made as in June 1972 at Stockholm Mrs. Indira Gandhi remarked "poverty is the greatest polluter."

Along with state, individual should also share the responsibility. As under art. 51-A of the Indian Constitution, it is a citizen's duty to protect and improve natural environment including forests, lakes, rivers, and wild life and to have compassion for the living creatures. This should act as a torch bearer to the individuals elsewhere. Mahatma Gandhi once opined that nature provides enough for everyone's need but not for everyone's greed. So individual needs to lead a life which pays respect to nature that is- a life which teaches self restraint in fulfilling one's desires in order to sustain human life. Gandhian sermon of "simple living high thinking" needs to be incorporated into actual life. In India an innovative idea and practice is emerging in some parts when devotees are giving plants, as blessings after religious rituals, particularly in Hindus.

Moreover, yellow journalism and sensational journalism should give way to green, journalism which advocates consistent and transcendental relation between human society and environment. Water, air and environment are the basic need of a society which ensure the human existence. In the age of communication revolution, media can help in promoting the "green-cause". This is happening in China, Kenya, Mozambique, Thailand and Indonesia."[35] Recently World Metrological Organization (WMO) has recommended correctly "to incorporate climate change as a discipline of study not only at degree and P.G. level but also to start M.PhiL and D.Phil courses in it, specially in agricultural Universities. According to W.M.O. such a step must be initiated particularly when climate related datas of the last 100 years are available. The WMO also found that in developing countries research activities on global warming and climate change has not received its due course and share which is why the environmental challenges are in an indifferent state in these countries."[36]

Conclusion

The concept of environmentalism is a reaction against undue exploitation of nature, in the later 20th century. We are living in a world in which we all will swim or sink together. Environment is facing grave challenges today, threatening the very human existence itself. Life is the very basis of organised civil society. Today the "right to life" itself is at great stake. The idea of "good life" demands many hindrances to be hindered at the earliest. Feeling for nature needs to be aroused and enhanced, for that the idea of sustainable development must be cherished and consumerist culture must be discouraged. The urgent need is to take drastic action-plan towards these ends, now and by all. Delay would mean that the cost of addressing the problems would be significantly grave and grave for all of us. The maxim of "think globally act-locally" needs to be adhered to, by all. To conclude with these words: "Shoot for the moon, even if you miss, you will land among the stars."

References

1. Lectures of Prof. V.K. Jha on 03.12.03 in 2nd Refresher Course in Political Science, D.D.U. Gorakhpur University, Gorakhpur.
2. *The Hindu,* 16.07.06.
3. Padam Nepal, Oct-Dec. 2004, *Indian Journal of Political Science* (I.J.P.S.) p. 603.
4. Young World, *The Hindu,* 10.11.2006
5. Prof. R.P. Pathak, *I.J.P.S.,* July-Sept. 2004, p. 369.
6. Dr. RD. Sharma, *Hindustan Times,* 25.08.02.
7. Dr. G. Mishra, *Hindustan Times,* 16.12.04.
8. Prof. R.P. Pathak, *I.J.P.S.,* July-Sept. 2004, p. 369.
9. *The Hindu,* 02.12.05.
10. *The Hindu,* 24.03.07.
11. Prof. Hari Vishnu Gautam, *Dainik Jagran,* 03.02.04.
12. Ibid..
13. *The Hindu,* 16.02.07, p. 11.
14. Jan Egeland, *The Hindu,* 30.10.04.
15. *Amar Ujala,* 02.04.07.
16. Sir Nicholas Stern, *Hindustan Times,* 02.11.06
17. John Vidal, *The Hindu,* 17.12.05
18. David Adam, Dylam Evans; *The Hindu,* 22.12.05.
19. Ibid.

20. Eureka, *Hindustan Times*, March 2000.
21. Report of World Commission on Environment and Development, Oxford University Press, 1987.
22. Ibid.
23. *Hindustan Times*, 18.09.02.
24. John Egeland, *The Hindu*, 30.10.06.
25. Ramesh Thakur and Collin Bradford, *The Hindu*; 10.02.07.
26. Robin Mac Kie, *The Hindu*, 12.12.05.
27. *The Hindu*, 10.02.07.
28. *Amar Ujala*, 03.04.07.
29. *The Hindu*, 04.03.07.
30. Ibid., 22.03.07.
31. Krishna Mahajan, *Yojana*, Aug. 1997, p. 119.
32. William J. Broad, *The Hindu*, 30.06.06.
33. Robin Mac Kie and Ned Temko, *The Hindu*, 19.09.06.
34. Arbinda Ghosh, *Yojana*, Aug. 97, p. 75.
35. Amarendra Kishore, *Hindustan Times*, 17.12.06, p. 12.
36. *Amar Ujala*, 04-04.07, p. 02.

7. WOMEN IN INDIA'S INTELLECTUAL TRADITION

Chandrakala Padia

My paper has three clear sections. First, it seeks to show that ontologically, or as human *beings,* women have all along been given an equal status in the Indian intellectual *tradition;* second, that in respect of character and contribution to cohesion and welfare of society, they have even been regarded superior to man; and thirdly, that it is unwarranted to hold the opposite view (of some critics) that the intellectual traditions of India have never thought highly of woman. Be it noted that, as demanded by the precise phrasing of the subject, my concern will be with *tradition* all along, *and not with things as they are at present;* and further that I will be focusing on *intellectual* tradition, that is, how women have been *thought of and written about* in the past, not on what their actual state of living and experience was in that period of time.

I

Now, to begin with woman's equality in respect of ontological status as visualized in our ancient texts, I may straight away refer to the Rg *Veda* commonly regarded as the earliest available text of Indian thought. This Veda speaks of a common source from which the diversity of life has emerged. *The Nasadiya sukta (Mandal 10, Rg 129)*[1] visualizes the state before creation,—even before the emergence of light, shade or form; and speaks of a process through which the One Will manifest itself in many forms, including the male and the female ones. Now, this very thought of a *common* origin recalcitrates the idea of *inequal* importance of the forms that emerge into existence. It is, in this context, relevant to point out that quite a few saints in India have also argued for the equality of all human beings on the ground that they are all alike the product of the five elements *(panch-bhutas)*. The *Kathopanisad* (II, ii, 15) sounds a similar note where it says that before creation began, there was nothing, neither light nor darkness, neither day nor night, no sky, no stars, no earth—nothing; only when the primal Will—crystallizing itself as the golden cosmic egg, *hiranyagharbham—split* itself, that all this diversity of forms came into being; and that, as in respect of its emergence, so in dissolution too, this diversity will lapse back into the one and common Essence, or Being.[2] So all that prevails on the earth is of equal significance, and also alike in impermanence.

It is noteworthy that such a non-discriminatory view of origin and dissolution continued to be held upto the times of *Dharm 'asastras*. Thus, *Manusmrti*, which is widely acknowledged as the earliest *Dharmasastras* text, more or less repeats the view in question (Manu I, 13-39) adding that the process of self-division of the one included gender differentiation as well. The One, we are told, split itself into two halves, and assumed the male form with one half and the female form with the other (I, 32). The implication here obviously is that though at the ontological level *gender-differentiation* there certainly is, it is surely not the same thing as gender *discrimination*.

The Upnisads, too, speak of human beings generally, not of man as opposed to woman. They formulate problems of life and offer thoughtful solutions for the whole of humanity. What is more, the solutions are based on the faith that an overriding principle is at work in all alike, the faith that *all* living beings are evolving towards *Mukti*, or spiritual liberation. The evolutionary process is described as a passage from the physical to the spiritual, and, collaterally, from the mundane to the divine, all along making for the realization that, more than a mind-body complex, the individual is 'the spiritual principle.' This supreme objective (of self realization) is held to be accessible to man and woman alike. Nor is such a view merely a thing of the past. Swami Vivekananda has spoken for it vigorously. Our psychology, too, insists that both men and women are basically spiritual; that body and mind are, but helpful instruments; and that it is the *atman* (the Self), which is the *tattva* (or Essence), and also the real *Karta* (or/agent) which is seeking *moksha*. The *Kathopanisad* visualizes the selfsame thought in the form of a beautiful image. The body (it says) is the chariot, the mind is the reins; and the *atman* is the driver which directs the chariot and keeps it running-in the direction of *moksha*.[3]

Even in the post *Samhita* period, we may note, woman was regarded as *ardhangini*, that is, one half of the very being of man and in no way subordinate to him. Another significant term that is used for her is: *sahadharmini*, that is, a co-participator in discharging the obligations of life and fully capable of taking her own decisions. Of all the different women mentioned in *Vedic Samhita* texts, Maitreyi is perhaps the most illustrious example of a woman's ability to exercise her own judgment in respect of a question of values. The relevant situation is, in brief, as follows; *Maharsi* Yajnavalkya wishes to embrace *sannyasa* (renunciation, the fourth stage of life). He duly seeks his wives' permission for the change, adding that he was quite willing to divide his property between his two wives. Thereupon, exercising both her individual sense of values and freedom to disagree, Maitreyi emphatically refuses to share the property and pleads instead for being granted the imperishable treasure of self-knowledge or *atman-jnana*.[4] This case clearly shows that women in the *Vedic* age were educated and free enough to exercise their own judgment on vital matters. Nor is Maitreyi a solitary example of capable womanhood. There were the following other ladies of substance as well, namely, Rsika Ghosa who had earned this name just because she was fond of emphasizing the value of the *Vedas* everywhere; Dakshina, so called because she would never tire of stressing the significance of *dana* (gift, offering, endowment); Romsa, Lopamudra, Vagabhrni, all of whom excelled in giving accounts of the process of creation, and Juho who became known for her sharp intellect. All these women of the *Samhita* period enriched the *Vedic* lore; and, in the process, added to the intellectual status of women in general.

The *Samhita* literature speaks of women as *Kulpalak* (family nurturer), *Dhruva* (steadfast), anchor of the whole society, the guiding agent of life, *Siva* and *Kalyani* that is the source of welfare and prosperity in general.

I turn now to show how in the Indian intellectual tradition woman has even been regarded as superior to man in many a way.

Thus see the following from *Rgveda* (V-61-6):

> "... Many a woman is more steadfast and better than the man who turns away from God... and [does not offer] prayers".[5]

The Satapath Brahman argues for the pre-eminence of women by saying that, as mothers, they are the best and the foremost preceptors of children.

The vasistha Dharmasutra heightens the emphasis even more by observing that woman is hundred times superior to man in instructing and elevating a child (XIII-48). *Parasarsmrti* declares that wife is the refuge of her husband in times of trouble, and that, therefore, she should not be made the victim of exploitation and oppression by him. It adds (Ch. IV. 33) that as a snake-catcher can pull out a snake from its hole, similarly a pious woman can redeem her husband-from moral turpitude. Another law-giver of ancient India, Apastamba has a different, yet commonly acceptable way of arguing for the superiority of woman. He argues that in so far as a mother serves her son in numberless ways and quite selflessly, he should not desert her even if, for some reason, she happens to take to devious ways. He is quite emphatic in honouring the fair sex where he says that all must make way for a woman when she is treading a path. *(Apastamba, Dharmasutra* II-5-11-7)

Manu, who is regarded as the highest authority on social matters, unequivocally assigns to women the status of presiding deities in the home. According to him, there is no difference whatsoever, (Manu, IX-26) between wives who are destined to bear children and who provide the blessings of love and caring, *and* those *idols* that are put in the houses of men for worship, as symbols of good fortune and holiness.[6] He adds that where the female relatives are unhappy, the family soon perishes. He lays even greater emphasis on the need to honour women by declaring, in one of his very well-known verses, that the gods are pleased with those who honour women; and that where they are not honoured, even sacred rites do not yield the desired result.

The same sentiments have been variously expressed by other writers of *Dharmasastras.* Yajnavalkya, for instance, extols women so much as to call them earthly embodiments of all divine virtues. The typical qualities of women, we are told, are god-given gifts to them. The god *Soma* is supposed to have bestowed purity on women, *Gandharvas,* sweetness of speech; and *Agni,* all his warmth that quickens life. A more or less similar laudatory attitude to women is to be found in our epics. Our most impressive epic, *Mahabharata* looks on woman as the light and the very life of a home, and as the pre-eminent source of family happiness. She has even been regarded as the presiding deity of prosperity and happiness, an embodiment of virtues like patience and forbearance, and therefore as the very diadem of a family. What is more, the *Mahabharata* looks on women as the anchor not only of family life, but of the social organism. The very future of a country is said to depend on women, essentially because it is they who beget, and nurture children and impart the right *samskaras* (or value based dispositions) to them. However, the most emphatic and comprehensive exaltation of the value of woman comes from the sage Visavmitra, who says categorically that ideally (or in principle) a wife is eminently helpful in enabling her husband to strive successfully after all the four principle objectives of life, namely, righteous living, securing material resources, gratification of desires, and spiritual emancipation. Here are some other relevant utterances from our sacred texts:

a. 'Wives can elevate men from the mundane world.' *(Durga Saptsati, Arglai Strotam,* 24).[7] "One *acarya* surpasses ten ordinary teachers; one father surpasses one hundred *ācārya;* and above all, mother surpasses a thousand fathers" in respect of imparting a right sense of values to children *(Manu,* II, 145).[8] The *Mahabharata* sounds a note which is easier to follow when it says: 'Sweet-tongued wives are their husband's friends on the occasion of joy; fathers, on occasions of religious observances; and mothers in hours of illness and woe" *(Mahabharata, Adiparva.* 74/43).[9]

Indeed, in the domestic life, women used to reign supreme. In regulating activities at home, her word would be final. Immediately after her marriage, she had to go to the house to be a mistress there *(Rgveda, X-85-26)*[10] and to exercise full loving sway over her husband's father, mother, brothers and sisters (Ibid, X-85-46).[11] In *Atharva Veda* she is repeatedly addressed as the queen of the house, who rules over all the members of the family 'as an ocean rules over ... the rivers ...' by embracing them, so to say, open-heartedly. *(Atharva, XIV,* 1/43).[12]

In *Vedic* India, indeed, woman occupied a very proud position in the household. She was the very axis on which the wheel of household life turned. It may here be added, in passing, that the words *Pati* and *Patni* as used in *Rgveda* simply mean *master* and *mistress* respectively, and that this implies only a *difference* of sex, and does not at all hint as to which of the two is *superior* to the other. And if there is any talk of such superiority, the reference is not to man but to woman, as in the following from *Mahabharata:* "Women, O King, should always be adored and treated with honour. [In a way], there the very gods are said to be propitiated, where women are treated with respect" *(Mahabharata, Anusasan Parva,* XVI-5). Here is something more in the same vein, from *Mahabharata* again:

> "Those houses which are cursed by women meet with destruction and ruin, as if scorched by some Atharvan rites. Such houses lose their splendour. Their growth and prosperity cease". *(Mahabharata, Anusasan Parva,* XVI-6)

I may here add that scholars like Macdonell and Keith support the view that in ancient India women in homes were indeed treated with honour and due consideration. Incidentally, there were two main reasons for the importance attached to women in domestic life. First, it was believed that man was born with three principal debts, namely, to the *rsis* or sages *(Rsi rna),* to the deities *(Deva rna)* and to the ancestors *(Pitr rna);* and that these debts could be repaid in three ways, respectively; by studying the *Vedas,* offering sacrifices, and by begetting children *(Mbh.* XII-28-55). The last of these clearly highlights the value of women. Secondly, only a man with a family could provide proper hospitality to guests and holy men. This is why the *grhastha asram* was regarded as almost a mother in respect of giving shelter to all. As the sea received all rivers so a good house wife welcomes every one *(Mbh.* XII-269-6). It was believed that in the family life alone one could perform great penance, that is by serving the needy in society.

It is important to note that in ancient India society's attitude even towards a fallen woman-say, a prostitute-was quite different from what it is today. She was even considered auspicious enough to be invited to ceremonial occasions, the reason being that such a woman was regarded as the preserver of some of the sixty-fourt arts, specially music and dance. This indeed is what made her welcome at republican assemblies and royal courts.

With a fall in the status of women, the country also began

to lose in character. So says *the Mahabharata* (XIII, 46.6)

स्त्रियां यत्र च पूज्यनते
रमन्ते तत्र देवताः ।।
अपूजिताश्च यत्रेताः
सर्वास्तत्राफलाः क्रियाः ।।

Here we find a clear agreement of views between Manu and *Mahabharata.* What is most striking is the fact that even Lord Siva is said to become a *Sav* (dead body) without' *Sakti'* because it is a woman's caring attitude which quickens one in difficult times. To quote *Saundarya Lahri,* Verse I

शिवः शक्त्या युक्तो यदि भवति शक्तः प्रभवितुम् ।
न चेदेवं देवो न खलु कुशलः स्मन्दितुमपि ।।

II

However quite a few Western and Indian scholars have alleged that women occupied a very insignificant place in India's intellectual tradition (Susan Wadley, 'Women and the Hindu Tradition' in Rehana Ghadially (ed.), *Women in Indian Society,* New Delhi, Sage Publications, 1988, p. 30). Here are the main points which they focus on:

(a) The birth of a girl was always regarded as an unwelcome event.
(b) Women were not given proper education; so they were less qualified than men. There was no co-education.
(c) Women had no right in matters of divorce and remarriage. My answer, here, is as follows:

1. Our *Vedic* literature indicates that there were people in ancient times who really wished the birth of a daughter; and so in one of the early *Upnisads,* a certain ritual has been recommended to a householder for ensuring the birth of a scholarly daughter. *(Brhadaranyaka Upanisad,* IV, 4-18)[13]

Cultured parents were often as anxious to get daughters as sons.

Some thinkers have even pointed out that a talented and well behaved daughter could prove to be better than a son *(Saṃyutta Nikāyā,* IIIc). Such a daughter was regarded as the pride of the family.[14] *(Kumarasambhava, VI,* 63).

The *Vanparva* of *Mahabharata* (293, 17) contains the following assurance: "with the grace of lord Brahma a powerful daughter (तेजस्विनी) will be born to you."[15] In a particular verse of *Yajurveda* the gods are blessing a bride by wishing her birth of both a son and a *daughter.*[16]

These citations indicate that the unfair view that the daughter is less desirable than the son was surely not accepted by all Indian social thinkers. There were quite a few people who realized that the view in question could inflict great harm on society and felt strongly that it had to be counteracted. They therefore championed the daughter's cause partly on the quite valid ground that patricides had always been a monopoly of the male sex, and that no father was ever known to have been killed by a daughter. There are cases on record where daughters like Kunti and Lopamudra are said to have saved their parents from dire calamities. In the *Kathasaritsagara* by Somadeva it is said that one has no right to be, elated at the birth of a son and depressed at the birth of a daughter.

Now, turning to the criticism that less importance was given to the education of daughter, I may counter it as follows:

We have instances of lady poets in pre- *Vedic* period who were themselves composing hymns, some of which were even included in the *vedic Samhitas.* According to the orthodox tradition itself, as recorded in *Sarvanukramanika* there are as many as twenty women among the "seers" or authors of *Rgveda.* Some of these may well have been mere mythical figures, but internal evidence shows that Lopamudra, Visvavara, Sikata, Nivavari and Ghosa, the authors of the *Rgveda* 1.79, V. 28, VIII. 90, IX. 81. 11-20, and X. 39 and 40 respectively, were women in flesh and blood, who once actually lived in Hindu Society. The authors of X. 145 and 159 are undoubtedly ladies, though it may be doubted whether their real names were Indrani and Sachi, as recorded by tradition. Among the authors and scholars to whose memory a daily prayer of respect is enjoined, a few ladies also figure such as Sulabha, Maitreyi, Vadava Pratithyi, and Gargi-Vachaknavi *(Asvalayana Grhyasutra,* III, 4, 3).[17]

Women students were divided into two classes *Brahmvadinis*

and *Sadyovadhus.* The former were *lifelong* students of theology and philosophy; the latter used to prosecute their studies only till their marriage at the age of 15 or 16. *Brahmviidinis* used to aim at a very high excellence in scholarship. Besides studying the *Vedas,* many of them used to specialise in *Purva Mimamsa,* which discusses the diverse problems connected with *Vedic* sacrifices. *Mahabhasya* speaks of a theologian named *Kasakritsana* who composed a work on *Mimamsa* called *Kasakritsni;* and lady scholars who used to specialise in it, were designated as *Kasakritisnas.*

In a congregation of philosophical debate held under the auspices of king Janaka, the most subtle philosophical questions were initiated for discussion by the lady philosopher Gargi. She launched her attack on Yajnavalkya with admirable coolness and confidence. The topics of her inquiry were so abstruse and esoteric in character, that Yajnvalkya declined to discuss them in public. The searching cross-examination of Yajnavalkya by Gargi shows that she was a dialectician *par excellence* (Br. Up. III, 6 and 8). Of a few distinguished poetesses who appear to have composed poetry of a really high order, Silabhattarika, we learn, was famous for her easy and graceful style. Vijayanka's fame was second only to that of Kalidasa. She seems to have attained a really high position among Sanskrit writers, for a distinguished critic and poet like Rajasekhara; likens her to goddess Saraswati herself.

The third charge can be easily refuted by pointing out that women have been granted the right to divorce and remarriage in a number of our *Dharmasastras.* Even Manu, who has been the most frequent target of glib criticism, has declared that a wife is not to be censured where she abandons her husband if he is impotent or suffering from an incurable or contagious disease (IX, 79), and that she may well remarry if her previous marriage has not consummated (IX, 175176). Again, in his *Arthasastra,* Kautilya says that the childless wife of a husband who has gone abroad, without making any provision for her proper maintenance, and who does not return even after 8 years, should be allowed to remarry (28). Similarly, Parashar has expressed the view that if the husband has been away for long and remains untraced, is dead, or has taken to *sannyasa* (that is, the life of renunciation) and so has gone away for good; or if he has been convicted for some misdeed, the wife may well remarry (28). Kautilya has ruled that a husband cannot divorce his wife without her consent, and that divorce is permissible if both husband *and wife* have ill will for each other. In respect of a widow; the intellectual tradition has allowed three options: first, to remain unmarried and practice celibacy; second, to have a child through *niyoga;* and third, to remarry. Several heroes whose account appears in the *Mahabharata* and *Puranas* were born out of *niyoga,* though Manu does not allow this option to a widow who already has a son to support her. Further, though it was surely not imposed on them, celibacy was surely recommended as an ideal for widows. *(Parasar,* 29). At the same time, due attention was also paid to provision of proper economic relief for widows. *(Mahabharata, Santiparva,* 24; 86). Gautam proposed that a widow may be regarded as a co-heir of her husband's property along with other close relatives *(Spindas).* Visnu goes to the extent of saying that if her sons desert her, the whole estate should go to the widow (XVII, 43). It was, however, Brhaspati who championed the right of widow to inherit the property most strongly. He pointed out that the *Vedas,* the *Smrtis,* and sages of antiquity have unanimously declared that husband and wife are the joint owners of family property and that they together constitute one legal personality.

It is, therefore, quite wrong to say, as has been contended by Kurnkum Roy *(Women's Studies in India: Contours of Change,* pp. 98, 99) that women in ancient India had no right of inheritance. Indeed, if we consider the socio-cultural context of that time, we would be led to believe that with some limitations, women enjoyed equal property rights with men. They were debarred from getting the property of their fathers only if their own brothers were alive. At the same time, in the event of her mother's death, she was regarded as the sole inheritor of the latter's property. Most of the *Smrtikaras* have categorically asserted that the transfer of *streedhan* should be towards the women. inheritors only, and that where a man has no son, the entire property must go to the women inheritors. This has been openly asserted by Manu and others at several places. This clearly proves that our ancient system of inheritance had more of a horizontal than a vertical structure.

Let me also cite those two verses of *Yajnavalkya* where he has clearly suggested that wives and daughters should be given preference in case where a man has no sons: *(Yajnavalkya,* II. 135-136),[18] His view, which is very significant, may be put thus. The lawfully wedded wife; the daughter (and the daughter's son); the parents; the brothers, their sons, cognatic relatives,—all have to be regarded as rightful claimants to a man's property *in this order of succession* in case he does not leave any male issue behind him. (P. V. Kane, *History of Dharmasastras,* Vol. III, 1946 edition, p. 701).[19] *Yajnavalkya* and Visnu among *Smrti* writers were probably the first to clearly enunciate the rule that the wife was the foremost heir of a man if he died without leaving a male issue. Brhaspati makes the wife the first heir of a sonless man and supports his opinion with reasons. He says:

> "In the *Veda* and in the doctrines of the *Smrtis,* as also in popular usage, the wife is regarded as one-half of a husband's being, and equal in sharing the consequences of his good and evil acts. How then can any body except his widow be regarded as a lawful heir of his property."?

Again, a text attributed to Vrddha Manu says,

"The wife alone, if she has no son and no illicit sexual relations with anyone and leads a life of religious observances, may offer *pinda* to her deceased husband *and take his entire estate" (Vrddh Manu quoted by Mitaksara on Yajnavalkya.* II, 135, *Dayabhag* XI. 1.7, *Vivadaratnakar,* p. 589)[20]

Even Manu asks, suggestively, how can another person except the daughter (along with son) take the wealth of the deceased when she, who is the very self of the deceased, lives. (Manu, Chapter IX, Verse 30. English Version taken from P. V. Kane's *History of Dharmasastra)*[21] The most emphatic assertion comes from Prajapati where he says that the king should punish as thieves those relatives who try to prevent a widow from getting her husband's estate. *(Prajapati quoted by Smrti Chandrika II,* p. 294, *Vivadachintamani,* p. 151. English version from P. V. Kane's, *History of dharmasastras,* Vol. III, 1946, edition, p. 712).

I may point out, in passing, that quite a few criticisms levelled against the place of women in India's intellectual tradition arise from a clear misinterpretation of our ancient texts.

Of the several examples that I can give in support of what I here say, let me draw readers' attention to just one.

> क्षेत्रभूता स्मृता नारी बीजभूतः स्मृतः पुमान–
> सेना बीज समायोगात्संभवः सर्वदेहिनाम् ।। (Ch. IX Verse 33)

"Woman may be taken as a field, and man as a seed. All living beings arise from the union of the field and seed."

Focussing on verse 33 of chapter IX of *Manusmrti*, Kum Kum Roy interprets it as follows:

> "Here, the womb is equated with the field, in which men sow *seed*, [the precise] offspring being determined by the nature of *the latter*, with the former conceived as a [merely] passive, supportive receptacle. The field, moreover, is ideally owned by a man, and, by extension, the produce of the field is his."

Hence, the critic concludes, man may well be regarded as superior to woman. (Kum Kum Roy's essay in *Women and the Hindu Right*, ed. Tanika Sarkar and Urvashi Butalia, Kali For Women, New Delhi, 1995, p. 18).

Now, to my mind, even a casual look at the verse in question shows that here there is not the slightest hint of the categorical view that, by virtue of being a mere "field", woman is inferior to man. How, indeed, can we decide as to which of the two is of greater value-the seed or the field? The seed remains merely itself until it impregnates the field, so to say; and the field is a mere stretch or receptacle until it is fertilized by the seed. What is more, the very next verse (no. 34) of *Manusmrti* makes it clear that, according to Manu, the seed or the male person is more important in some contexts; *and the .field (or woman) in quite a few others.* (Chap. IX, verse no. 34). Here we also have the additional suggestion that where the seed and the field *alike* contribute to the act of begetting or production, the maternity involved is commendable. I may, in the end, cite the following powerful words of P.V. Kane:

> "Hindu law does not favour the distribution of a deceased man's estate among the several relatives, as some other systems do. It is greatly to the credit of the ancient Hindu law that it boldly gave all the separate property of a deceased male to women, viz. to the widow and after her to the daughter, in preference to the man's own father or brother or nephew. (P.V. Kane, *History of Dharmasastras*, Vol. III, 1946, edition, p. 711).

References

1. नासदासीन्नोसदासीत्तदानीं नासीद्रजो नो व्योमा परोयत्।

किमावरीवः कुह कस्य शर्मत्रम्भः किमासीदृगहनं गभीरम्।।
ऋ. X/ 129.1।।
न मृत्युरासीदमृतं न तर्हि न रात्र्या अन्ह आसीत प्रकेतः।
आनीदवातं स्वधया तदेकं तस्माद्धान्यत्र पुरः किं चनास।
ऋ. X/129/2

2. न तत्र सूर्यो भाति न चन्द्रतारकं, नेमा विद्युतो भान्ति कुतोऽयमग्निः
तमेव भान्तमनुभाति सर्व, तस्य भासा सर्वमिदं विभाति।। (कठोपनिषद, II, ii, 15)
3. आत्मानं रथिनं विद्धि शरीरं रथमेव तु
बुद्धिं तु सारथिं विद्धि मनः प्रग्रहमेव च।। (कठोपनिषद, I, iii, 3-4)
इन्द्रियाणि हयानाहुर्विषयान् तेषु गोचतन्।
आत्मेन्द्रियमनोयुक्त भोक्तेयाहु र्मनीषिणः
4. See, Brthdaranoyak Upnisad/IV/V
5. उतत्वा स्त्री शशीयंसी पुंसो भवती वस्यसी।
अदेवत्रादराधसः।।
6. प्रजनार्थ महाभागः पूजाहा ग्रहदीप्तयः
स्त्रियः श्रियश्चः गेहेषु न विशेषोऽस्ति कश्चन।
7. पत्नीं मनोरमां देहि मनोवृत्तानुसारिणीम्।
तारिणीं दुर्गसंसार सागरस्य कुलोद्भवाम्।। (दुर्गा सप्तशती, अर्गला स्तोत्रम्, 24)
8. उपाध्यायान्दशाचार्य आचार्याणां शतं पिता।
सहस्त्रं तु पितृन्माता गौरवेणतिरिच्यते।। मनुस्मृति, अध्याय II, 145
9. सा भार्या सा गृहे दक्षा सा भार्या या प्रजावती।
साभार्या या पतिप्राण सा भार्या या पतिव्रता।।
अर्ध भार्या मनुष्यस्य भार्या श्रेष्ठतमः सखा।
भार्या मूलं त्रिवर्गस्य भार्या मूलं तरिष्यतः।।
भार्यावन्तः क्रियावन्तः सभार्या गृहमेधिनः।।
भार्यावन्तः प्रमोदन्ते भार्यावन्तः श्रियान्विताः।।
सखायः प्रविविक्तेषु भवन्त्येताः प्रियंवदाः। आदिपर्व 741-40-43
10. पूषा त्वेतो नयतु हस्तगृह्यश्विना त्वा प्र वहतां रथेन।
गृहान् गच्छ गृहपत्नी यथासो वशिनी त्वं विदथमा वदासि।। Rgveda X/85/26
11. सम्राज्ञी श्वशुरे भव सम्राज्ञी श्वश्र्वां भव।
ननान्दरि सम्राज्ञी भव सम्राज्ञी अधि देवृषु।। Rgveda X/85/46
12. यथा सिन्धुर्नदीनां साम्राज्यं सुषंवे वृषा।
एवा त्वं सम्राज्ञ्येधि पत्युरस्तं परेत्य।। अथर्ववेद XIV/1/44
सम्राज्ञ्येधि श्वशुरेबु सम्राज्ञ्युत देवृषु।
जनान्दुः सम्राज्ञ्येधि सम्राज्ञ्युत श्वश्रवाः।। अथर्ववेद XIV/1/44
13. अथ य अच्छेद् दुहिता में पंडिता जातेय, सर्वमायुरियादिति तिलौदनं पाचरित्वा

सर्पिष्मन्तमश्नीयातामीश्वरौ तनयितवै।।
बृहदारण्यक उपनिषद 4.4.17

14. एतेवयममी दाराः कन्येयं कुलजीवितम्।
ब्रूत येनात्र वः कार्यमनास्था बाह्यवस्तुषु।। कुमार VI/63
15. प्रसादाच्चैव तस्मात् ते स्वूयम्भु विहिताद् भुवि।
कन्या तेजस्विनी सौम्य क्षिप्रमेव भविष्यति।। Vanparva: 293/17
16. हृदे त्वा मनसे त्वा दिवे त्वा सूर्याय त्वा।
उर्ध्वमिममध्वरं दिवि देवेषु होत्रा यच्छ।। (यजुर्वेद 6/25)
17. सुयन्तुजैमिनिवैश्म्पायन पैलसूत्रभाष्यभारतमहाभारतधर्माचार्या–
जानन्तिवाहविगार्ग्य गौतमशाकल्यवाभ्रव्यमाण्डव्यमाण्डूकेया
गार्गीवाचक्नवी वडवाप्रातीथेयीसुलभामैत्रेयी–आश्वलायनगृह्यसूत्रम् 2 अध्याय, खंड 4, सू. 3.
18. याज्ञवल्क्य समृति, व्यवहाराध्याय, श्लोक 115
19. पत्नी दुहितरश्चैव पितरौ भ्रातरस्तथा।
तत्सुता गोत्रजा बन्धु शिष्यसब्रह्मचारिणः।। याज्ञवल्क्यस्मृति व्यवहाराध्याय 135
एषामभावे पूर्वस्य धनभाूक्तरोत्तरः।
स्वर्यातस्य ह्यपुत्रस्य सर्ववर्णेष्वयं विधिः।। 136
20. वृद्धमनुरदि पत्नयाः समग्रधन संबंध वक्ति–'अपुत्रा शयनं यर्तुः पालयन्ति
पत्न्येव दघात् तत्पिण्डं कृत्स्नमंशं लभेत च'।।–व्रते स्थित। मिताक्षय याज्ञवलक्य V-135
21. यवैवात्मा तथा पुत्रः पुत्रेण दुहिता समा।
तस्यामात्मनि जीवन्तयां कथमन्यो हरेद्धनम्।। विवादरजाकर 84/1070

8. DEMOCRACY IN THE ERA OF GLOBALIZATION

Vimla Vyas

Ending the colonial rule of British imperialism, India won its independence and established itself as a sovereign, secular, socialist, democratic republic on January 26, 1950. In the last half century India experienced three wars, two year-long national emergency and severe natural and man-made calamities. Yet, India's maturing democracy and its multi-ethnic, pluralistic character weathered those 50 years.

Independent India's first prime minister, Jawaharlal Nehru, put forward the still relevant idea of "unity in diversity". His socialist credentials and pro-Soviet Union stance had great influence among India's poor and working masses. Nehru even adopted a five year plan for development projects and public sector enterprises. The public sector flourished. Money from these enterprises went to the development of social services.

This scenario lasted until 1991, when the Congress Party government under Prime Minister P.V. Narasimharao and Finance Minister Manmohan Singh adopted "neo-liberal" globalization policies dictated by the International Monetary Fund and World Bank. The private sector was touted as the only remedy for the ailments of the Indian economy. Without any public debate or discussion, even in Parliament, they opened the doors for foreign, as well as Indian monopoly corporations to dominate the economy. The role of the public sector became minimal and public enterprises began to close. "Profit" became the slogan for not only business but the government as well.

The collapse of the Soviet Union was another reason for this drastic change. Indian rulers tossed out any ideas of socialism and swung to the other extreme-market capitalism. The ruling parties, who once administered the national economy on the basis of socialist thinking, turned "reformers."

Successive governments continued these policies. When the extreme far right Hindutva (Hindu nationalist) forces jumped into the government driver's seat, "reform" gave way to a more extreme situation.

The official line from the former Prime Minister Atal Behari Vajpayee's Economic Advisory Council is unequivocal, arguing, "Globalization is an unavoidable process which is taking place independent of us. It forces us to cope with it. There is no room in a globalized world for an economy delinked from world trade and foreign investment." The advisory council candidly says, "The truth is that if we do not reform rapidly and position ourselves to compete, we will be marginalized. There is no divine dispensation that gives India alone the power to survive and prosper as an isolationist island in a globalized world." Under the new prime Minister that conviction is undiminished. Nonetheless, universal consensus on this view is far from apparent; as a Financial Times columnist wrote in October 2004, "Globalization means many things to many people, particularly in India, which is host to probably the widest range of anti-globalization groups in the world. (Jessica Einhorn, 2005)[1]

There are plenty of experts to tell all who listen, that globalization opens up tremendous potential for growth and poverty alleviation, and an outward-looking model frees up entrepreneurs to innovate and invest. Such expert advice from outside is not, however, necessary in India, whose political system already has important groups of reformers who do not need to learn from foreign experts, but who need external support in legitimizing the reform agenda that they wish for the country to embrace. Most importantly, they need the backing of India's elite and politicians to carry through tough reforms.

Presently in India, we are witnessing the simultaneous growth of two forces- one of globalization, the other of localization, one driven by global corporations, the other driven by local communities and grassroots movements, one moving power upwards, the other moving it downwards.

The New Economic Policy of 1991 is an example of the tendency towards globalization. This policy was the result of the World Bank and the IMF Structural Adjustment Programme. Globalization processes underwent an acceleration with the completion of the Uruguay Round of GATT and the establishment of the World Trade Organization.

The Panchayat Raj Amendment and grassroots movements for democratic control over the resources necessary for survival are examples of the tendency towards localization.

The Relationship between the Community, the State and the Corporation: A Global Perspective

The post-Cold War project of globalization is changing the established notion of liberal democracy and local governance. The political autonomy of the liberal state is being increasingly compromised in favour of market forces and local governance more and more exposed to direct penetration by global and corporate power structures. This change has far-reaching implications for the future of democracy, particularly in the Third World. Aware of this challenge, new social movements in India, active at the grass roots of politics, are resisting global penetration of local communities, using new political spaces opened up by the retreat of the state from socio-economic arenas. Through an inventive politics of struggle over issues concerning local communities and their empowerment, they articulate a vision of democracy as a creative political process, operative primarily at the local level. Their politics is addressed to establishing direct access and control of people over their immediate environment-economic, social, and cultural. To ensure that, they seek to transcend old dichotomies between state and society, global and local, political and social and open up new possibilities for democracy in India.[2]

With international "free trade" agreements such as NAFTA, GATT and FTAA, the giant transnationals have been elevated above the sovereign powers of nation states. These agreements endow anonymous international trade committees with the authority to prevent, overrule, or dilute any laws of any nation deemed to burden the investment and market prerogatives of transnational corporations. These trade committees- on which the World Trade Organization (WTO) is a prime example- set up panels composed of "trade specialists" who act as judges over economic issues, placing themselves above the rule and popular control of any nation, thereby insuring the supremacy of international finance capital. This process, called globalization, is treated as an inevitable natural "growth" development beneficial to all. It is in fact, a global coup d'etat by the giant business interests of the world.

Free trade is not fair trade; it benefits strong nations at the expense of weaker ones, and rich interests at the expense of the rest of us. Globalization means turning the clock back on many twentieth-century reforms: no freedom to boycott products, no prohibitions against child labour, no guaranteed living wage or benefits, no public services that might conceivably compete with private services, no health and safety protections that might cut into corporate profits.[3]

> A Noble-prize winning US economist has warned that public services could suffer in countries like India as a result of globalisation.[4]
>
> Professor Stiglitz said that:
>
> "A decline in tariff leads to less money for the governments to spend on its people,"
>
> Professor Siglitz emphasized that globalization had played an important trigger in the buoyant Indian economy- it grew at over 9 per cent in the six months to this September [2006]. But it had been given too much credit for the growth.
>
> In his opinion "Much of India's early growth [after liberalizing the economy in 1991] came from a change in internal government policies- from anti- business to market friendly policies".
>
> He stated categorically "that some excess credit was given to external liberalization rather than internal liberalization for India's economic growth."

Globalization has rendered totally fluid the relationship between the community, the state and the corporation. For more practical interpretation, we can use Marc Nerfin's more colourful categories, the relationship between the citizen, the prince and the merchant.

The appeal of globalization is usually based on the idea that globalization implies less red tape, less centralization and less bureaucratic control. It is celebrated because it implies the erosion of the power of the state.

Globalization does mean "less government" for regulation of business and commerce. But less government for commerce and corporations can go hand in hand with more government in the lives of people. As globalization allows increasing transfer of the resources from the public domain-either under the control of the communities, or under the control of the state, discontent and dissent necessarily increases, leading to law and order problems. In such a situation even a minimalist state restricted only to policing and law and order will become enormously large and all pervasive, devouring up much of the wealth of society, and intruding into every aspect of citizens lives.

Most of the ideological projection of globalization has focused on the new relationship of the prince and the merchant, the state and the corporation, the government and the market. The state has been stepping back more and more from the regulation of commerce and capital. Reflecting this ideology or deregulation, our then, finance minister Manmohan Singh had stated that "Power should move to the Boardroom", i.e. power should move from the state to corporations.[5] However, the shift from the rule of the nation-state to corporate rule does not imply more power to the people. If anything, it implies less power in the hands of people both because corporations, especially transnational corporations, are more powerful than governments and also because they are less accountable than governments to democratic control.

In recent years, the economic and political power of transnational corporations has been increasing dramatically. Corporations are driving the globalization agenda: Trans-National Companies control one third of the world's wealth. Global production by TNCs exceeds world trade. Trade within firms, rather than between them, takes a growing proportion of world commerce.

In terms of size, corporations dwarf countries. In 1980 the sales of each of the top ten multinationals were over $28 billion, more than the GDP of eighty-seven countries. Since then, there has been a proliferation of small states, and the fracturing the larger ones, while corporations have expanded exponentially. This has probably made the competition even more unequal. Exxon's sales in 1980 were larger than the GDP of ninety-six countries, well ahead of Austria, Denmark and Norway. The order has changed over the decade, with Exxon losing out a little to finish between Indonesia and South Africa and Austria gaining some ground; but a report by the Conference Board of New York shows that if General Motors was a country, it would have the world's twentieth largest economy. Ford comes in just behind Denmark and IBM behind Thailand. The point that the Conference Board makes is that there are more TNCs in the top hundred and fewer countries, 47 to 53, in the 1990 list with only 39 to 61 in 1980.[6]

As Barnet and Muller have stated:

> "The men who run the global corporations are the first in history with the organization, technology, money and ideology to make a credible try at managing the world as an integrated economic unity..... What they are demanding in essence is the right to transcend the nation-state, and in the process, transform it."[7]

The erosion of the power of the nation-state from outside and above leads to a concentration of power in the hands of corporations. It does not devolve power to the people. It does not move power downwards into the hands of communities. In fact, it takes power away from the local level and transforms institutions of the state from being protectors of the health and rights of the people to protectors of the property and profits of corporations. This creates an inverted state, a state more committed to the protection of foreign investment and less to the protection of the citizens of the country. The inversion of the state is well exemplified in a recently announced proposal that foreign security experts would train the Indian police to protect the "life and property of foreign investors."[8]

Another example is the recent decision of the government to lower the health standards and raise the permissible level of MSG (Mono Sodium Glutamate) in order to not allow people's health concerns interfere with the expansion of fast-food chains like KFC (Kentucky Fried Chicken). MSG has been proven to cause severe health problems such as asthma.[9]

As noted writer and social activist Vandana Shiva stated in "stolen Harvest".

"The right of corporations to force-feed citizens of the world with culturally inappropriate and hazardous foods has been made absolute [in the globalizing economy]. The right to food, the right to food, the right to safety, the right to culture are all being treated as trade barriers that need to be dismantled.... we have o reclaim our right to nutrition and food safety. We have to reclaim our right to protect the earth and her diverse species. We have to stop this corporate theft from the poor and from nature. Food democracy.... is the new agenda for ecological sustainability and social justice."

Another example, worth citing is a chapter in Stolen Harvest, "Mad Cows and Sacred Cows," about attempts by developed countries to increase meat consumption in the South- even in historically vegetarian India- in which Shiva makes a compelling economic and ethical case. She argues that the slaughter of increasing numbers of Indian cows for export to the Gulf States (exports of meat from India have increased 20 times since 1995, to nearly 140,000 tons per year) is creating more poverty than wealth. Her calculation; because so many cows are being exported, less dung is available for manure and fuel. (Eighty million cattle meet two-thirds of the energy needs of Indian villages). In addition, to replace the "energy and fertility" cows provide for free, India must import more fertilizer, fossil fuels, tractors and trucks. The result? While meat exports earn India Rs. 10 million per year (about %330,000), the lost wealth cows provide costs the country Rs. 150 million ($ 5 millior) annually- a balance sheet no rational economist would accept.

And this is part of Shiva's main point, when it comes to food production and so much else, globalizers ignore both context and consequences. They argue for "modernization"- more, bigger, faster- without evident concern for what's left behind: strip-mined seas, deserted villages, rural people in thrall to corporate agri-business for their seeds and markets, and a stunning loss of diversity in agriculture.[10]

Globalization as the expansion of the economic space controlled by corporations therefore runs into conflict with the democratic space for citizens to determine and influence the conditions for their health and well-being.

The expansion of corporate control is often made to appear as the expansion of the democratic space for citizens on the basis of "consumer choice". However, choice within a predetermined option offered, a set up of corporate rule, is not freedom because it involves the surrender of the right to determine the context of living and the values that govern society. The apparent widening of individual consumer choice for the elite in matters of automobiles and junk food is based on the shrinking of the rights of communities to control their local natural resources and a shrinking of social choice through democratic public process.

Globalization is creating more freedom for corporations. But this is not translating into more freedom for citizens.

Deregulation of commerce is not the same as reduced interference by the state in the lives of citizens. The end of the "Licence Raj" might imply more freedom for corporations to invest freely. But it also heralds the beginning of a "Patent Raj"- in which governments are forced to play a new role of interfering in the lives of citizens- shall producers, the farmers and craftsmen, to protect what big corporations have claimed as their "intellectual property"- seeds and medicinal plants.

Concentration of Ownership of Natural Resources: A Big Question Ahead

Biodiversity: Rights & Sustainability

Biodiversity, land and water are the three vital resources that the majority of our people depend on for their livelihood and survival.

GATT and subsequent free trade agreements allow multinationals to impose monopoly property rights on indigenous and communal agriculture. In this way agri-business can better penetrate locally self- sufficient communities and monopolize their resources. Ralph Nader gives the example of the neem tree, whose extracts contain natural pesticidal and medicinal properties. Cultivated for centuries in India, the tree attracted the attention of various pharmaceutical companies, who filed monopoly patents, causing mass protests by Indian farmers. As dictated by the WTO, the pharmaceuticals now have exclusive control over the marketing of neem tree products, a ruling that it being reluctantly enforced in India. Tens of thousands of erstwhile independent farmers must now work for the powerful pharmaceuticals on profit-gorging terms set by the companies.

A trade agreement between India and the United States, the Knowledge Initiative on Agriculture (KIA), backed by Monsanto and other transnational corporate giants, allows for the grab of

India's seed sector by Monsanto, its trade sector by Archer Daniels Midland and Cargill, and its retail sector by Wal-mart. (Wal-Mart announced plans to open 500 stores in India, starting in August 2007) This amounts to a war against India's independent farmers and small business, and a threat to India's food security. Farmers are organizing to protect themselves against this economic invasion by maintaining traditional seed-banks and setting up systems of communal agrarian support. One farmer says, "We do not buy seeds from the market because we suspect they may be contaminated with genetically engineered or terminator seeds."[11&12]

In a similar vein, the WTO ruled that the U.S. corporation Rice Tec has the patent rights to all the many varieties of basmati rice, grown for centuries by India's farmers. It also ruled that a Japanese corporation had exclusive rights in the world to grow and produce curry powder. As these instances demonstrate, what is called "free trade" amounts to international corporate monopoly control.

Such developments caused Malaysian prime Minister Mahathir Mohamad to observe:

"We now have a situation where theft of genetic resources by western biotech TNCs [transnational corporations] enables them to make huge profits by producing patented genetic mutuations of these same materials." What depths have we sunk to in the global marketplace when nature's gifts to the poor may not be protected but their modifications by the rich become exclusive property?

If the current behavior of the rich countries is anything to go by, globalization simply means the breaking down of the borders of countries so that those with the capital and the goods will be free to dominate the markets.[13]

"Intellectual property rights" are emerging as an important mechanism for taking away the living resources and biodiversity from the people and converting them into corporate monopolies. Seeds, medicinal plants, neem plant- based pesticides which have been the basis of people's livelihoods in agriculture and health care are being appropriated through new patent regimes enforced through GATT.

These companies have pushed for intellectual property protection in GATT "to prevent extensive losses to worldwide industry due to inadequate and ineffective national protection of intelelctual property." The third World has been repeatedly accused of "piracy" by the industrialized countries. In a 1986 survey, U.S. companies stated that they lost US $23.8 billion due to inadequate or ineffective protection of intellectual property. The U.S. agrochemical industry estimates that it loses over $200 million in sales per year from inadequate and ineffective patent protection. The U.S. pharmaceutical industry claims it has lost US $245 millions. They do not assess how much the Third Word loses due to their claiming of "Third World Bio resources and Third World Knowledge" as their "intellectual property" as in the case of neem patents, and patents on micro organisms, plant-based medicines and seeds. As the team of RAFI, (Rural Advancement Foundation International) has shown, if the contribution of Third World biodiversity and the innovation of peasants and tribals are taken into account the roles the pirate and dramatically reversed. The U.S./ is then found to owe US $202 million in royalties for agriculture and US $5097 million for pharmaceuticals to Third World countries.

Ironically it is the companies that accuse the Third World of piracy and have created TRIPs to stop this piracy who are themselves engaged in large scale piracy of the biological wealth and intellectual heritage from the Third World. Thus Pfizer, Bristol Myers and Merck who are aware on the Intellectual Property Committee which was responsible for initiating and successfully introducing IPRs into GATT have patents on biomaterials collected from the Third World without any permission or payment of royalties to the original owners of the biological material.

Similarly W.R. Grace and other corporations have taken patents on neem biopesticide, Agracetus, a subsidiary of Grace, has claimed monopoly rights on rice, soyabean, cotton. Patents have become a means for corporations to establish monopoly control on food crops.

In response, people are putting forward alternatives to IPRs, especially in the area of biodiversity. This includes the Collective Intellectual Rights Movement started on Independence Day, 15 August 1993, by the Karnataka "Rajya Ryota Sangha", the Research Foundation and the Third World Network. Collective intellectual rights are aimed at protecting people's rights to their biological resources including seeds, medicinal plants and protecting the integrity of their collective heritage.

Challenges to patents based on Indian knowledge have also been filled in the U.S. and the European Patent Offices.[14] While the transnational corporations might have succeeded in getting a TRIPs agreement in the final text of the Uruguay Round, they cannot be at all sure of forcing unethical and unjust IPR systems on people. Movements against patents on life are growing everywhere, and in India, the "Seed Satyagraha", the movement to conserve indigenous seeds and to protect farmer's rights to seed in response to TRIPs is spreading and gaining strength.

Land Reforms: The Global Impact

The Indian people still largely depend on the agricultural sector for their livelihood. Agricultural growth leads to rural prosperity, which in turn leads to more buying power, and that triggers higher industrial growth. But during the current corporate globalization process agriculture has seen negative growth, despite campaign promises by many bourgeois political parties to help the agricultural sector. Capital invested in Indian agriculture has declined from 17 per cent in 1980 to 9 per cent now. This trend has had a negative impact across the economy.

The displacement of rural and tribal peoples- as in the case of the anti-people Narmada dam project, where hundreds of thousands of people will be displaced- is also part of the neo-liberal picture. Although the movement of the people of Narmada carries considerable moral power, this alone is unable to get them redress. Their democratic resistance is often brutally attacked not only by the ruling class but in particular by rightwing political organizations.

Land and water too are being appropriated. Land reform laws which had attempted to undo concentration of land ownership under Zamindari are themselves being undone. These changes are part of the Structural Adjustment Programme. One of the major targets of the World Bank agricultural reforms is the removal of land ceiling laws. Land ceiling was a mechanism to disallow the continuation or emergence of monopolies in land ownership of the kind that the country had faced in colonial India as the Zamindari system.

Under the Permanent Settlement of 1793, the British made Zamindars, the proprietors of these estates, subject to a permanent fixed payment to the government. The revenue of the government was fixed at about ten-elevenths of what the zamindars received as rent from the ryots: the remaining one-elevenths was left as the share of the zamindars. As years passed, the landlord became more and more a rent receiver, living on the proceeds of other's labours and investing no resources on the land.

As the Uttar pradesh Zamindari Abolition Committee reports:

> "Millions of people were by these settlements, deprived of rights that they had enjoyed for well over two thousand years; hereditary cultivating proprietors of land were turned into rack-rented tenants-at-will, and conditions were thus created that led to continuous social discord and economic deterioration and decay of agriculture."

The growth of a class of non-productive rent receivers was accompanied by the dispossession of impoverished peasants with small holdings. As land increased in value, the number of land transfers rapidly increased. The expropriation of peasants posed as political danger and the Land Alienation Act of Punjab was passed in 1900, which sought to restrict the sale of agricultural land and its sale to non-agriculturists.

Free trade in land leads to monopolies which dispossesses small producers of their land rights. The situation in the US where only 2.4 per cent of the population survives as farmers is proof of this failure of the market to protect land rights of producers.

In 1776, nine out of ten Americans worked in agriculture. In 1929, there were seven million farmers in the US and over thirty-five million farm residents. Since the 1950s the number of farms has diminished from six million to under two million today with only 2.4 per cent of the US population on farms.

Almost half of US farmland today is owned by non-farmers. Very large industrial farms today dominate agriculture in the US. These superfarms have very negative environmental impacts, from draining aquifers to poisoning the soil and to compacting the soil with heavy equipment and reducing biodiversity through monocultures. It was projected that by the year 2000, just one per cent of the farms will produce half of the nation's food. Huge grain dealers are subsidized by the government to purchase their commodities for substantially less than the farmers cost of production. This cheap grain has driven off many Third World farmers from their land and contributed to food insecurity.

The model of large corporate farms is now being introduced in India.

Today under trade liberalization, states are told to change land ceiling laws in order to allow the corporate sector to acquire vast tracts of land. Peasants are thus losing their right to land. The government has already given agri-business the go-ahead for contract farming, which means that the farmer has to sell the produce to the corporation at a price determined exclusively by corporate and trade monopolies and not by farmers.

The removal of limits in ownership of land is detrimental to both justice and sustainability. Only small farmers can use land sustainably replenishing the organic fertility of their soil with internal inputs. Only small farms can provide food security to millions of rural people.

The recent amendment of the Karnataka Land Reforms Act (1961) is aimed at undoing the Land Reforms Act of Karnataka, Land ceiling has been removed for agriculture in the Uttara Kannada and Dakshina Kannada district. Horticulture, floriculture and agro-based industries have also been made exempt of ceiling laws.

Water Trading : A Crucial Issue

The World Bank policy paper recommends the creation of "markets in tradeable water rights." It is argued that "rights to the delivery of water can be freely bought and sold, farmers with new crops or in new areas will be able to obtain water provided they are willing to pay more than its value in deciding on what and how much to produce."

This institution of tradeable water rights is a guarantee for diverting water from small farmers to large corporate super farms. Tradeable water rights will lead to water monopolies. In the logic of the market, tradeable rights have a tendency to be sold to the highest bidder and hence lead to water-power linked to concentration of wealth. It will also lead to over-exploitation and misuse of water, since those who deplete water resources do not have to suffer the consequences of water scarcity as they can always buy water rights from other farmers and other regions. Besides aggravating the already severe ecological crisis in water resources, tradeable water rights will destroy the social fabric of rural communities and create discord and disintegration. The social breakdown in Somalia can be traced, in part, to the privatization of water rights according to the World Bank policy. Tradeable water rights are based on the assumption that no ecological or social limits should be placed on water use. Such use without limits leads to abuse. The World Bank proposals on tradeable water rights are a prescription for social and ecological disaster.

The World Bank policies on the privatization of water have already been implemented. For example, in the new Agriculture Policy of Karnataka, the section on reforms of the irrigation sector talks of a shift from "top down to bottom up" approach. The privatization and tradeable water approach is definitely a bottom up policy and not in the sense of democratic control. It is bottom up, since it moves the control over water resources upwards from small and marginal farmers to large corporations and agri-business interests who can buy up the "water equity shares" of "water users associations" and establish monopoly control on water. This has already happened in Sri Lanka, where export corporations have purchased shares from farmers, thus leading to displacement of farmers from agricultural activities and livelihoods.

Corporate Control or Community Control of Natural Resources: Which Way Forward for a Sustainable Future?

The major democratic issue emerging in India is the right to survival of the large number of poor people who derive their livelihood from natural resources- land, water and biodiversity. In each sector a major conflict is emerging between corporate control and community control of natural resources.

People's movements are demanding that power should not be concentrated in institutions of the centralized nation-states but should be distributed throughout society and should be dispersed through a multiplicity of institutions, with more power at the local level, controlled by local communities and their institutions. However, while the TNC driven globalization agenda requires that power move from centralized control to nation-states to even more centralized control of global corporations and global institutions like WTO, the World Bank and IMF, the people's democratically driven agenda is for greater localization, both political and economic. Political localization implies more decisions being transferred to the local space. Economic localization implies that whatever can be produced locally should be part of the local economy so that both the livelihoods and the environment are protected.

While the international financial and trade organizations coerce and push the government into a blind and indiscriminate experiment with globalization, the Indian people are responding with a new politics of "localization". They are engaging in an enlightened response to put globalization in its ecological and social context. In region after region where foreign investment is diverting local resources from the survival needs of the local people to the limitless appetite of global markets, people are putting investment to the test of ecological and social accountability. They are also redefining the principles of governance on the basis of decentralized democracy. The rule of the World Bank and the WTO have implied rule by super-state institutions serving the one-sided interests of commerce and beyond the democratic control of people. As the state withdraws from environmental and social regulation in the "free-trade" era, local communities are getting organized to regulate commercial activity by asserting their environmental rights to natural resources- land, water and biodiversity and their democratic rights to decide how these resources are used. They are redefining democracy in terms of people's decisions in their everyday lives. They are redefining the nation in terms of people, not in terms of the centralized state.

Another example of people's concern is the citation by Vandana Shiva in Stolen Harvest: She has documented the work of community and small non-governmental organizations in the developing world to counter the corporatization and monopolizatiion of food. She also includes the voices of people at the grassroots level living with the consequences of private sector and their own governments' decisions to globalize and mechanize. Here is the voice of just one, an Indian villager living in a coastal area full of large-scale shrimp farms: "We have lost all our drinking water, where earlier there used to be nine wells .... we no longer live in this village as all the houses have collapsed because of dampness and salinity five hundred families have been displaced."

The irony is that traditional systems of shrimp cultivation practiced in India for over 500 years- but viewed as backward and small scale by India's technocrats and global corporations, intent on "modernization" and higher and higher shrimp yields- have little negative environmental impact, do not require chopping down coastal trees, and, Shiva argues, are as profitable as the intensive shrimp farms. A major theme that runs throughout the book is that methods of food production developed over thousand of years by rural peoples are not only more profitable than the globalizers' preferred methods, but are more effective at promoting food security. They also have far fewer negative environmental impacts, keep control of food supplies in local hands, promote crop diversity (as opposed to industrial agriculture's focus on monocrops) and support local and national economics.

This trend towards localization has in fact, been born along with the trend towards globalization. If globalization is the corporate driven agenda to corporate control, localization is the counter-vailing citizens agenda for protecting the environment and people's survival and people's livelihood. In the absence of regulation by national governments, citizens are creating a new politics for introducing ecological limits and social responsibility in this process of globalization. The ecological and democratic response of localization has built into it an environmental component of the control and ownership of local resources a decision making component about the utilization of these resources and an economic component to resist the destruction of local economics by the global economy and international trade.

Localization does not imply autarchy or insularity. It involves subjecting the logic of globalization to the test of sustainability, democracy and justice in each concrete instance of foreign investment. It also involves reclaiming the state to protect people's interest and not allow it to be reduced to being a mere instrument for foreign investors even while returning to people the power and authority the state had usurped from them. No society can live without governance or government. The issue is not whether nation-states should exist or disappear or wether they should be more or less of the state. The real issue of our times is how to reinvent the state and make it different from the centralized bureaucratic and controlling state that had taken away the functions and roles of civil society. It would be an error to imagine that protection for the environment and for the weaker members of the society can be provided by leaving environmental decisions and decisions of distribution of goods and services to unregulated and unaccountable market forces. Social regulation of the market requires social policy and this is not the same as individual consumer choice. The contest between the transnational corporations, the force behind globalization and the citizens and local communities, and the force behind localization spins off into a contest over what kind of state will regulate corporations while creating and enhancing freedom for citizens, freedom from want, from hunger and homelessness and the denial of basic needs is the most fundamental freedom without which there can be no other. How this freedom will be ensured by deepening of democracy, strengthening of civil society and the creation of a different kind of a state is the project of democracy in our times.

Movements for localizations are giving rise to a new people's protectionism which is different from the old protectionism in the fact that power and authority to make environmental and economic decisions move from centralized states to self- governance structures at the local level and citizens and community organizations decide which roles and functions the state should have. It is also different from corporate protectionism in which all institutions of society- the courts, police, government departments- are distorted to protect the interests of transnational corporations, sacrificing the interests of citizens, of small producers and small traders.

The largest corporations of the world have found new investment opportunities in India since 1991, under a combination of strong-arm tactics of the 301 clauses of the U.S. Trade Act, the IMF/ World Bank pressures for liberalization and the Uruguay Round GATT which have combined to shape the government's new economic policies that put the interests and rights of foreign investors above the interests and rights of the citizens of India. And in each sector, the biggest multinational corporation has been forced to recognize that it is the clearance from citizens, not just a clearance from the government that is necessary for democratic functioning.

Whether it is Cargill and Grace in Karnataka, Dupont in Goa, or KFC in Delhi and Bangalore, the entry of TNCs which threaten people's livelihoods, resources and people's health is questioned by local communities and grassroots struggles. Local communities are raising a common voice "We will decide the pattern of investment and development. We will determine the ownership and use of our natural resources." As this message resonates in village after village, from one investment site to another, a new environmental philosophy based on democratic decentralization of control over natural resources is emerging. The pressure of the people is forcing the government to remember its role as protector of the public interest and the country's natural and cultural heritage, not merely the interests of foreign investors. The tendency towards localization and deepening of democracy is aimed at taming the excesses of globalization, including the political excesses of deregulation.

Now the question arises, is there an inherent contradiction between democracy and globalization? Some anti-globalization protesters might say yes. And their pro-free trade opponents might also agree. But upon careful consideration, write philosopher and political scientist Pratap Bhanu Mehta, it is clear that the debate between democrats and globalizers is often too stylized. "The constraints on democracy, in reality, stem from the political structures of states themselves, "Mehta says, while" As part of a rhetorical battle, globalization gets saddled with causing ills it is not patently responsible for." Yet despite the sometimes dubious arguments made against globalization, he argues, the recent elections in India remind us that voters who protest globalization at the polls are "asking legitimate questions about the distribution of risks this process entails. Why should particular classes of labour be made more vulnerable by globalization than holders of capital? Why should the low-yield, but risk-averse farming strategies of an Indian farmer with a small plot of land give way to large-scale commercial farming that takes the land away from him?" These compelling questions deserve the attention of people at all levels of society, he says, and their democratic resolution could benefit a citizenry's economic and political life. Even though the political processes of democratic countries can be cumbersome and slow, Mehta concludes, democracy is still "the only way of ensuring that all the relevant consideration have been taken into account in creating a new architecture for the world."[15]

The pattern that seems to be emerging is for environmental governance beyond the centralizing state and super-state systems, which work unidirectionally for the corporate interest.

Localization is emerging as an antidote to globalization and to unrestrained commercial greed.

The challenge before us is to build on these movements for localization to bring substance into Panchayati Raj by establishing community control over natural resources and over the economy. It is this search for democracy in the age of globalization towards which we must all strive, for which we must all struggle, in diverse ways, at multiple levels.

References

1. Jessica Einhorn, "Millons of Indians Await Benefits of Globalization", Yale, *Global*, February 25, 2005.
2. D.L. Sheth, "Democracy and Globalization in India: Post-Cold War Discourse *Annuals of the American Academy of Political and Social Science,* Volume 540", pp. 24-39, July, 1995.
3. See the report by the United Nations Development Program referenced in *New York Times*, July 13, 1999.
4. Soutik Biswas, "India Warning on Globalization", *BBC News,* Delhi, December 20, 2006.
5. Quoted in *The Hindu*, October 1, 1995.
6. See the report by the Conference Board of New York, 1992.
7. Barnet, Richard J. & Muller, Ronald E., *Global Reach: The Power of the Multinational Corporation*, New York, Simon & Schuster, 1994.
8. Quoted in *The Indian Express*, August 25, 1995.
9. George Schwartz, *In Bad Taste: The MSG Syndrome*, 1995.
10. Vandana Shiva, *Stolen Harvest: the Hijacking of the Global Food Supply*, Cambridge, MA: South End Press, 2000.
11. Quoted in *Real News*, Project Censored, April 2007.
12. Arun Shrivastava, "Genetically Modified Seeds: Women in India take on Monsanto", *Global Research*, October 9, 2006.
13. Quoted in *People's Weekly World*, December 7, 1996.
14. Historic Legal Challenge on IPR Laws, Dossier published by Research Foundation for Science, Technology and Natural Resource Policy September 14, 1995.
15. Pratap Bhanu Mehta, "Globalization Requires the Legitimacy only Democracy can give", Yale, *Global*, June 17, 2004.

9. SECULARISM AND THE CONSTITUTIONAL FRAMEWORK

H.K. Sharma

The basic constitutional provisions that give shape to the concept of the secular state, and their interpretation by the Indian High Court and Supreme Court are being examined under this article.

The term 'Secular State', it should be noted, does not appear in the constitution itself. The late Professor K.T. Shah, a member of the Constituent Assembly, attempted on two occasions to secure the inclusion of the word 'secular' in the fundamental law, but without success. His second attempt took the form of a proposed new article that read in part: "The State in India being a secular state shall have no concern with any religion, creed or profession of faith".[1] Shah argued that in view of the tragic result of communalism in India, it would be well to emphasize the secularity of the state in the most explicit terms.

His amendment did not receive the support of the law minister, however was rejected by the Assembly. The inclusion of such an article in the Constitution however laudable the intention behind it, would certainly have produced a conflict with Article 25 which, permits extensive state intervention in matter connected with religion in the interest of society.

We shall now examine the Indian constitution in terms of the three components of this conception.

Freedom of Religion, citizenship and separation of State and religion.

Freedom of Religion

The Indian Constitution provides for the religious liberty of both the individual and associations of individuals united by common beliefs, practices and discipline. The individual and collective aspects of religious liberty shall be discussed in this order.

Individual Freedom of Religion

The basic guarantee of this right is found in Article 25(1):

Subjects to public order, morality and health and to the other provisions to this part, all persons are equally entitled to freedom of conscience and the right freely to profess, practice and propagate religion.

In discussion of the origin of this article, attention is frequently drawn to its similarity to the following provision of the 1937 constitution of Eire: "Freedom of Conscience and the free profession and practice of religion are, subject to public order and morality, guaranteed to every citizen."[2] There were however other sources nearer at hand. The language of the Indian constitution is very similar to that of the resolution on fundamental rights adopted at the Karachi Congress in 1931: "Every citizen shall enjoy freedom of conscience and the right freely to profess and practice his religion, subject to public order and morality.[3]

The freedom of religion guaranteed by the Indian Constitution is not confined to citizens but extends to all persons', including aliens. This point, underlined by the Supreme Court in Ratilal Panchand Vs. State of Bombay (now Mumbai), is of special interest because of the substantial number of foreign Christian missionaries in India, some of whom are exclusively engaged in propagating their faith among the adherents of other religions.[4]

The constitution thus declares that every person has a fundamental right not only to hold whatever religious beliefs command themselves to his judgment (Freedom of conscience) but also to manifest his beliefs in such overt acts as are prescribed by his religion and to propagate its tenets among others (right to profess, practice and propagate religion). The exercise of this right, is however, 'subject to public order, morality and health'. Here the constitution specifically expresses the limitations on religious liberty that have been evolved by judicial pronouncements in the

US and Austraalia. In a long series of cases the US courts have held that : Polygamy may be prohibited by legislation although it is,

(1) Sanctioned by a religious body.
(2) religious propaganda on the streets is subject to regulation, etc.

Strictly speaking, the language of the Indian Constitution makes freedom of conscience as well as the right to freely profess, practice and propagate religion subject to state control in the interest of public order, morality and health. This is however, simply a case of inaccurate drafting, and the courts have made it clear that the state can have no power over the conscience of the individual. This right is absolute.

The necessity of the state's power to preserve public order was pointedly enunciated when the US Supreme Court asked: "Suppose that one believed that human sacrifices were a necessary part of religious worship, would it be seriously contended that the civil government under which he lived could not interfere to prevent a sacrifice.[5] The Indian Penal Code (Sects. 295-8) makes it a Crime to injure or defile a place of worship or to disturb a religious assembly etc. even though, their actions might be sanctioned by the offender's own religion. Practices like Sati, or devdasi dedication that frequently led to temple prostitution, may have some basis in Hindu religion, but the state still has constitutional power to ban them.

The right to freedom of religion is subject not only to public order, morality, and health but to the other provisions of Part III Therefore, the practice of untouchability [Forbidden in Art. 17] could not be protected under Article 25. Land can be compulsorily acquired by the State with compensation under Article 31, despite the fact that it is part of a religious endowment.

The Indian courts have sketched out other areas in which freedom of religion is not absolute. It was held that Article 25(1) did not give a Hindu student the right to perform the ceremonies of his religion in the compound of a Christian college. [Sanjib Kumar Vs. St. Paul's College]

In another case the Supreme Court held that an optimal religious practice need not be protected by the constitutional guarantee of freedom of religion. Thus a Muslim accustomed to sacrificing a cow at Bakar ID would be compelled to obey a law prohibiting cow slaughter for Islam recognizes as equally valid the sacrifice of goat.

Limitations Imposed by Indian Constitution

The restrictions on freedom of religion based on considerations of public order, morality, and health are obvious ones and have many parallels in the constitutional law of the West. Article 25(2), however, imposes drastic limitations on the rights just guaranteed in 25(1) and reflects the particular needs of Indian Society.

Nothing in this article shall affect the operation of any existing law or prevent the state from making any law:

(a) regulating or restricting any economic, financial, political or other secular activity which may be associated with religious practice.

(b) Providing for social welfare and reform or the throwing open of Hindu religious institutions of a pubic character to all clauses and Sections of Hindu.

Laws providing for the very extensive supervision by the state of temple administration (Hindu religious endownment Acts) have been enacted by virtue of this provision.

The same constitutional provision permits legislation opening Hindu religious institutions of a public character to all classes and Sections of India. Harijan temple entry laws have been enacted by many of the state legislatures. The central untouchability (offences) Act of 1955 provides inter alia that any attempt to prevent Harijans from exercising their rights of temple entry is punishable with imprisonment, fine or both.

Article 25(2) thus authorizes the state to regulate any secular activity associated with religion, to legislate social reforms, and force open the doors of Hindu temple to Harijans. C.H. Alexandrowicz wrote: "The above clause constitutes in itself a revolution in the traditional conception of religions in India".

Another aspect of the revolution envisaged by this clause is, however, the assumption by the state of vast powers of control over the financial administration of Hindu religious institutions.

Individual freedom of religion, basically guaranteed in Article 25 is further strengthened by Article 27, which declares that no person shall be compelled to pay taxes for the support of any particular religion. The Interpretation of this provision is considered in another Section, 'Taxation and Religious Education'. The protection of the individual's freedom of conscience is also the object of article 28(3), which forbids compulsory religious instruction or worship in educational institutions recognized or aided by the State.

Collective Freedom of Religion

Religious denominations as well as individuals have certain important rights; collective freedom of religion is spelled out in Article 26.

Subject to public order, morality, and health, every religious denomination or any Section thereof shall have the right-

(a) To establish and maintain institution for religious and charitable purposes;
(b) to manage its own affairs in matters of religion;
(c) To own and acquire movable and immovable property;
(d) To administer such property in accordance with law.

The conflict between the internal autonomy of a religious denomination and the role of the State in social reform was most dramatically manifested in the case of Taher Saifuddin Vs. Tyebbhai Moosaji.[6] The Bombay prevention of excommunication Act 1949 prohibits the expulsion of a person from any community of which he is a member; thus depriving him of his rights and privileges. The rights and privileges referred to are those that are legally enforceable by a civil suit and include the right to office or property or to worship in any religious place, and the right of burial or cremation. The head priest of the Dawoodi Bohra community which were later declared to be void, illegal, and of no effect by virtue of the prevention of Excommunication Act. The Bombay High Court in this case upheld the constitutionality of the Act which, according the head priest, deprived his religious denomination of the right 'to manage its own affairs in matters of religion'.

It is in the interest of the secular state to strengthen the internal autonomy of religious denominations, although this is little realized by the various legislatures. The demand for social reform and religious reform is so pressing that little attention is paid to the principle of separation of state and religion.

Under Article 26(b), therefore, a religious denomination or organization enjoys complete autonomy in the matter of deciding as to what rites and ceremonies are essential according to the tenets of the religion they hold and no outside authority has any jurisdiction to interfere with their decision in such matters.

Thus, the right of collective freedom of religion guaranteed by Article 26 does not provide the kind of protection from the state interference which is found in a secular state in the west, the U.S. for example. Article 30 deals with another aspect of collective freedom of religion:

1. All minorities, whether based on religion or language shall have the right to establish and administer educational institution of their choice.
2. The state shall not, in granting aid to educational institution's discriminate against any educational institution on the ground that it is under the management of as minority, whether based on religion or language.

The Supreme Court made it clear that, with the exception of certain Anglo-Indian Institutions provided for under Article 337 Private educational Institutions had no constitutional right to receive any grant from the state. Nevertheless, the situation was such that without state aid practically none of their institutions could operate. The court declared:

"No educational institution can in actual practice be carried on without aid from the state and if they will, by compulsion of financial necessities, be compelled to give up their rights under Article 30(10)."[7]

Citizenship

The second component of the secular state, the concept of citizenship, is based on the idea that the individual, not the group, is the basic unit. The individual is confronted by the State which imposes duties and responsibilities upon him, in return the state guarantees rights and grants privileges to the individual. The sum total of these individuals- state relationship constitutes the meaning of citizenship.

No State Discrimination on Ground of Religion

In the Indian Constitution there are many provisions dealing with the citizen's relations with the state. After guaranteeing in Article 14 the right to equality before the law and the equal protection of the laws, the Constitution goes on in Article 15(1) to provide: "The State shall not discriminate against any citizen on grounds only of religion, race, caste, sex, place of birth or any of them".

The Bombay High Court upheld the severe penalties on the ground that they were necessary to make the law socially effective. Laying emphasis on the word only in Article 15(1), it held that the legislation did not single out the Hindus on the ground of religion only. The legislature had to lake into account the social customs and beliefs of the Hindus and other relevant considerations before deciding whether it was necessary to provide special legislation making bigamous marriage illegal. The state was entitled to consider, for example the relative educational development of the Hindus and the Muslims. "One community might be prepared to accept and work social reform; another may not yet be prepared for it... The state may rightly decide to bring about social reform by stages, and the stages may be territorial or they may be community wise."

In a similar case arising under the Madras Hindu Bigamy prevention and Divorce Act of 1949, it was held that the Act did not discriminate between Hindus and Muslims on the ground of religion[8] while only Hindus were affected by the legislation, 'the essence' of that classification is not their religion but that they have all along been preserving their personal law peculiar to themselves which was derived from the Smirit, Commentaries, custom and usage. According to this interpretation, they did not discriminate on the ground of religion since it applied not to those who profused Hindu religion, but to those who were governed by Hindu law. The Madras High Court here indulged in a bit of pure sophistry.

The strained interpretations of the courts notwithstanding, there is absolutely no doubt that such legislation is discriminatory and contrary to Article 15(1). This is not to suggest that the courts should have declared these laws uconstitutional. During this transitional period when India is struggling to become a modern state, it is precisely the function of the courts to concot such ingenious interpretations in order to harmonize the permanently valid principle, Article 15(1) in this case, with the dynamic urge for social reform which has yet to find expression within the antiquated framework of religious civil law. Not only the Hindu Bigamous Marriages Act, but the whole system of Hindu Muslim personal law is contrary to Article 15(1). It is only when there is a uniform civil code that the courts will be able to afford the luxury of a natural and straight forward interpretation of this fundamental constitutional principle of the secular state. While the existence of different personal laws contradicts the principle of non-discrimination by the state contained in Article 15(1) the constitution itself contradicts this principle in dealing with the problems connected with the caste system. In its special provisions for the scheduled caste, scheduled tribes, and other backward classes, the constitution "Introduced what may be called protective discrimination in favour of those sections of the community which require urgent support, for, if the Principle of equality was applied without any exception, the reorganization of Indian society and the uplift of its hitherto neglected strata would be difficult if not impossible."[9]

One of the problems was the constitutional one, namely of reconciling the principles of protective discrimination and non-discrimination by the state. In certain specific areas this adjustment had already been made in the constitution as adopted in 1950, but contained in Article 15(1). Adverse court decisions necessitated the 'first Amendment Act, 1951, which inter alia inserted Article 15(4):

> Nothing in this article or in clause (2) of article 29 shall prevent the state from making any special provisions for the advancement of any socially and educationally backward classes of citizens or for the scheduled castes and the Scheduled Tribes.

The state is thus permitted to discriminate among citizens on grounds of religion, caste, etc. when providing for the advancement of certain sections of the population.

Applying the Principle of Non-discrimination

It seems clear that the fundamental conception of citizenship as a relationship between the individual and the state is being seriously undermined by the attempt to deal with the problem of the under privileged on the basis of the group, especially the caste. Article 15(1) lays down the basic democratic principle that the state shall not discriminate against any citizen on grounds only of religion, caste. This general principle is then applied to three specific areas:

1. Pubic employment or office
2. Admission to state educational institutions
3. Voting and representation in legislatures

However, just as Article 15(1) is qualified by a major exception, there are similar exceptions to the principle of non-discrimination in each of these specific areas.

In regard to public employment the guarantee is stated both positively and negatively. Article 16(1) asserts the principle of equality of opportunity for all citizens in matters relating to employment or appointment to any office under the State. Negatively, according to Article 16(2): 'No citizen shall, on grounds only of religion, race, caste, sex, descent, place of birth, residence or any of them, be ineligible, or discriminated against in respect of, any employment or office under the state'.[10]

The Constitution provides for one exception to the principle of no religious qualifications for public office. Article 16(5) permits law requiring that the incumbent of an office connected with the affairs of a religious institution be an adherent of that religion. Thus the commissioner and all of his subordinates in the Madras Hindu Religious Endownments Department must be Hindus. Although there are all officers of the secular state, the religious qualification is allowed by this clause.

Another exception to the general principle of non-discrimination is found in Article 16(4).

Nothing in this article shall prevent the state from making any provision for the reservation of appointments or posts in favour of any backward class of citizens which, in the opinions of the state is not adequately represented in the services under the state.

Article 335 of the constitution states that the claims of the members of the Scheduled Castes and Scheduled Tribes shall be taken into consideration in the making of appointment to government posts and services. Such special consideration must be made 'consistently with the maintenance of efficiency of administration'. Article 16(4) refers to 'any backward class of citizens', which includes the Schedule castes and Tribes as well as others. Further more, it goes beyond the vague provisions of Article 335 by permitting the state to reserve certain posts and appointments for these sections of the population.

Non-discrimination in Political Functions

The third application of the principle of nondiscrimination among citizens is in the area of voting and representation in the legislature. Article 325 states.

There shall be one general electoral roll for every territorial constituency for election to either House of Parliament or to the either House of the legislature of a state and no person shall be ineligible for inclusion in any such roll or claim to be included in any special electoral roll for any such constituency on grounds only of religion, race, sex or any of them.

The first important provision to be noted here is that there can be no religious or caste requirements for voting. Article 326 states the principle positively and simply by declaring that elections 'shall be on the basis of adult suffrage'.

The second aspect to be noted is that the system of separate communal electrorates, first established in 1909, as abolished. "There shall be one general electoral roll for every territorial constituency....' Under the old system each of the larger minority community is (Muslims, Christians, Sikhs etc.) had its electoral roll and a number of reserved seats in the legislatures. Thus, only Muslims voters could vote for Muslim candidates standing for election to seats specifically reserved for Muslims in the legislatures.

While the system of separate electorates was abolished, the constitution does provide for the reservation of seats for the scheduled castes and scheduled tribes[11] in the central and state legislatures (Article 330 and 332). According to the original Article 334 the reservation of seats was to cease after a period of ten years from the commencement of the constitution, or in 1960. The 8th amendment, however, extended this reservation for another ten years.

Difficult constitutional problems have arisen over this arrangement, especially under the system of double member constituencies (one reserved and one general seat). In V.V. Giri

Vs. D.S. Dora the Supreme Court upheld the election of Scheduled Tribe candidates to both the reserved and the general seats.[12]

In 1961 Parliament enacted legislation providing for the division of two member constituencies. While this will eliminate certain problems, it will undoubtedly create others. Thus a non Scheduled Class person residing in a constituency for which there is reserved seat will be unable to stand for election to that seat. If he is a person of limited financial resources it will be very difficult for him to conduct an effective election campaign in another constituency where he is less well known.

The provision for joint electrorates in Articles 325 refers specifically to elections to the central and state legislatures only. The questions arose whether a state law could provide for separate electorates for the members of the various religious communities in election to local legislative bodies. The Supreme Court in Nainsukh Das Vs. State of U.P. held that such a law went counter to the non-discrimination principle of Article 15(1). The court observed "Now it cannot be seriously disputed that any law providing for elections on the basis of separate electorates for members of different religious communities offends against article 15(1). The constitutional mandate to the state not to discriminate on the ground inter- alia of religion extends to political as well as to other rights.[13]

In concluding this section on the constitutional basis for the concept of citizenship in the Indian secular State, a few generalizations may be made. It is obvious that the fundamental provisions of equalling and nondiscrimination in the state's relationship with the individual citizen is seriously compromised in several areas. Almost all of the difficulties have their roots in the state's commendable recognition of its special responsibilities towards those sections of the population which in the past have been the victims of exploitation. However the approach to the problem has too often identified special need with a caste designation, and there is no doubt that caste consciousness has thereby been strengthened.

Separation of State and Religion

Separation of state and religion is the principle that preserves the integrity of the other two relationships, freedom of religion and citizenship. Once the principle of separation of state and religion is abandoned, the way is open for state interference in the individual's religious liberty, and for state discrimination against him if it happens to dissent from the official creed.

Even today in some of the democratic states of Western Europe, the state church system retains vestiges of these consequences. In actual practice the separation is not absolute. But it is clear that such a thoroughgoing separation of state and religion does not exist in India. The important areas in which state interference in religious matters is permitted by the constitution:

1. The financial administration of temples and maths,
2. The admission of Harijans into Hindu temples.
3. The practice of excommunication from religious communities,
4. The modification of religious personal law.

The chief reason for such state interference is that Hinduism lacks the kind of ecclesiastical organization necessary to set own house in order; the tremendous urge for effective social and religious reform that characterizes present day India can only be satisfied by state action.[14] The organizational deficiency of Hinduism is indeed a serious problem. How can there be separation of church and state where there is no church?

The firmly established principle in the US that the courts will not decide controversies over matters of religious doctrine or ritual has a pale reflection in Indian judicial decisions of some years ago. In 1935 the Bombay High Court held that a civil court is competent to decide whether a particular name or mark should be placed on an idol's forehead was one pertaining to religious ritual and as such was excluded from the cognizance of a civil court.[15] Since 1950, however, the courts have frequently had to deal with doctrinal questions in defining the scope of freedom of religion guaranteed in Article 25 and 26. For example, the courts have had to determine the correct interpretation of scriptures that forbid the entry of untouchables into temples, the doctrine basis for the practice of polygamy in Hinduism, and similar matters. These cases have of course, not involved religious controversies between individuals, but between individuals and the legislating state.

There are, however, other aspects of the principle of separation of state and religion that are supported by the Indian Constitution:

1. There is no provision regarding an official State religion
2. There can be no religious instruction in state school
3. There can be no taxes to support any particular religion.

What the constitution does not say is just as significant as what it does say. There is no mention made of any official state religion. There is no explicit prohibition of the adoption of a state religion, as in the Constitution of America, but it is inconceivable that such a radical step would be attempted without a constitutional amendment. Not only is there no state religion in India but no official recognition is given to the religion of the majority. By way of contrast, the Constitution of Burma before 1961 declared : "The state recognize the special position of Buddhism as the faith professed by the great majority of the citizens of the union.[16]

India has no state religion, nor does it give any constitutional recognition to Hinduism as the religion of the majority of citizens. It is also important to note that there is no Ecclesiastical Department in the central government, such as existed during the British period. Before 1927 the bishops of the established church of England in India were appointed by the crown. Right upto 1948, however, the Ecclesiastical Department continued to pay a large number of Christian chaplains and maintain Christian churches out of the public revenues of the country. The unstated principle embodied in the Indian constitution is that found in the 1931 Karachi resolution of the Indian National Congress: 'The state shall observe neutrality in regard to all religions'.

Taxation and Religious Education

Article 27 of the constitution states: "No person shall be compelled to pay any taxes, the proceeds of which are specifically appropriated in payment of expenses for the promotion or maintenance of any particular religion or religious denomination.[17]

Several writers have very erroneously equated this provision with the principle laid down in such rigid terms by the US Supreme Court in the Everson case. 'No tax in any amount, large or small, can be levied to support any religious activities or institutions, whatever they may be called, or whatever form or whatever form they may adopt to teach or practice religion. ' The differences of constitutional position on this point between the US and India are considerable.

First, the Indian Constitution forbids only taxation for the benefit of any particular religion. Non discriminatory taxes for the benefit of all religions would be perfectly constitutional. Such an arrangement would in fact, be in accord with the general traditions of the Hindu state. It would however, seriously undermine the fundamental principle of separation of state and religion as it has here been defined. Separation means that it is not the function of the state to aid one religion or to aid all religions.[18] The secular state will not coerce any individual (by taxation or any other mans) to support any religion.

Second, Indian and American law very greatly differ in their treatment of educational institutions managed by religious bodies. While in the US public funds may be used to support parochial schools only in very limited ways (bus transportation, free lunches, text books for the pupils) in India the system of government grants to privately managed schools has over a century of history behind it and is still very important.

Third, in the US no government grants of money may be made to religious institutions.[19] The Indian constitution explicitly provides for state contributions to Hindu temples and shrines. This surprising provision is found in Article 290A.

Article 28 deals with the question of instruction in these different types of education institutions. The first provision refers to institutions that are of a completely public nature.

Class (1) lays down:

"No religious instruction shall be provided in any educational institution wholly maintained out of state funds."[20]

The prohibition here is absolute; neither the state nor any private agency may provide religious instruction in state educational institution.[21] Here we have a stricter adherence to the principle of separation of state and religion than in the previous article examined.

Article 27 would permit taxation for the benefit of all religions but not for any particular religion? The logical counterpart in the field of education would be a provision enabling the state to provide instruction in all religions but not in one particular religion alone. But such is not the case; there is to be 'no religions instructions' in state educational institutions.

Article 28(2) deals with a second special type of educational institution in which the state functions in the role of trustee.

'Nothing in clause (1) shall apply to an educational institution which is administered by the state but has been established under any endowment or trust which requires that religious instruction shall be imparted in such institution.

The Banaras Hindu University and the Aligarh Muslim University were established under endowments which require that instruction be imparted in Hinduism and Islam respectively. Although administered by the central government, religious instruction in these Universities is permitted by clause (2).

The third type of educational institution is the state aided denominational school. As we have seen every religious group has the right to establish and administer its own educational institutions, the state may not discriminate against those managed by minority groups. The principle involved in Article 28(3) is that the state cannot become a party to the active propagation of religion in state aided institutions by permitting compulsory religious instruction.

No person attending any educational institution recognized by the state or receiving aid out of state funds shall be required to take part in any religious instruction that may be conducted in such institution or in any premises attached thereto unless such person or, if such person is a minor, his guardian has given his consent thereto.

Protection of Interest of Minorities

Article 29 guarantees to "every section of the citizens" residing anywhere in India and " having a district language, script or culture" the right to conserve the same. No citizen can be denied admission to any educational institution maintained or aided by the state on grounds only of religion, race, caste or language.

Although the marginal heading of the article uses the term 'minorities', it has not been mentioned in the text of the article and it has been held that it is equally available to any section of citizens- whether in minority or majority.[22]

Rights of minorities to establish and administer educational institutions

The constitution does not anywhere define the term 'minorities'. Article 30(1) says that all minorities, whether religious or linguistic, shall have the right to establish and administer educational institutions of their choice. Clause 1(A) added by the 44th Amendment, in effect provides that if the property of any such institution is acquired, the compensation paid would be proper and adequate so that the right given by the article remains meaningful. Clause 2 provides that in the matter of aid, the state shall not discriminate against minority - managed institutions.

Article 30 is strictly in the nature of a minority right, i.e. one intended to protect the rights of minorities. Autonomy of a minority institution cannot be taken away completely. It is quite wide in as much as it is not confined like article 29 only to conversation of language, script and culture. (Rev. Father proost 'Vs. State of Bihar, AIR 1969 SC 465; Ahmedabad St. Xavier's College Society V. State of Gujarat, AIR 1974 SC 1389; St. Stephen's College V. University of Delhi, (1992) SCC 558). Also, the right of minorities under this article to 'establish and administer' educational institutions" of their choice' includes the right to choose the medium of instruction, curricula, subjects to be taught etc. (D.A.V. College Bhatinda V. State of Punjab, AIR 1971 SC 1731; In Kerala Education Bill, AIR 1958 SC 956).

The right to administer, however does not mean right to maladministration. The right is subject to regulatory power of the state. Legislation in the interest of social welfare, industrial relations, academic standards, efficiency, discipline, health sanitation, public order, morality, reasonable regulation to prescribe syllabus etc. does not violate article 30 so along as it does not deprive the minority of its right to manage the institution. A law made to safeguard the service interests of teachers and regulate their conditions of service in the matter of dismissal, removal or reduction in rank did not violate article 30 (In Kerala education Bill, AIR 1958 SC 936; Ahmedabad St. Xavier's College Society V. University of Delhi (1992) 1 SCC 558; State of T.N.V. Joseph, (1991) 3 SCC 87; Frank Anthony Public School Employees' Association V. Union of India, (1986) 4 SCC 707; Virendra Nath V. Delhi (1990) 2 SCC 307; All Saints High School V. Government of Andhra Pradesh, AIR 1980 SC 1042).

Also, educational institutions must be genuinely an educational institution of the minorities to be entitled to the right given by article 30(1). The government, the University and the court could go behind the claim of a minority institution where the claim was a mere clock or pretension and the real motive was business adventure, the protection of article 30(1) would not be available (A.P. Christians Medical Education Society V. Government of A.P., AIR 1986 SC 1490).

In T.M.A. Pai V. State of Karnataka [(2004) 1 SCC 86] and Islamic Academic V. State of Karnataka, [(2003) 6 SCC 697] the Supreme Court in their judgements of 31 October, 2002 and 14 August 2003 held:

1. Private educational institutions have a right to determine their own fee structure but education cannot be made a means of personal profit or help in other profession or business. Every state shall constitute a committee which will settle the appropriate fee structure for every private educational institution. It will be impermissible to ask for additional amounts in the name of donation or capitation fee.
2. It will not be correct to say that under article 30 minority educational institutions do not have any special rights which are not available to educational institutions of the majority community. The protection of article 30 is not for members of the majority community.
3. National interest must stand above the fundamental rights of individuals. Therefore, it is necessary that in professional (medical, engineering etc.) colleges- whether of the majority or minorities- the basis for admission should be merit alone.

   In non-minority professional institutions, with the exception of seats reserved for the management, all admissions should be on the basis of merit determined through common entrance tests conducted by official agencies. Even in professional institutions established and administered by minority communities, admissions should be on the basis of merit but this merit has to be determined among the candidates of the concerned minority community only. The number of seats that should be reserved for minority candidates would depend upon the particular requirements of the minority community in each state. Such college can select meritorious candidates on the basis of private common admission tests.

4. Every state shall set up a standing committee to see that the admission procedure and tests etc. are transparent and just.

Article 30 has been criticized inter alia on the ground that the right to establish and administer educational institutions of their choice available to the minorities is denied to the majority community. Also since the term 'minority' has not been defined in the constitution anywhere and there are advantages in belonging to the minority, groups within the majority Hindu fold have started claiming minority status e.g. Arya Samaj in Punjab. The Ram Krishna Mission in Bengal had to declare that it is not Hindu at all but represented an independent minority religion. All this became necessary to claim the protection and benefits of Article 30 for the DAV and Ramakrishna Mission institutions.

Protection of Linguistic Minority Rights and Non-Discrimination on Grounds of Religion

Article 30 seeks to protect the rights of all minorities based on religion or language to establish and administer educational institutions of their choice. The state is enjoined not to discriminate against any educational institution on the ground of this language or religion based management

Article 350 A inserted by the Seventh Amendment provides for local authorities in every state endeavouring to extend adequate facilities for instruction in the mother tongue at the primary stage of education to children belonging to linguistic minority group send for the President necessary directions to any state. The term 'linguistic minority group' has been interpreted to mean a group of people who are in a numerical minority in a state as a whole as distinguished from any particular area or region thereof (in Kerala Education Bill, AIR 1958 SC 956).

Article 350B provides for the appointment by the president of a Special officer for linguistic minorities to investigate matters concerning safeguards for linguistic minorities and to report to the president at such intervals as the president may direct.

Conclusion

In the Indian constitution, the state is neutral to all religions. At the same time, every individual has the freedom to profess and practise his own religion. Therefore, secularism in India is neither a religion nor an indifference towards any religion but it stands for equal respect to all religions.

In fact, the provisions of secularism in the Indian constitution combined the position of both Mahatma Gandhi and Jawaharlal Nehru on secularism. Nehru's secularism was based on a commitment to scientific humanism tinged with a progressive view of historical change, while Gandhi's secularism was based on a commitment to the brotherhood of religious communities based on their respect for and pursuit of truth. By making the state neutral towards all religions the Indian constitution incorporated the Nehruvian concept of secularism, whereas by giving equal respect and opportunity to the followers each religion it incorporated the Gandhian concept of secularism or 'sarva-dharma sambhava'. The provision of secularism is a reflection of the basic character of Indian society that is the peace loving and tolerant character of the Indian public.

Notes and References

1. *Constituent Assembly Debates,* Vol. 7, p. 815.
2. Article 44(2)
3. Sadiq Ali (ed.) *Congress and the Problem of Minorities,* (Law Journal Press: Allahabad, 1947), pp. 19, 129.
4. 1954 Supreme Court Appeals, p. 546.
5. Reynolds V. United States, 1878, 98, US, p. 145.
6. A.I.R. 1953, Bombay, p. 183.
7. In Kerala Education Bill, 1957, A.I.R. 1958, S.C., p. 983.
8. Srinivasa Aiyar V. Saraswati Ammal, A.I.R. 1952, Madras, p. 193.
9. Alexandrowicz, op., cit., p. 289
10. Similarly, the Government of India Act, 1935, Provided that no subject of his majesty domiciled in India shall on grounds of religion, place of birth, descent, colour or any of them be ineligible

for office under the crown in India.

11. As has been noted above, the constitutional (Scheduled Castes) Order provides that no person who professes a religion different from the Hindu or Sikh religion shall be deemed a member of a Scheduled Caste. In S. Michael V.S. Venkateswaran, the Madras High Court upheld this Order under which a Christian convert from a Scheduled Caste was denied the right to stand for election to a reserved seat in the legislature. *A.I.R.* 1932, Madras, p. 474. The Constitution also make provisions for the special representation of the anglo-Indian Community in the Central and State legislature.
12. *A.I.R.*, 1959, S.C., p. 1318. See S.S. Nigam, 'Equity and the Representation of the Scheduled Classes in Parliament', *Journal of the Indian Law Institute*, Vol. 2, pp. 297- 320, 1960.
13. A.I.R. 1953, S.C. p. 383.
14. Earlier it has been argued that Hinduism's lack of organization is a factor which is favourable to the development of a secular state. While this is basically true. The greater opportunity for state intervention in religious affairs constitutes the negative aspect of the situation.
15. Devchand Totaram V. Ghansham, *A.I.R.* 1933, Bombay, p. 361, Aiyanchariar Sadagopachariar, *A.I.R.* 1939, Madras, p. 757.
16. *Constitution of Burma,* Article 21(1). In August 1961 this was Amended to read as follows: "Buddhism being the religion professed by the great majority of the citizens of the Union shall be the state religion."
17. Article 21 of the 1956 Constitution of Pakistan presents an interesting contrast: 'No person shall be compelled to pay any special tax proceeds of which are to be spent on the propagation or maintenance of any religion other than his own'.
18. This sentence, and my general approach throughout represent the 'wall of separation' approach to the problem. American constitutional law is by no means settled on this fundamental question, and court decisions fluctuate between this.
19. Protestant, catholic and Jewish Chaplains, however, serve in the armed forces of the US as commissioned officers. Similarly, in the larger defence service establishments in India, qualified 'Religious Teachers' of the Hindu, Muslims, Sikh, and Christian faiths are either engaged as civilians or hold a rank corresponding to that of junior commissioned officers. They conduct religious services and rites and assist at attestation parades when the oath of obedience and discipline is administered to trained recruits.
20. The 1956 Constitution of Pakistan would permit religious

instructions in state schools, and such instructions could be made compulsory for those who profess the religion or religions taught. Article 13(1): "No person attending any educational institution shall be required to receive religious instruction, or take part in any religious ceremony, or attend religious worship, if, such instruction, ceremony or worship relates to a religion other than his own.

21. *Constituent Assembly Debates,* Vol. 7, p. 871.
22. Ahemdabad St. Xavier's College Society V. State of Gujarat, *A.I.R.*, 1974 SC 1389; DAV College Bhatinda V. State of Punjab, *A.I.R.*, 1971 SC 1731.

10. INDIA'S FOREIGN POLICY SINCE THE END OF THE COLD WAR

Subhash Shukla

In 1991, with the end of the Cold War and the disintegration of the erstwhile U.S.S.R., the world had become unipolar in military terms with the U.S.A. being the only superpower but in economic terms the world had become multipolar with the emergent power centers being, the U.S.A.. Western Europe, Japan and China. Human rights; disarmament and arms control; good governance and democracy; management of the global environment; and the structuring of an economic order ruled by free market economy principles and globalization were the principles governing the new world order. Internally, the Indian economy was passing through a heavy balance of payments crisis. Heavy commercial borrowing since the 1980's had led to tangible increase in debt service payments, steep rise in the import of oil, industrial raw material and military hardware, and stagnant exports had resulted in a decline in India's credit worthiness. It was against this background that the Narasimha Rao government charted its foreign policy course.

Narsimha Rao Government

With the disintegration of the U.S.S.R., India lost a strategic and a very beneficial trade partner. Therefore, it was a conscious attempt on the part of Prime Minister Narasimha Rao to initiate new links with the emerging power centers. Hence. India initiated a process of more intense and extended interaction with the U.S.A..

Western Europe, Japan and ASEAN.

One of the important beginnings made under his regime in the Indo- U.S. relations was the growing cooperation between the two countries in the field of security. Indo-American joint naval exercises were started—a proposition inconceivable under the previous regimes in New Delhi. India and the U.S.A. signed an agreement on cooperation in defence production, The agreement also called for a close military contact. This agreement was signed by U.S. Defence Secretary, Mr. William Perry, and the Union Home Minister, Mr. S.B. Chavan in January 1995.[1] This led to a comprehensive security relationship between the U.S.A. and India which was due to a growing realization by the two countries about the convergence of their security concerns and interests in the region.

Another area of mutual interest to both India and the U.S.A. was the sphere of economic relations. India needed the capital, business, and technology of the U.S. to make its economic reforms a success; whereas the U.S. was interested in the big Indian market which was identified by it as one of the top ten big emerging markets of the world. Prime Minister Rao, during his visit to the United States in 1994, made it absolutely clear that the reforms in India were irreversible. Yet, all was not well in this sphere. Though, 'the U.S. was the largest foreign investor in India the flow of its investments into India lagged far behind its investments in China and the other South East Asian countries. The Americans, on the other hand, complained about inadequate liberalization. The intellectual property rights issue emerged as the most formidable irritant in the economic ties between the two countries.

Other areas of concern between the two countries were human rights, US policy towards Pakistan, nuclear non-proliferation and missile technology. India came under extensive criticism from the State Department and other non governmental organizations of the U.S. over the alleged abuse of human rights in Kashmir and Punjab. However, what was unacceptable to India was the one-sided criticism of the government of India and its security forces. Therefore, the Narasimha Rao government, since 1994, allowed various human rights groups to visit India which not only stemmed the barrage of American criticism but also contributed towards frustrating Pakistan's attempt to humiliate India.

As regards the U.S. policy towards Pakistan was concerned,

where the support to the Shimla agreement by the U.S., imposition of arms embargo to Islamabad under the Pressler amendment were welcomed by India; the questioning of Kashmir's accession to India by the U.S. Assistant Secretary of State Ms. Robin Raphael in 1993[2] and Washington's decision to sell $368 mn worth of arms to Pakistan under the Brown amendment were not received well by the Indian government. But, it can be said that the U.S. tried to straighten its tilt towards Pakistan and maintain equidistance from both New Delhi and Islamabad after the end of the Cold War which led to the strategic importance of Pakistan.

The most contentious aspect of the Indo-U.S. relations during this time was the difference between the two countries relating to Nuclear Non-Proliferation Treaty (NPT) and the Missile Technology Regime (MTCR). However, after the initial years of the Narasimha Rao government certain subtle shifts took place in the respective positions of both Washington and New Delhi on the issue of nuclear non-proliferation in the sub-continent. Washington, insisted on pressing New Delhi to sign the NPT and on capping the existing nuclear capabilities of India and Pakistan. However, the trouble centered on Washington's decision to extend its 'cap, reduce destroy' policy to India's missile development programme as well. Washington was, actually, afraid of the emergence of 'a commercial competitor in the lucrative missile and satellite communications market, as Indian technology was cheaper.

To sum up, the Indo- U.S. relationship under the Narasimha Rao government was a mixed bag of success and disappointments. But on the whole, Indo-U.S. relationship was informed by a sense of realism and maturity. New Delhi had realized that sustaining a stable working relationship with Washington was ultimately in its interest. Washington, also, gave up its traditional myopia which harped on differences alone and it took care to ensure that disputes in one area do not spoil the other aspects of the relationship.

Recognizing the priority that economic issues received over the security issues in international affairs after the end of the Cold War, the Narasimha Rao government tried to improve relations with the West European countries. India's approach towards Western Europe was influenced by three factors. Firstly, apart from Britain, France and Germany should also become the focus of attention of India's European policies in terms of expansion of bilateral relations. Secondly, India should cultivate relations with Belgium, Holland, Portugal and Spain for establishing a substantive equation with the European Community. Thirdly, a careful assessment of India's relations with countries such as Switzerland, Austria and the Scandinavian nations should be made and to calibrate them to become responsive to India's economic and technological needs. Consequently, India, first, concentrated on the expansion of bilateral relations with the larger and more important countries of Europe and, secondly, strived for greater economic coordination between European Community and India. While the Narasimha Rao government was conscious of establishing economic links with the European Community, it was equally aware of the policy orientations of its member countries on issues such as nuclear non-proliferation, disarmament transfer of dual use technology and human rights, therefore it made it clear to these countries that it would not compromise on its policies on these issues just for the sake of furthering economic relations.

Before the advent of the Narasimha Rao government, South East Asia counted among the neglected areas of India's foreign policy. A strong economic underpinning predominated the South East Asian nations' foreign policy, while New Delhi had always accorded priority to politics over economics in its foreign relations. India's proximity to the U.S.S.R also had an adverse effect. The Narasimha Rao government followed the 'Look East' policy to become engaged with the regional forums like ASEAN, APEC and ARF, making a sharp break from the tradition of Indian foreign policy. India advanced its bilateral relations with Malaysia and Singapore, both in security and economic terms. Even those countries that were traditionally not close to India, like Thailand, also became more accommodative towards India. Economic dynamism of the South East Asian region and the alluring prospect of expansion of trade and investment led India to take interest in this area. The ASEAN countries, too, recognized the trading and commercial opportunities unfolded by India's liberalization programme, India's relations with the ASEAN as well as Japan focused more on economic cooperation, as they had reservations about the Indian stand on certain political and security issues.

Despite the attempts to cultivate extended interaction with the western countries after the end of the Cold War, the Narasimha Rao government, at the same time, did not ignore the importance and value of Russia in its foreign policy scheme. After the initial hiccups, the visit of President Yeltsin to India in 1993 and the visit of Prime Minister Narasimha Rao to Russia in 1994 put the Indo-Russian relations back on track. During the 1993 visit of President Yeltsin, the vexed rupee-rouble issue was resolved along with the issue of the supply of defence spares and ammunitions. The Indo-Russian Treaty of Friendship and Cooperation was also signed during this visit but it did not contain the vital security clause of the Indo- Soviet Treaty of 1971. India recognized that Russia could now provide cooperation based on mutual interest. However, Russia reiterated its support to India's position on Kashmir and it also supported India's claim to become a permanent member of the U.N. Security Council. But, it has to be said that India did not enjoy the same special position as it had enjoyed with the erstwhile U.S.S.R.

The Narasimha Rao government continued further the process of normalization of relations with China which had begun with the path breaking visit of the former Prime Minister Rajiv Gandhi to Beijing in December, 1988. Between 1991 to 1993, New Delhi and Beijing took positive steps to move forward towards the solution of the Sino-Indian boundary dispute. Both India and China undertook a detailed re-examination of their respective: negotiating stances on the boundary issue in late 1950's and early 1960's and realized that both sides had adopted rigid postures which resulted in the breakdown of negotiations. India suggested a step by step approach to resolve the boundary dispute. The first step to be taken, as suggested by India, was the stabilization of the situation on the Line of Actual Control (LAC), and to delineate it more precisely in those sectors where differences of opinion existed between India and China. The second step to be taken was to come to a mutual agreement to maintain peace and tranquillity on the Line of Actual Control. The third step to be taken was to put in place the expanding mutual confidence building measures which could create an atmosphere of peace and normalcy on the Line of Actual Control, after which both sides could proceed to address the substance of the Sino-Indian boundary dispute. This approach was mutually agreed upon and after four rounds of negotiations between 1991 and 1993, a Sino-Indian Agreement on 'Maintenance of Peace and Tranquility' along the Line of Actual Control was signed during Prime Minister Narasimha Rao's visit to Beijing in September, 1993.[3] The gains from this agreement were two fold: First, there was a sizable reduction in the troops' level on the Sino-Indian frontier. Secondly, a practical approach came to be adopted in defining the Line of Actual Control, itself. However, not much progress was made after 1993. The lack of progress could be attributed to the fact that although the Chinese had no problem with the status quo continuing, on the other hand the Indian public was not yet prepared to agree to a realistic solution. In the meantime both sides agreed to expand economic, scientific and cultural interactions as a confidence building measure.

The Narasimha Rao government adopted a more conciliatory approach towards its neighbours. The signing of the Mahakali Treaty with Nepal, the decision to remain distant from the Tamil problem in Sri Lanka, the Tin Bigha accord with Bangladesh and the decision to resume talks with it on the sharing of the Ganga waters, despite the fact that Bodo and ULF A militants were taking shelter there, were examples of this conciliatory approach of this government towards its neighbours. However, relations with Pakistan continued to be adversarial with no let up in Islamabad encouraging subversive activities in Jammu and Kashmir. Prime Ministers' Narasimha Rao and Nawaz Sharif met each other six times between 1991 and 1993. However, things could not make much headway with the destruction of the Babri mosque in December 1992 and the subsequent bomb blasts in Bombay in March 1993 making things further bad for the governments of both the countries. Even then, New Delhi submitted to Islamabad six working papers in January, 1994, suggesting a new set of confidence building measures on Siachen, Jammu and Kashmir, the nuclear issue, Tulbul navigation project, and the activation of the committees set up within the framework of the Joint Commission set up in July, 1989, at Islmabad.[4] Pakistan rejected these proposals made by India. Pakistan's attempt to internationalize the Kashmir issue proved to be abortive as India rejected any third party mediation. The impasse continued for the remainder of the tenure of the Narasimha Rao government which, however, succeeded in preventing bilateral tensions degenerating into a conflict situation.

Among the other new initiatives that were taken by the Narasimha Rao government was the establishment of formal diplomatic relations with Israel. Taking special note of the emerging realities, Prime Minister Rao took the decision to recognize and also to establish full fledged bilateral relations with South Africa, along with the necessary institutional back-up. The Indian embassy was opened in South Africa in May, 1994. Keeping in view the strategic importance of the Central Asian Republics for India's security in the entire area stretching from Iran to the eastern borders of Kazakhstan, the large market in Central Asia, the region's requirements of investment and technologies, India's new interest in Central Asia's energy and mineral resources, to counter the possibility of these states becoming theocratic and to reduce the influence of Pakistan, Prime Minister Narasimha Rao promptly decided to give recognition to all the Central Asian Republics.

The Narasimha Rao government called for the restructuring of the U.N. Security Council so as to make it more representative, and for reforms in the decision making process in order to make its functioning more democratic and transparent. The Indian government staked its claim for the permanent membership of the Security Council on the grounds of size and population of the country; economic and regional considerations: and a proven track record of commitment to the U.N. Charter, and participation in the U.N. peace keeping, social and developmental activities and the fulfilment of the financial obligations to the U.N. every year. However. India's refusal to sign the NPT, its basic differences on a number of global issues with the permanent members of the U.N. Security Council and its marginal inputs to the U.N. finance rendered its chances slim.

The Narasimha Rao government tried to adopt a calibrated non- confrontationist policy in dealing with the U.S. and other nuclear weapon powers on nuclear non proliferation, arms control and disarmament. The indefinite extension of the NPT was a setback but India did not succumb to the pressure generated by it and it did not sign it. Though India had initially supported the CTBT, it did not sign it because it allowed for further testing of the nuclear weapons states through computer simulation.

Economic Diplomacy was given utmost and primary importance by Prime Minister Narasimha Rao in the conduct of the foreign policy during his tenure. He visited all the major 'business centers and nations of the world to attract foreign investment and technology to India. The government of India set before itself two primary tasks: conducting bilateral and multilateral trade negotiations and mobilizing foreign capital resources. In seeking financial assistance from the West, India had to face stiff resistance from the African and the Latin American states on the one hand, and from the new states of Eastern Europe and the erstwhile U.S.S.R on the other. It also had problems in accessing the markets of the western world because of the weak growth experienced by the Western countries and the resultant protectionism in their economic policies. It also had to face stiff competition from China and the ASEAN countries who had liberalized their economies more than a decade ago. The momentum of the economic aspects of India's foreign policy slowed down, also, because of the electoral politics within the country and the populist policies of the political parties in India.

Prime Minister Narasimha Rao adopted a consensual approach in the evolution of India's foreign policy. He was patient and was willing to listen to the opinion of all concerned, therefore at times, he used to take time to take a decision. This led to the impression that he procrastinated and dithered, and that he was disinclined to take definite decisions. He had a quiet diplomatic style of his own, unlike the diplomatic flair of Pt. Nehru and Mrs. Indira Gandhi. The innovations he made in the Indian foreign policy were to a large extent necessitated by the exigencies of the post Cold War world. But it has to be said that he was astute enough to grasp the demands of the changing times and chart a new course in the country's foreign policy accordingly.

United-Front Government

In mid 1996, Mr. H.D. Deve Gowda succeeded Mr. Narasimha Rao as the Prime Minister of India. Mr. Deve Gowda was heading the United Front government which had the outside support of the Congress party. Mr. I.K. Gujral, the external affairs minister under this government who later on became the Prime Minister in April 1997, was more or less solely responsible for the foreign policy of the country. He, basically, continued the same policies of the Narsimha Rao government.

However, Mr. I.K. Gujral outlined a bolder regional policy which came to be known as the Gujral Doctrine. He was willing to go the extra mile to resolve problems with neighbours without insisting on reciprocity. The Gujral doctrine was based on five principles:

Firstly, with neighbours like Nepal, Bangladesh, Bhutan, Maldives, and Sri Lanka India did not ask for reciprocity but would give all it can in good faith and trust.

Secondly, no South Asian country would allow its territory to be used against the interest or another country of the region.

Thirdly, none would interfere in the internal affairs of another.

Fourthly, all South Asian countries would respect each other's territorial integrity and sovereignty.

Fifthly, all of them would settle all their disputes through peaceful bilateral negotiations.[5]

Broadly, the Gujral doctrine implied that India was prepared to extend unilateral concessions to its smaller neighbours. This policy was dictated by three factors. Firstly, the Economic imperative forced India to follow this policy. India having launched itself on the path of economic reform, it had realized the importance of regional cooperation among the countries of the Indian sub-continent. Secondly, it realized that it could not fulfill its aspirations of becoming a global power as long as it was involved in regional conflicts. Thirdly, there had been a gradual increase in the influence of the U.S.A. and China in India's neighbourhood. Therefore, the Gujral doctrine was dictated by India's self interest and real politics,

Though, the Gujral doctrine cosmetically improved the regional political atmosphere and India's relations with all its neighbours in general terms but the optimism embodied in the Gujral doctrine about unilateral goodwill and generosity did not bring about the desired results in the management of the security problems which remained. Despite the signing of the Ganga Waters Treaty with Bangladesh and the signing of hydroelectric projects with Nepal, negative under currents still remained. Pakistan's support and promotion of crossborder terrorism continued unabated. The adversarial and confrontationist approach of Pakistan towards India continued during the tenure of the United Front government, thus impeding the normalisation of relations.

The Comprehensive Test Ban Treaty (CTBT) was firmly opposed by the United Front government because of its discriminatory provisions. India had long supported the concept of CTBT as an important step towards disarmament but as its drafting was being done our policy makers realized that the treaty was driven more by non proliferation concerns than those relating to disarmament. Its motive was to limit the nuclear capabilities of the threshold states like India because it would close an Indian option to test. The United Front government considered the option of nuclear testing but it backed off as it felt that the political and economic costs of it would be very high.

NDA Government and the Aggressive Foreign Policy

However, the Atal Behari Vajpayee government decided to end the long standing nuclear ambiguity of our country by conducting two rounds of nuclear tests on 11th and 13th May, 1998, respectively. After these tests, India had to rework its nuclear diplomacy. From being a protestor against discrimination, India was now ready to support the existing nuclear order and called for its incremental reform. The Vajpayee government announced a unilateral moratorium on nuclear testing after the two tests. It also declared the policy of no first use. It was also ready to negotiate with the great powers to become a party to the CTBT but it also insisted that India would not accede to it without reciprocal concessions from the great powers. The government had to face state opposition parties on signing the CTBT. However, with the rejection of the CTBT by the U.S. Senate in 1999, there was no pressure on the Indian government to sign the CTBT.

The Vajpayee government tried to build on the foundations laid by the Narasimha Rao government of a new foreign policy based on establishment of good relations with the West. Immediately after coming to power, Prime Minister Vajpayee declared in his speech at the Asia Society in New York that India and the United States were natural allies. America's lack of sensitivity for India's security concerns was cited by him as the reason why both the nations could not work together in the past; however he conceded that India would be America's newest ally in the 21st century even though America had reacted very angrily to the Indian nuclear tests of 1998.[6]

After the nuclear tests, not only did the Clinton administration impose mandatory sanctions itself but also mobilized other nations, like Japan, to do the same. It was also instrumental in the passing of the U.N. Security 'Council Resolution 1172 which laid down a full set of conditions for India which included signing the NPT and addressing the root cause of

Indo- Pakistani tensions- the Kashmir dispute. However, within a month after the nuclear tests, the U.S.A. and India agreed to initiate a dialogue through their representatives, Strobe Talbot and Jaswant Singh, to reconcile India's security concerns with the non- proliferation objectives of the U.S. After many rounds of discussions, the essence of the deal boiled down to the signing of the CTBT by India, but with the U.S. Senate refusing to ratify the CTBT the deal could not be clinched.

Besides differences on nuclear non-proliferation, one other thing that divided India and the United States was the American attitude towards the Kashmir issue between India and Pakistan. President Clinton repeatedly referred to Kashmir as a nuclear flash point and his urging India and Pakistan to end the world's most dangerous military confrontation seemed to reflect a hidden American agenda in the sub-continent. However, during the Kargil crisis in May-June 1999, Washington not only supported India's military action but also exerted diplomatic pressure on Pakistan to restore the sanctity of the LoC. The Clinton administration rejected Pakistan's sinister design of questioning the LoC or to link its withdrawal from Kargil to negotiations with India on the Kashmir dispute. The U.S.A. not only insisted that Pakistan should withdraw from Kargil unconditionally but it also asked Saudi Arabia to pressurize the Pak authorities to withdraw unilaterally from Kargil. It also restrained China from giving any support to Pakistan. President Clinton invited the Pakistani Prime Minister Nawaz Sharif to visit Washington in July 1999 and asked him to announce the withdrawal. This was for the first time that the United States supported India in its various conflicts with Pakistan.

The shift in American thinking was clearly discernable when the U.S. Secretary of State Madeleinc Albright, asked for tangible steps to be taken to respect the LoC and she also reaffirmed at the same time the American opposition to changing the territorial status quo in Kashmir by the use of force.[7] President Clinton, in his visit to India in March 2000, outlining the U.S. policy on Kashmir asked for the respect of the LoC; stopping of violence by third parties in Kashmir; negotiate; and there was not a military solution to the problem of Kashmir. While encouraging India to address the grievances of the Kashmiris, President Clinton suggested that the LoC should be the basis for an eventual settlement of the Kashmir dispute.[8]

When President Bush came to power in 2001, he made an early decision to build a long term strategic partnership with India. The Bush administration no longer treated India and Pakistan as Siamese twins. It wanted to make India the centre piece of its policy in Asia. It saw China as a potential competitor and therefore aimed at balancing it by increasing the strategic role of India in Asia. In its first comprehensive articulation of its world view, the Bush administration stated that the U.S. interests of a free flow of commerce, in fighting terrorism, and in creating a strategically stable Asia require a strong relationship with India, politically, economically and militarily.[9]

After the terrorist attack on the World Trade Centre in New York on 11th September 2001, India expected an American confrontation with the sources of international terrorism in Pakistan but as Washington mobilized support from Islamabad to oust the Taliban from Afghanistan there was deep disappointment in India. There was an apprehension in India that Pakistan would be able to insulate its own support of terrorism in Kashmir from the broader declared objectives of American war on terrorism.

However, Washington was determined not to undermine its new relationship with India, even as it reached out to Pakistan. President Bush sought to assure the Indian government that there would be no double standards in battling terrorism, though there would be priorities in dealing with it. He promised that the Indian concerns on terrorism in India would be addressed once the immediate threat from Afghanistan was settled. To a series of terrorist attacks in India such as on 1st October. 2001 in Srinagar on 13th December, 2001 on the Indian Parliament in Delhi, on 14th May. 2002 in Kaluchak the Bush administration exerted pressure on President Musharraf to proclaim that Pakistani soil would not be allowed to export terror to any part of the world and obtained formal commitments from Pakistan to end cross border infiltration and not to disrupt the impending elections for the Jammu and Kashmir assembly. It also rejected the demand of Pakistan that India should engage in talks on Kashmir immediately. On the contrary it supported the Indian position that cross border violence had to be stopped first before talks could start.

The U.S. mission in India took an active part in observing the elections of the Jammu and Kashmir assembly that were held in 2002 and was quick to assert that the polls were by and large free and fair. These elections were acknowledged by 'Colin Powell,' the then Secretary of State of the U.S., as a step forward in determining the will of the Kashmiri people.[10] After the 11th September. 2001 terrorist attacks the U.S. was no longer interested in an independent Jammu and Kashmir because it felt that this would create a weak state and a potential haven for Islamic extremists.

The Bush administration lifted the sanctions imposed by the Clinton administration in 1998 after India's twin nuclear tests. This cleared the ground for renewed defence cooperation between the two countries. The Bush administration was prepared to sell weapons required by India such as weapon locating radafs, engine and systems for the Light Combat Aircraft, multi mission maritime aircraft and jet trainer engines. India and the U.S. agreed to work together to maintain peace and stability in the Indian Ocean. This new convergence of interests in the Indian Ocean was reflected in the decision of India to provide naval escort to American military assets transiting the Malacca Straits during Operation Enduring Freedom in Afghanistan in 2002. India was one of the first countries to have supported the missile defence programme of the Bush administration against weapons of mass destruction.

Keeping with its intention of developing a strategic relationship with India, the Bush administration signed the 'Next Steps in Strategic Partnership' with India in January, 2004. Under this agreement, both the countries agreed to extend cooperation in the areas of civilian nuclear technology, space exploration, missile defence and high technology trade.[11] This agreement by America was based on its own assessment that by 2025 India would be one of the world's five largest economies, having an enormous pool of a highly educated and young people which would establish India as a force to reckon with in the 21st century.

Despite developing a natural strategic alliance with the U.S.A.. the Vajpayee government tried to preserve India's strategic relationship with its traditional friend, Russia as well Initially, after the nuclear tests of 1998, the Yeltsin administration was very angry with the Indian administration for not having informed the Russian leadership about the impending nuclear tests. The message from the Russian administration was that India could not take it for granted and to gain its support Indians would have to keep it informed on vital issues of mutual concern. However, the anger did not last for long, Russia, along with France worked hard to limit the collective action against India.

When President Putin visited India in October 2000, the common threats of religious extremism and terrorism identified by Narasimha Rao and Yeltsin, earlier, were no longer theoretical. Just as India was facing militancy and terrorism in Kashmir, the same was being faced by Russia in Chechnya, therefore New Delhi and Moscow stepped up bilateral cooperation in countering terrorism. After President Putin's visit to India, Russia renewed its interest in helping India in its civilian atomic energy programme. Russian nuclear cooperation with India was based on the principle that India was already a nuclear weapons power therefore, denying it advanced technologies to prevent proliferation of nuclear weapons made no sense. During his visit to India in 2002, President Putin assured India of selling additional nuclear reactors within the framework of its international obligations in the nuclear field. He also made a distinction between India and Pakistan's nuclear weapons in the sense that he expressed his concern at the danger of Pakistani nuclear weapons falling in the hands of militant extremists.[12]

Prime Minister, Vajpayee visited Russia in November, 2003. During this visit, Prime Minister Vajpayee and President Putin signed a political declaration on global challenges and threats to world security. This declaration aimed at further enhancing political cooperation between the two countries in dealing with challenges and threats faced by the world which included terrorism, transnational organized crime, drug trafficking, money laundering, environment and developmental challenges.[13]

However, there was still an element of unpredictability in Indo-Russian relations because of the relations of both countries with the U.S. and China and the changing Pakistan-Russia relationship. Given the uncertainty in the Sino-Indian relationship, the deepening of the Sino-Russian relationship, which culminated in the singing of a strategic partnership agreement in July 2001, is of concern to India. But Moscow's continued effort to renew its ties with Pakistan was also a concern for New Delhi. Under President Putin, Russia has tried to improve its relations with Pakistan which was reflected in President Putin refraining from saying anything on Indo- Pakistani relationship or Kashmir that would be offensive to Pakistan, during his visits to India. Besides this, there was also stagnation in the economic and social ties between the two countries.

Prime Minister Vajpayee, in his letter written to President Clinton and other world leaders, had justified the two nuclear tests of 1998 on the ground that India had an overt nuclear state in the form of China which had helped its another armed neighbour, Pakistan, to become a covert nuclear power. This had antagonized the Chinese leadership of that time. India was surprised by China's intensely negative reactions because China had nuclear weapons since 1964 and it had also helped Pakistan in acquiring these weapons. China accused India of deliberately raising the Chinese bogey with the United States because Washington was all set, to proclaim Beijing as a strategic 'partner at that time. However, despite this mistrust it was only a matter of time before both sides began the painful process of re-engaging each other. India down played the significance of the Vajpayee letter and affirmed its intention of not pursuing an arms race with China. After this a series of bilateral exchanges set the tone for the normalization of relations.

The Vajpayee government was determined to accelerate the talks with China on the boundary issue. The then foreign minister, Mr. Jaswant Singh, in his visit to China in 1999 and in a letter to his counterpart expressed the desire for the stepping up of the pace of talks on the clarification of the Line of Actual Control (LAC). On Sikkim, there were signals from Beijing throughout the mid 1990's that it was prepared to recognize it as a part of India. China had shown its readiness to grant an indirect recognition in a border agreement between China's Tibet and India's Sikkim. During his visit to China in 2002, the external affairs minister. Jaswant Singh, took up the issue of Sikkim with his Chinese counterpart, Tang Jiaxuan.[14] He was assured that during the next visit by the Chinese premier, an announcement would be made. This assurance was fulfilled during the visit of Chinese Premier, Wen Jiabao, to India in 2005. Trade between the two countries grew by leaps and bounds at the turn of the century to reach 4.5 billion dollars in 2002 which was agreed by both sides to be raised to 10 billion dollars in a few years, during Premier Zhu Rongji's visit to India in 2002. Prime Minister Vajpayee also paid a visit to China in the year 2003 during which he concentrated upon the improvement of trade and business ties between the two countries.

However, the growing proximity between the United States and India and the transfer of nuclear and missile technologies to Pakistan were casting shadows on future Sino-Indian relations. Though the nuclear tests of May 1998, have given India the nuclear equivalence, if not parity with China, still managing the growing Chinese political influence in the Indian sub-continent remained a big challenge for India.

The most difficult task of the Vajpayee government was the containment of Pakistan which was based upon the assumption that the ruling establishment in Pakistan was committed towards unremitting war of terror against India. The objective of this policy was to engineer through external pressures, an internal transformation or Pakistan that puts an end to the sources of compulsive hostility towards India.

Continuing with his viewpoint that a country can choose its friends but not its neighbours, Prime Minister undertook his famous bus visit to Lahore in February 1999. Outlining his philosophy of live and let live, he proclaimed India's stake in a peaceful and prosperous Pakistan. During this visit, the Lahore Declaration was signed between the two countries which underlined that the establishment of peace and the development of peaceful relations and friendly cooperation were in the interest of the people of the two nations. It reaffirmed its faith in the Shimla Agreement of 1972. It was agreed that both the governments would make an effort towards resolving all the outstanding issues including the issue of Jammu and Kashmir.

However, the trust shown by Prime Minister Vajpayee was betrayed by the Kargil intrusion of the Pakistani army in May 1999. The Pakistani chief of Army Staff, Gen. Pervez Musharraf, had got the Pakistani Prime Minister Nawaz Sharif to sign on the papers authorizing the Kargil invasion before the signing of the Lahore Declaration. India responded with full military force on its own side of the Line of Control (LoC) and got its territory evacuated from Pakistan. The unambiguous call from the United States to restore the status quo ante unconditionally, China's reluctance to help Pakistan in any meaningful manner and the lack of support from Saudi Arabia also helped in pushing the Pakistani authorities to a cease-fire. The Indian decision to not to cross the LoC won widespread international acclaim in contrast to the .criticism of the Pakistani adventurism. While India was seen as a state offering the prospects of a successful economy, Pakistan was being seen as a failing state. Both the counties agreed to a cease-fire in July. 2000. But here was a political stand off between the two countries.

This political stand-off was broken after two years when Prime Minister Vajpayee extended an invitation to President Musharraf to visit India which was readily accepted by him. In his letter of invitation, Prime Minister Vajpayee pointed to the common enemy of poverty and expressed India's willingness to discuss the Kashmir issue. He emphasized that there was no alternative to reconciliation and urged Musharraf to walk the high road with him. To demonstrate the seriousness of purpose, the Vajpayee government came up with a series of confidence building measures on the eve of the summit which included easing of punishment for Pakistani fishermen who got caught in Indian waters, opening up the Line of Control in Jammu and Kashmir to facilitate the movement of Kashmiris across the divide, offer of fellowships for Pakistani students in Indian technical institutions, unilateral reduction of tariffs on Pakistani goods and the readiness to send the Director General of military operations to make the border a peaceful one. This was done by India in good faith. Pakistan felt that this might have been done to divert attention from what it saw as the core issue-the issue of Jammu and Kashmir.

The Agra talks focused on the primary issue of cross border terrorism and Kashmir, besides the overall relationship between the two countries. After two days and two nights of negotiations at Agra, both the countries could not agree on the draft of the Agra Declaration. Prime Minister Vajpayee's another attempt to find a breakthrough with Pakistan failed again. Although the two sides covered considerable political ground, the non fulfilment of the initial expectations of a final declaration created a sense of failure in the minds of the Indian public which led to the government being blamed for not doing its homework properly.

There were unresolved differences between the two countries on three sets of issues because of which both nations could not agree on a final declaration. The first issue was the insistence of the Pakistani side that the core issue of Kashmir had to be first addressed for the overall improvement in bilateral relations. India, on the other hand, focussed on the totality of the overall relationship. The second issue was the issue of cross border terrorism. If Kashmir was the core issue for Pakistan, the immediate stopping of the Pakistani support to cross border terrorism in Kashmir was the core issue for India. Pakistan did not agree with the Indian accusation of Pakistani support to terrorists in Kashmir, instead it accused India of indulging in state terrorism and human rights abuses in Kashmir. India made it abundantly clear that the promotion of cross border terrorism and violence must be stopped immediately. The third issue on which there were differences between the two countries was the importance of the previous agreements. The Pakistani side wanted that the Agra Declaration should be the basis for future negotiations between the two countries because the Shimla and Lahore declarations did not place enough emphasis on solving the Kashmir issue. But the Indian side insisted that Agra was simply a continuation not only of the Lahore process but also of the agreement laid down in Shimla.

The Agra talks failed primarily because of the Pakistani reluctance to accept the Indian accusation that terror was being exported from its soil to Kashmir and other parts of India which had to be stopped for a meaningful dialogue to take place between the two countries. The Indian stand was Vindicated when terrorists attacked the Indian parliament on 13th December, 2001, following the attack previously on 1st October, 2001 on the Jammu and Kashmir state assembly. This forced India to adopt a new strategy which involved a head—on confrontation with Pakistan. India delivered a formal demarche to Pakistan on 14th December, 2001, demanding an immediate crackdown on the operations of terrorist organizations on its soil. At the same time, India launched its biggest military mobilization and to reinforce this military threat it called back its envoy from Pakistan; sought a reduction of staff at the Pakistani High Commission in New Delhi; restricted the movement of the Pakistani staff that stayed back and terminated rail, road and air transportation links with it. India also considered scrapping of the Indus Waters Treaty of 1961. In response to all this, Gen. Musharraf threatened serious repercussions if India was to launch an attack on Pakistan.

As expected, the U.S. and the U.K. got involved in an intensive diplomatic engagement with India and Pakistan. Under the combined Anglo- American pressure, President Musharraf in his speech on 12th January, 2002, declared that the Pakistani soil would not be allowed to be used to promote terrorism anywhere in the world and that he would not allow the fomentation of violence in the name of the Kashmir cause.[16] India's response to the speech was positive, but it insisted that there must be evidence of the cessation of cross border terrorism on the ground before it could resume engagements with Pakistan. India suggested that the evidence would become clear only after the winter months by judging the trends of cross border infiltration and cross border sponsored violence. At the same time, India also desired that Pakistan should hand over the twenty criminals who were in Pakistan.

The crisis which was expected to ease after Gen. Musharraf's speech got exacerbated with another terrorist related violence in May, 2002 against the armed forces and their families at Kaluchak. This led to Indian forces being moved to high alert so that they could go to war in a few hours notice. As India prepared for a war, President Bush sent the Defence Secretary, Donald Rumsfeld, and the Deputy Secretary of State, Richard Armitage to the Indian sub-continent to ease the tension. Richard Armitage was successful in extracting the commitment from Gen. Musharraf that Pakistan would end cross border infiltration permanently, which was conveyed to India. In response, India agreed to pull back some of its naval forces from the Arabian Sea, reduced the alert level of its armed forces, lifted the restrictions imposed on Pakistani over .flights and named a new envoy to Islamabad but it expressed its unwillingness to resume political dialogue with Pakistan until it implemented its promises. The U.S. also pressed Pakistan to desist from' disrupting the elections to the Jammu and Kashmir assembly in September, 2002. After the successful completion of elections to the Jammu and Kashmir assembly, India announced the redeployment of its troops from the border.

India made significant gains from its coercive diplomacy on the issue of cross border terrorism which included the unambiguous international characterization of violence in Kashmir as terrorism; getting the western powers to hold Pakistan responsible for it and obtaining assurances from it to end cross border terrorism; and to get America to endorse the fairness of the elections to the Jammu and Kashmir assembly which was a step forward in determining the wishes of the people.

This process of rebuilding the mutual confidence between the two countries resulted in the issuing of the Indo-Pak Joint Statement of 6th January, 2004 during the SAARC summit at Islamabad in which leaders of both the countries welcomed the recent steps towards non-nationalisation of relations between the two countries and expressed the hope that the positive trends set by the CBMs (confidence building measures) would be consolidated. Prime Minister Vajpayee said that in order to take forward and sustain the dialogue process, violence, hostility and terrorism must be prevented. President Musharraf reassured Prime Minister Vajpayee that he will not permit any territory under Pakistan's control to be used to support terrorism in any manner. President Musharraf emphasized that a sustained and productive dialogue addressing all issues would lead to positive results, To carry the process of normalisation forward the President of Pakistan and the Prime Minister of India agreed to commence the process of the composite dialogue in February 2004. The two leaders were confident that the resumption of the composite dialogue would lead to peaceful settlement of all bilateral issues, including Jammu and Kashmir, to the satisfaction of both sides.[17]

The foreign policy of the Vajpayee government has to be viewed as a more purposeful implementation of the policies of the Narasimha Rao government but was based more on realism than on idealistic principles. While there was some autonomy to foreign policy making, all its key decisions, except the decision on nuclear testing, were subject to the consensus building process in the country through consultations with various political parties and taking into account the public opinion. The reorientation of the Indian foreign policy during the 1990' s and at the beginning of the 21st century was a response to the changes within the international system after the end of the cold war.

U.P.A. Government and the Foreign Policy of Tomorrow

In May, 2004, the United Progressive Alliance (U.P.A.) government came to power with Dr. Manmohan Singh becoming the next Prime Minister of India. The Common Minimum Programme (CMP) of the UPA government did not show any marked departure from the policies of the Vajpayee government. In continuance of the policies of the Vajpayee government, the UPA government continued to build upon the natural alliance with the U.S.A. Prime- Minister Manmohan Singh and President Bush had a meeting in New York in September, 2004 during the annual U.N. General Assembly session there and both of them reaffirmed the strategic partnership between the two countries.

In July, 2005, Prime Minister Dr. Manmohan Singh visited the U.S.A. In the Joint Statement issued on 18th July, 2005 it was stated that the two leaders agree that the new relationship between India and the United States will promote stability, democracy, prosperity and peace throughout the world. Building on their common values and interests the two leaders resolved:

- To create an international environment conducive to promotion of democratic values and to strengthen democratic practices in societies which wish to become more open and pluralistic.
- To combat terrorism relentlessly. They applauded the active and vigorous counter terrorism cooperation between the two countries and support more international efforts in this direction. The two leaders strongly affirmed their commitment to the conclusion by September of a UN comprehensive convention against international terrorism.

The Prime Minister's visit coincided with the completion of the Next Steps in Strategic Partnership (NSSP) initiative, launched in January 2004. The two leaders agreed that it provided the basis for expanding bilateral activities and commerce in space civil nuclear energy and dual-use technology. Recognizing the significance of civilian nuclear energy for meeting growing global energy demands in a cleaner and more efficient manner, the two leaders discussed India's plans to develop its civilian nuclear energy program.

President Bush conveyed his appreciation to the Prime Minister over India's strong commitment to preventing WMD proliferation and stated that as a responsible state with advanced nuclear technology, India should acquire the same benefits and advantages as other such states. The President told the Prime Minister that he would work to achieve full civil nuclear energy cooperation with India as it its goals of promoting nuclear power and achieving energy security. The President also assured that he would also seek an agreement from Congress to adjust U.S. laws and policies, and the United States would work with friends and allies to adjust international regimes to enable full civil nuckar energy cooperation and trade with India, including but not limited to expeditious consideration of fuel supplies for safeguarded nuclear reactors at Tarapur. In the meantime, the United States will encourage its partners to also consider this request expeditiously. India has expressed its interest in ITER and a willingness to contribute. The United States will consult with its partners considering India's participation. The United States will consult with the other participants in the Generation IV International forum with a view toward India's inclusion.

The Prime Minister conveyed that for his part, India would reciprocally agree that it would be ready to assume the same responsibilities and practices and acquire the same benefits and advantages as other leading countries with advanced nuclear technology, such as the United States. These responsibilities and practices consist of identifying and separating civilian and military nuclear facilities and programs in a phased manner and filing a declaration regarding its civilians facilities with the International Atomic Energy Agency (IAEA): taking a decision to place voluntarily its civilian nuclear facilities under IAEA safeguards; signing and adhering to un Additional Protocol with respect to civilian nuclear facilities; continuing India's unilateral moratorium on nuclear testing; working with the United States for the conclusion of a multilateral Fissile Material Cut Off Treaty: refraining from transfer of enrichment and reprocessing technologies to states that do not have them and supporting international efforts to limit their spread; and ensuring that the necessary steps have been taken to secure nuclear materials and technology through comprehensive export control legislation and through harmonization and adherence to Missile Technology Control Regime (MTCR) and Nuclear Suppliers Group (NSG) guidelines.

The President welcomed the Prime Minister's assurance. The two leaders agreed to establish a working group to undertake on a phased basis, in the months ahead, the necessary actions mentioned above to fulfil these commitments. The President and Prime Minister also agreed that they would review this progress when the President visits India in 2006. In light of this closer relationship, and the recognition of India's growing role in enhancing regional and global security, the Prime Minister and the President agreed that international institutions must fully reflect changes in the global scenario that have taken place since 1945. The President reiterated his view that international institutions are going to have to adapt to reflect India's central and growing role.[18]

Before the Prime Minister's visit to the U.S. in July, 2005, the Indian Defence Minister, Mr. Pranab Mukherjee and the U.S. Defence Secretary, Mr. Donald Rumsfeld signed a ten year defence deal which for cooperation in such areas as technology transfer, cooperation in defence trade and research. It envisaged the conducting of joint exercises and exchanges, and collaboration in multinational operations in common interest.[19]

The nuclear deal signed by the U.S.A. and India in July, 2005, was a major step forward in the history of Indo - U.S. relations. The U.S.A. recognized India as a nuclear weapons power, getting the same benefits as other nuclear weapons states. The modalities of this agreement were worked out during President Bush's visit to India in March, 2006 under which India put 14 out of its 22 nuclear reactors under the civilian category which were open to verification by the IAEA and the U.S.A. agreed to provide full cooperation to India in its civilian nuclear energy programme, even though the U.S. Government had to get Congressional approval for this.

This agreement will govern civil nuclear trade between the two countries and open the door for American and Indian firms to participate in each other's civil nuclear energy sector.

However, vehement opposition by the political parties, for their vested interests, has stalled any movement on this agreement by India. The UPA Government not only faces opposition from the opposition parties but from its own ally, the Communists, who oppose it because of their ideological differences with the West. They have even threatened to withdraw their support to the government that is dependent on their support for its survival.

At the same time India continued its strategic relationship with Russia. President Putin's visit in December, 2004, provided an opportunity to carry forward the relations to a higher level of interaction. Prime Minister Dr. Manmohan Singh visited Moscow on the anniversary of Russian victory over Nazi Germany. The two leaders discussed the prospects of Indo-Russian cooperation in the areas of civil nuclear technology, defence and information technology. Russia continuously affirmed its support to India's claim of permanent membership in the U.N. Security Council.

The eighth annual summit between India and Russia took place with the visit of Prime Minister Manmohan Singh to Moscow in November, 2007. Prime Minister Singh's discussions with President Putin were characterized by warmth, cordiality and unanimity on all issues of mutual interest. There was substantial forward movement on many of the issues that they had discussed at their last summit in January. They discussed ways to substantially upgrade the economic ties, which should form the bedrock of the strategic partnership between the two countries.

Both the leaders were able to satisfactorily resolve the long pending issue of the utilization of the rupee debt fund. They also agreed to redouble the efforts to achieve a bilateral trade target of 10 billion US dollars by 2010. The cooperation in the area of high technology is symbolized by the agreement on Chandrayan II, which will include a joint mission to the Moon involving an orbiter, a lander and a rover to carry out scientific studies.

Both countries continued their dialogue on energy. The Indian Prime Minister thanked ,the Russian President for his country's steadfast support in supplementing our nuclear energy programme, and its assistance in lifting international restrictions on nuclear cooperation with India that are still in place.

Defence cooperation is one of the pillars of our strategic partnership. The decision on the co-development and co-production of the Fifth Generation Fighter and the Multi role Transport Aircraft were major steps forward in this direction.

Sino-Indian relations improved during the U.P.A. government. During the Indian visit of the Chinese Premier Wen Jiabao in 2005 the Chinese formally recognized Sikkim as a part of India. The Joint Statement released during this visit agreed to establish a 'Strategic and Cooperative Partnership for Peace and Prosperity.' An agreement was signed which laid down the parameters and the guiding principles for the settlement of the border issue. It was agreed that the boundary question should not be allowed to affect the overall development of bilateral relations. Sino-Indian trade reached the 13 billion dollar mark in 2004 and it was agreed to increase it to the 20 billion mark by 2008.[20] The booming Sino-Indian trade, despite the border problem, was often cited as an example to Pakistan by the international community for the improvement of its relations with India, despite the Kashmir dispute.

President Hu Jintao of China paid a state visit to India from November 20-23, 2006. Both Governments attached great importance to this visit and made careful preparations. This was the first visit by a Chinese President to India since President Jiang Zernin's visit in November-December 1996. The visit was seen as imparting even greater dynamism to the on-going high-level exchanges between the two countries.

The visit highlighted the resolve of both countries to work towards the further consolidation and diversification of India-China relations. During the visit of the Chinese Premier to India last year, both countries had decided to establish a strategic and cooperative partnership. President Hu's visit offered the opportunity to add greater content and meaning to this partnership. This was reflected in the "tenpronged strategy" embodied in the Joint Declaration that was issued on behalf of the Prime Minister and the Chinese President during the visit. The range of these agreements reflects the evolving multi-dimensional nature of India's relationship with China.

Both Prime Minister and President Hu noted that India-China relations had transcended their bilateral dimension and acquired a global and strategic significance. President Hu characterized the present phase in the relationship as marking a "new historic beginning" and conveyed that his visit would send out a strong signal to the international community that India and China were willing to work hand in hand for long-term friendship and common development. He stressed that China had taken a "long-term and strategic view" of the relationship with India, desiring to build a strong and cooperative relationship based on shared and common interests. Prime Minister Manmohan Singh also highlighted that he would like India and China to work together as good neighbours and partners and to develop together in a mutually supportive manner while remaining sensitive to each other's concerns and aspirations. Both leaders agreed on the need for sustained efforts to exploit the full potential of strategic partnership and to resolve outstanding issues in a focused, sincere and problem-solving manner.

Economic cooperation emerged as a major thrust area of the visit, with both sides keen to send out a clear message in this regard, reflected in the signing of Bilateral Investment Protection Agreement, fixing of trade target of US$ 40 billion by 2010 and mandating the Joint Task Force already established by the two countries to complete its study on the feasibility and benefits of India-China Regional Trading Arrangement by October 2007.

Both sides also expressed the commitment that pending the final settlement of the boundary question, they would maintain peace and tranquility in the border areas and expedite the work of clarification and confirmation of the line of actual control.

India unambiguously- rejected the Chinese contention, stating that Arunachal Pradesh is an integral part of India. The matter was taken up immediately with the Chinese Government through the Indian Ambassador in Beijing and the disappointment and concern over the Chinese statement was clearly conveyed.

Prime Minister also had a useful exchange of views with President Hu on regional and multilateral issues. It was noted that as two most populous countries with rapidly developing economies, the development of India and China were important factors in the shaping of future global architecture. The two leaders noted that together India and China could make effective contributions in dealing with global issues of sustainable and equitable development, energy, security, peace and prosperity in Asia and in the world, environment protection and fight against terrorism and cross-border crimes. On the issue of the reform of the United Nations Security Council, President Hu Jintao reiterated the assurance given by the Chinese Premier to Prime Minister in April last year that China understands and supports India's aspirations to play a bigger role in the United Nations, including in the Security Council, and that China would be happy to see India succeed in its endeavour to become a permanent member of the UN Security Council.

The visit represented an important step forward in the process of developing a cooperative 'framework of engagement with China, notwithstanding outstanding issues. It highlighted the commitment of the two sides to add greater content to their strategic partnership and to develop an action-oriented template for the future development and diversification of India-China relations. It also offered an opportunity to send out a strong signal to the international community that as good neighbours and partners, there was enough space for India and China to develop together in a mutually supportive manner,' while remaining sensitive to each other's concerns and aspirations.

In 2007, both countries conducted their first ever joint military exercise to combat terrorism. However, the Chineses strikes on the Indian military posts in Sikkim, Tibet, Arunachal Pradesh and Bhutan have forced a serious rethinking to be done by India in view of the growing assertion by the Chinese of their economic and military power in global politics of late.

The Sixth India-Russia-China Trilateral Foreign Minister fleeting took place in February, 2007. It was the second time that the three Foreign Ministers met exclusively for a trilateral meeting after the first one in in June 2005. In July 2006, Prime Minister Dr. Manmohan Singh, President of the Russian Federation H.E. Mr. Vladimir Putin and President of the People's Republic of China H.E. Mr. Hu Jintao met in St. Petersburg for the first summit level trilateral meeting. They shared their thoughts on the political, economic and security aspects of the global situation, the present word order and recent developments in various areas of mutual concern. They agreed that cooperation rather than confrontation should govern approaches to regional and global affairs. They also agreed on the importance of the UN and that there was a need to make it more effective so that it reflects contemporary global realities. The three countries felt that their interaction would contribute to strengthening peace, security and stability in our region and the world. There was a coincidence of views against terrorism in all its forms and manifestations and on the need to address financing of terrorism and its linkages with narco-trafficking.

During the visit of the Japanese Prime Minister to India in August 2007, the two Prime Ministers shared the view that the visit of Prime Minister Singh to Japan as well as the decision to establish the Strategic and Global Partnership last December elevated the partnership between the two countries to a new level. India and Japan share universal values of democracy, open society, human rights, rule of law and market economy and share common interest in promoting peace, stability and prosperity in Asia and the world. Based on this recognition the two leaders reaffirmed that the India-Japan partnership is a bilateral relationship with the largest potential for growth. The two leaders reiterated that a strong, prosperous and dynamic India is in the interest of Japan and a strong, prosperous and dynamic Japan is in the interest of India and recognized that India and Japan share a congruence of interests.

A new dynamism for growth is being generated in Asia as a result of economic development in India and in other countries as well as heightened efforts towards regional integration. Asia is in the process of rapidly developing synergies/interaction among the different economies, societies, civilizations and cultures of the region while respecting existing diversity and enhancing' openness. Recognizing the current dynamism in Asia, the two Prime Ministers expressed their firm belief that the 21st century should be the century for peace, progress and democracy, and that the partnership between India and Japan, the two major democracies in Asia, is an essential pillar for the future architecture of the entire region. They resolved to work together to further promoting the new dynamism in Asia in a positive direction. Based on this recognition, they exchanged views on the future course of bilateral relations, and set-forth a Roadmap for New Dimensions to the Strategic and Global Partnership. They reaffirmed their willingness to build a strong and enduring partnership through the following Roadmap Political, Security and Defence Cooperation.

The two leaders recognized that India and Japan share common interests in such fields as maintaining the safety and security of sea lanes in the Asia Pacific and the Indian Ocean regions, and fighting against transnational crimes, terrorism, piracy and proliferation of Weapons of Mass Destruction. The two leaders directed respective authorities to study future course of cooperation in the security field between the two countries and to report to them by the time of Indian Prime Minister's visit to Japan.

The two sides recognized the importance of deepening and broadening strategic dialogue through various channels. The two leaders welcomed the launching of the annual Strategic Dialogue at the Foreign Minister level in March 2007. The Foreign Minister of Japan will visit India for the second Dialogue in 2008 before the Indian Prime Minister's visit to Japan'. The two sides will continue to hold regular dialogues through the National Security Advisor of India and the Japanese counterpart. The two sides will commence bi-annual Foreign Secretary/Vice Minister level dialogue. The two sides will also launch an exchange programme of young diplomats in order to promote mutual understanding between the two Foreign Offices.

The U.P.A. Government continued the peace process revived by the Vajpayee Government. The successful start of the bus service between Srinagar and Muzaffarabad in the Pakistan occupied Kashmir has been hailed as a landmark in the Indo-Pak peace process. Musharraf visited India from April 16-18, 2005. During this visit, both countries agreed to carry the bilateral relationship forward. A lot of progress was made in the bilateral relationship, between the two countries through confidence building measures, people to people contacts and by enhancing the areas of interaction. It was agreed to restore the rail link between Kokhrapar and Munnabao which was started in 2006 along with the bus services from Amritsar to Lahore and Nankana Sahib respectively.

President Musharraf and Prime Minister Singh discussed the issue of Jammu and Kashmir in a positive atmosphere. Prime Minister Singh emphasized that while there would be no redrawing of borders, all measures that could bring the people on both sides together, including increased transport linkages to facilitate greater traffic of people and trade across the border and the Line of Control would be taken to help the process and create an atmosphere of trust and confidence. President Musharraf stressed the importance of addressing the Jammu and Kashmir issue. However, he agreed that the confidence building process had made significant progress which would create a general sense of trust and understanding between the two countries which in turn would be conducive in creating an environment for a just, fair and mutually acceptable solution of all outstanding issues.[21]

However, with the detection of Pakistani involvement in the serial blasts that took place in the local trains of Mumbai, the foreign level secretary talks were suspended by India. This led to renewing of tensions between the two countries once again.

Other priority areas of the U.P.A. Government were to carry forward the 'Look East' policy started by the Narasimha Rao Government and the mobilization of international support for India's bid for a permanent seat in the restructuring of the U.N. Security Council. The document of India-ASEAN Partnership for Peace, Progress and Prosperity was adopted at the Indo ASEAN summit in November, 2004. However, the Special Commission set up by the U.N. Secretary General to go into the expansion of the Security Council did not advocate the right of veto to India in the two ways it suggested for the expansion of security Council.

Overall, the foreign policy of the U.P.A. Government was guided by a sense of realism in response to the emerging global and domestic environment.

References

1. *Asian Recorder,* volume 41.1995, p. 24562.
2. J.N. Dixit. *My South Block Years: Memoirs of a Foreign Secretary,* New Delhi, 1996, p. 194.
3. *Annual Report,* 1993-94, Ministry of External Affairs, New Delhi, p. 19.
4. J.N., Dixit. op. cit., p. 134.
5. I.K. Gujral, *A Foreign Policy for India,* New Delhi: Ministry of External Affairs, 1998, pp. 74-75.
6. *Foreign Relations of India: Select Statements, May 1998-March 2000,* New Delhi, Ministry of External Affairs, 2000, pp. 57-69.
7. Washington File, 16 March, 2000.
8. "Remarks by President Clinton", *Visit of the U.S. President to India,* p. 40.
9. http://www.whitehouse.gov/nsc/nssall.html
10. Washington File, 29 July, 2002.
11. http://meaindia.nic/ statement /2004/01113 .htm
12. Amit Baruah. "Concerns over Terrorists Acquiring Pak. Nuclear Arms Remain: Putin", *The Hindu,* New Delhi. 1 December. 2002.
13. htto:// meaindia.ric.in/ joint declaration/2003/11/13.htm.
14. C. Raja Mohan, "India China to Quicken the Pace of LAC Negotiation", *The Hindu,* New Delhi. 30 March, 2002.
15. *India-Pakistan Summit,* New Delhi, Ministry of External Affairs, 2001, pp. 1-2.
16. http:// www.forisb.org/CE-019.html.
17. http:/ meaindia.nic.in/ joint statement/2004/0 1/06. htm.
18. http://meaindia.nic.in/jointstatement/2005/07/18.htm.
19. hllp:!! www.indianembassv.org!press release/2005/June.htm.
20. http://meaindia.nic.inlspeech/2005/04/20ss02.htm
21. http://meaindia.nic.inlspeecdhrs/2005/04/20ss02.htm

11. IMPACT OF GLOBALIZATION ON INDIAN ECONOMY AND STATE

Sarika Dubey

Indian society has been an example of religious, and ethnic co-existence all along. Most of the major religions of the world-Hinduism, Islam, Christianity, Buddhism, Jainism are found here with their numerous cults, doctrines, ideals and ideas. In a world, India has always followed a pattern of cultural pluralism. The Indus Valley civilization, known to be the dawn of Indian civilization was also multi-ethnic in character. Hinduism draws largely on Brahmanical texts, such as the Vedas, the Upanishads and the Bhagavadgita. The normative principles of Hinduism are based on beliefs, ideals, and logic of permissiveness, liberalism, being and becoming, creation and destruction, hedonism, utilitarianism and spiritual transcendence (Singh, 1973).[1]

In Indian Vedic thought, man is throughout a bundle of Kama (desire). Possession of desires gives him second birth, but their absence makes him one with Brahma. The concept of globalization is inherent in the Hindu philosophy, and is very much related to sublimation and the blend represents the true nature of Karma (deed) which ultimately leads to Moksha (salvation). So altruism is the basic tenet of the Bhagvadgita. The core of Indian philosophy talks about divinity and salvation, about holy and sacred tradition, about global harmony, and cosmic rhythm, about spiritual transcendence, and morality irrespective of space, time, labour, and human qualities.

In traditional Indian society the issue of today's modernism i.e., space- time, the philosophers conceived linkage or space-over time concept. Hindu philosophy didn't preach syndicated Hinduism, or Hindu nationalism, rather it always advocated the doctrine of divinity, eternity, and universalism. Bhagavad Gita denotes the philosophy of today's globalism. "Him we salute.... salute to that supreme one who is bodied forth is Brahma." Bhagvad Gita also tells, "the right is to work only; but never to the fruits thereof," then the defoliation and disparity would not dominate our global economic scenario.

The ancient Indian tradition has the philosophy of "Vasudhai Kutumbakam," means the whole planet (Earth) is like a single unit or family. So this tells that our mythology believes in boundary less world which globalization claims today. In modern society, crisis and disparity arise mainly because of uneven distribution of wealth, comfort, and assistance. Our philosophy tells that only he, who looks with equal regard upon well- wishers, friends, foes, neutrals, the hateful, the relatives, the neighbors and the righteous and the unrighteous, attains "Universal self." The centre of global village is nothing but the "Universal self". It would be the "ideal type" model of a global village. So the globalization for India is not new, but this is different in terms of rules, and regulation, which are imposed by international economic organizations and the advancement of technology.

How was India Trapped?

Though globalization or the concept of global village was not new for India, it lies in the soul of Indian culture, yet economic globalization or the profit oriented western imperialism led capitalist globalization, is new to some extent. Now we examine the picture of early 1990s, when India decided to become a part of economic liberalization. India opened up the economy in the early nineties. Indian economy was in deep crisis in July 1991, when foreign exchange reserves had plummeted to almost $ 1 billion; inflation had roared to an annual rate of 17 per cent. Fiscal deficit was very high, and had become unsustainable; foreign investors, and NRIs had lost confidence in Indian economy. Capital was flying out of the country and was close to defaulting on loans. Under such critical situation we were forced to devalue our currency twice, pledge our gold, and accept IMF conditions for receiving assistance to tide over the balance of payments crisis. Such a kind of economic crisis, built up in the Indian economy left no choice but to act fast and bring major economic reforms, which could assist in revival of our economy. To control this crisis, Union Government decided to cut down fiscal deficit and to adopt a structural adjustment policy with liberalization, privatization and globalization in 1991. The two broad objectives of the measures introduced by Union Government were the re-orientation of the economy from centrally directed and highly controlled economy to what is known as a market friendly economy.

Major measures initiated as a part of the liberalization and globalization strategy in the early nineties included the following:

Devaluation: The first step was the announcement of the devaluation of the Indian currency by 18-19 per cent against major currencies in the international foreign exchange market.

Disinvestment : In order to accelerate the process of globalization smooth, privatization, and liberalization policies have been moving along as well. Under the privatization scheme most of the pubic sector undertakings have been sold to private sector.

Dismantling of the Industrial Licensing Regime: At present, only six industries are under compulsory licensing mainly on account of environmental safety and strategic considerations.

Allowing Foreign Direct Investment (FDI): to attract more FDI government is opening some sectors such as insurance (upto 26%); development of integrated townships (upto 100%); defence industry (upto 26%); tea plantation, etc.

Non-Resident Indian Scheme: The general policy and facilities for foreign direct investment available to foreign investors companies are fully applicable to NRIs as well. In addition government has extended some concessions especially for NRIs and overseas corporate bodies having more than 60 per cent stake by NRIs.

Throwing Open Industries Reserved for the Public Sector to Private Participation: Now there are only three industries reserved for the public sector.

Abolition of the (MRTP) Act.:

The removal of quantitative restrictions on imports.

The reduction of the peak customs tariff: From over 300 per cent (Prior to the 30 per cent rate that applies now.)

Wide-ranging financial sector reforms: In the banking, capital markets, and insurance sectors, including the deregulation of interest rates, strong regulation, and supervisory systems, and the introduction of foreign/private sector competition.

Impact of Globalization on Indian Economy

The implications of globalization for national economy are tremendous. Growing interdependence and competition between economies have changed the entire scenario. It has not changed our economic system alone but the socio-political system as well. Globalization in India had a favorable impact on the overall growth rate of the economy. India's growth rate in the 1970s was very low at 3 per cent and GDP growth in countries like Brazil, Indonesia, Korea and Mexico was more than twice that of India. Though India's average annual growth rate almost doubled in the eighties to 5.9 per cent, it was still lower than the growth rate in China, Korea and Indonesia. The pick up in GDP growth has helped improve India's global position. Consequently, India's position in the global economy has improved from the 8th position in 1991 to 4th place in 2001. At present India is the fifth largest economy and has the second largest among emerging economies, based on purchasing power parity (PPP). India also ranks as the 11th largest economy in terms of industrial output, and has the 3rd largest pool of scientific, and technical manpower. The gross Domestic product (GDP) growth accelerated to 5.3 per cent in 1992-93, and 6.2 per cent in 1993-94, and a growth rate of above 8 per cent was an achievement by the Indian economy during the year 2003-04. This shows that India is a growing economy. The advance estimates of GDP for 2006-07, released by the Central Statistical Organization (CSO) on 7 Feb., 2007, places the growth of GDP at factor cost at constant (1999-2000) prices in the current year at 9.2 per cent.[2] The overall growth of GDP during 2006-07 (as per the revised estimates of CSO) has been placed 9.4 per cent. Gradually increase in growth rate can be seen within last three years (See Fig. 11.1). This is the indication of growing, and stronger economy.

Structure of the Economy

Due to globalization, not only the GDP has increased, but also the direction of growth in other sectors as well has changed. Earlier

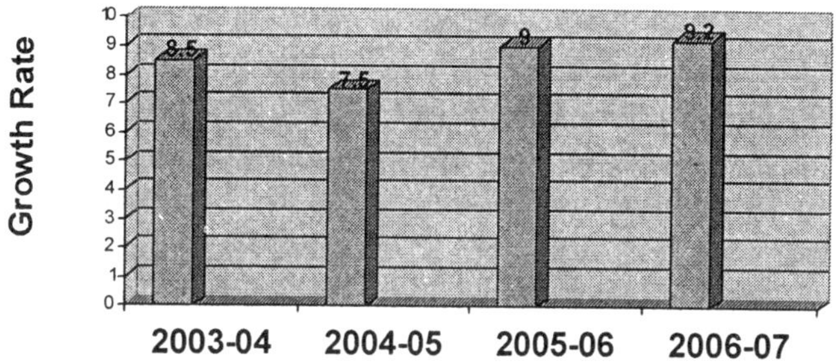

FIG. 11.1

the maximum part of the GDP in the economy was generated from the primary sector, but now the service industry is devoting the maximum part of the GDP. The service sector remains the growth driver of the economy with a contribution of more than 57 per cent of GDP. India is ranked 18th among the world's leading exporters of services with a share of 1.3 per cent in world exports.[3] The services sector, is expected to benefit from the ongoing liberalization of the foreign investment. Software and the ITES-BPO sectors have recorded an exponent growth in recent years. The service sector continued to record double digit growth of 10.6 per cent in April-June 2007.[4] Sub sectors of services trade, hotels, transport and communication services have continued to boost the sector. This entire happening rapidly because of the emergence of knowledge based society. Impressive Progress in information technology (IT), and IT-enabled services, both rail and road traffic, and fast addition to existing stock of telephone connections particularly mobiles, played a key role in such a growth. Growth rate in the GDP from major sectors of the economy can be seen from the following table 11.1.

Table 11.1 shows the clear-cut vision of growing Indian Economy. In 2006-07, while the share of agriculture in GDP declined to 18.5 per cent, the share of industry, and services improved to 26.4 per cent and 55.1 per cent respectively.

Foreign Direct Investment inflows

There was strong growth in foreign direct investment (FDI) flows

Table 11.1

SECTORAL REAL GROWTH RATES IN GDP AT FACTOR COST
(at 1999-2000 Prices)

Item	Percentage change over the previous year						
	2000-01	*2001-02*	*2002-03*	*2003-04*	*2004-05*	*2005-06*	*2006-07*
						(Q)	(A)
I. Agriculture & allied	0.2	6.3	-7.2	10.0	0.0	6.0	2.7
II. Industry	6.4	2.7	7.1	7.4	9.8	9.6	10.0
- Mining & quarrying	2.4	1.8	8.8	3.1	7.5	3.6	4.5
- Manufacturing	7.7	2.5	6.8	6.6	8.7	9.1	11.3
- Electricity, gas & water supply	2.1	1.7	4.7	4.8	7.5	5.3	7.7
- construction	6.2	4.0	7.9	12.0	14.1	14.2	9.4
III. Services	5.7	7.2	7.4	8.5	9.6	9.8	11.2
- Trade, hotels, transport & communication	7.3	9.1	9.2	12.1	10.9	10.4	13.0
- Financial, real estate & business services	4.1	7.3	8.0	5.6	8.7	10.9	11.1
- Community social & personal services	4.8	4.1	3.9	5.4	7.9	7.7	7.8
IV Total GDP at factor cost	4.4	5.8	3.8	8.5	7.5	9.0	9.2

P : Provisional
Q : Quick
A : Advance estimates

Source : Central Statistical Organization.

(net), with three-quarters of such flows in the form of equity. The growth rate was 27.4 per cent in 2005-06 followed by 98.4 per cent in April- September 2006. The total FDI inflow during April-September 2006 was 4.38 Billion US $. Going one step ahead of

South Korea, India got the fourth place in gaining FDI.[5] The top three FDI achievers are China, Hongkong and Singapore. In terms of FDI approval, New Delhi gets first place, than Bombay, Banglore, Chennai and Hyderabad. According to the latest World Investment Report 2007, released on 17 October 2007 by United Nations Conference on Trade and Development (UNCTAD), India would be the second Most Attractive location during year 2007-09, China and USA would be on Ist and 3rd place respectively.

According to the UNCTAD'S just released World investment Report 2007, India attracted US $16.88 billion in FDI during 2006, up by 152.86 per cent over the 2005 inflow of US$ 6.68 billion.[6] Global foreign direct investment FDI inflows amounted to US $ 1.306 billion, in 2006, up by 38 per cent over the 2005 level of US $, 946 billion. According to UNCTAD's report, FDI in 2006 was the largest since 2000, when it had touched US $ 1,411 billion[7] (See Figure 11.3). USA was the largest recipient country in the year, followed by the U.K, France, Belgium and China. India stood at the 21st Position getting US $ 16.9 billion. In 2005 the country had received US $ 6.7 billion in FDI. From the Figure 11.2, the FDI Inflow in India during years 1992 to 2006 can be seen clearly. It shows gradual increase from 1992 to 2005, and the sharp increase in 2006. This is the clear-cut impact of globalization and liberalization, over Indian economy, which is gaining strength day by day.

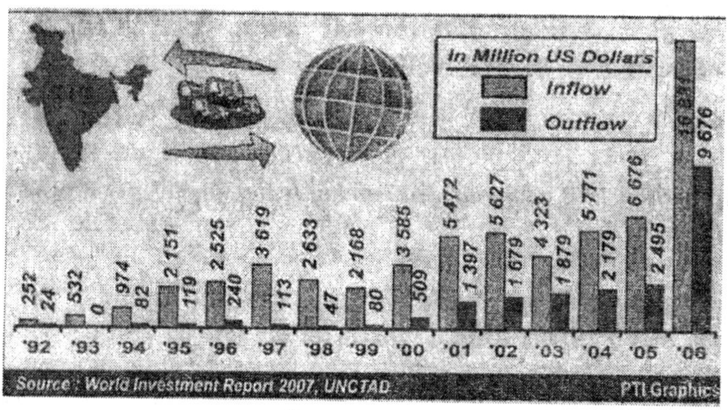

FIGURE : 11.2

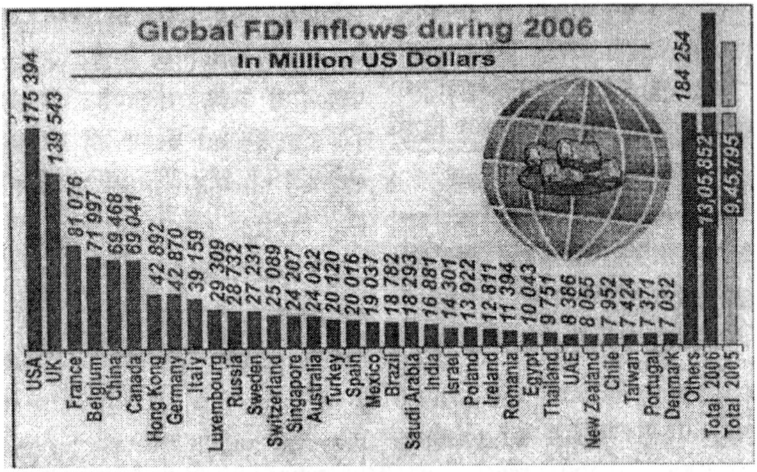

FIGURE : 11.3

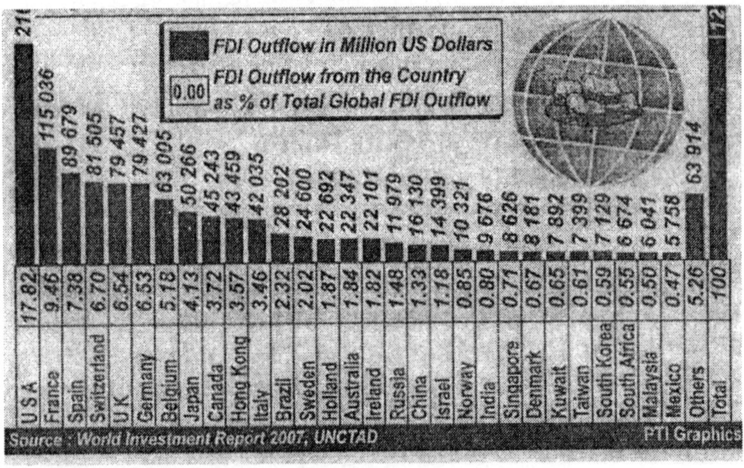

FIGURE : 11.4

Foreign Direct Investment Outflows: (Figure 11.3, 11.4)

Due to globalization, not only investment inflow has increased, but at the same time India's outflow has also increased sharply in the last year 2006. The year also saw substantial FDI outflow from the country, highlighted by Tata Steels US $ 11 billion acquisition of the Anglo-Dutch steel maker Corus. FDI outflow from India during 2006 amounted to the US $ 9.68 billion.[8] (See Figure 1.3) India ranked 21st in both inflow and outflow of FDI during the year. FDI outflows worldwide amounted to the US $ 1,216 billion in 2006, up by 45.2 per cent over the 2005 level of US $ 837 billion, according to UNCTAD'S Report 2007. USA was the largest host country for FDI outgo during the year, followed by France, Spain, Switzerland and U.K. (See Figure 11.4)

This is a matter of pride for us that in the present globalized world we are not only accepting FDI, but our outflows show that we are able to compete with the western market. This is the real picture of integrating economy and increasing dependency on each other. Our outflows indicates that Indian Big Business is also going abroad to launch its own business either through investments or acquisitions. Tata steel is working on mergers, and acquisitions in China, South East Asia and Far East for the emerging markets of Rs. 25,000 crore where demand for steel is potentially possible.[9]

If Tatas are going abroad for accumulation, and profits, Indians are reciprocating it by allowing foreign investors in its own firms. FIIs now own an average of 30 per cent stake in 10 top Indian Corporates, reflecting the growing role of foreign investors in driving investments. Their stake in the top 50 companies is now put at an average of more than 17.5 per cent up from 15 per cent just two years back.

Not only tata's but also other Indian companies are also performing well. The Reliance group, the Aditya Birla group, and IT companies like Wipro and HCL et al are scouting for business in foreign markets.

Tata Motors have also tied up with Daewoo commercial vehicles, Korea and signed the acquisition of company for the US $ 118 million.[10] It is estimated that Indian corporate businessmen have invested US $ 1048.78 million (Rs. 4.813 crore) abroad during 2002-03 as reported by the Reserve Bank of India on September 30, 2003 (See Table 11.2).

Social Implication of FDI Inflows and Outflows :

Globalization's Free trade policy is increasing integration among economies, and dependency to each other. So now, we are the part of global benefits, and global crisis, because of the direct Impact

Table 11.2

SOME NOTABLE OVERSEAS ACQUISITION DETAILS IN THE LAST YEAR

Reliance Industries	Flag Telecom (Oct 2003) : 100 per cent equity was acquired for $ 211 million. Flag is a global submarine cable network with a capacity of around 5000 gbps and a network length of 50,000 km. Access to 55 countries and high bandwidth will help-reliance realize its global ambitions.
Infosys	Export information services, Australia (Dec. 2003) : 100 per cent stake was acquired for $ 23 million. The acquisition will give infosys access to the Australian market.
Tata Motors	Daewoo Commercial Vehicles (March 2004) : Acquisition ($ 118 million) give Tata Motors a foothold in the lucrative South Korean markets besides facilitating its entry into china and other SE Asian Markets.
Bharat Forge	Forging business of CDP, Germany (Jan 2004): Acquisition of CDP (Euro 28 million) has made Bharat Forge the second- largest foreign company in the world.
Hindalco	Copper mines, Australia (march 2004) Two copper mines were bought for $ 72 mllion
Ranbaxy	Aventis's generic unit in France (Dec 2003) Acquisition price was $ 75 million. Though the French generic market is currently small, It is likely to witness significant growth over the next decade.
Tata Steel	11 billion US $ acquisition of the Anglo Dutch steel maker corus in 2007.
Sundaraman Fasteners	Precision forging unit of Dana Spicer (UK) (Dec. 2003): the unit was acquired for GBP 1.5 million.
Dabur	British cosmetics firm, Redrock Ltd. (Sep. 2003): Acquisition amount was $ 5 million. Redrock is a franchisee of Dabur in the Middle East. It entered into a licensing pact with Dabur India in 1991 and has since been producing and marketing Dabur Brands

Source: The Business Standard, New Delhi.

of these changes on national economies. Therefore we must be alert to the changes in global economy, and we will have to prepare our self towards the global competitiveness. Many national companies, and small-scale industries would not be able to compete, if they have not changed their mindset of traditional setup. Three basic things should be done in this regard—

1. Creating Work Culture
2. Competitiveness
3. Advancement in technologies.

D.S. Brar, Ranbaxy Laboratories CEO and MD, said "In India we are used to a lot of short cuts to get our work done, but such measures would not deliver in other countries. This is one area where we can stumble in the global market."[12]

We welcome FII Inflows, but we should be attentive too. A timely warning has been given by T.N. Ninan to globalised India, that the stock market boom has been fuelled essentially by the dramatic. Increase in FII inflows, a consequence of the excess money slashing around in the rest of the world. But how many among us understand, the drivers of this global liquidity, which determines our stock prices?

The Annual Report 2004-05 of Reserve Bank of India (RBI) also shows some positive aspects in Indian Economy.

- The current account deficit has hovered at less than 1 per cent of GDP in recent years.
- The strength of the external sector was reflected in a sizeable accumulation of India's foreign exchange reserves comprising foreign currency assets, gold, SDRs and the reserve position with the IMF which touched US $ 185.1 billion as on Feb. 9, 2007.
- The composition of debt is also favourable. Short-term debt amounts to 3.5 per cent of external debt, and concessional debt amounts to 36.5 per cent of total debt.
- The external debt burden looks sustainable according to a range of measures of indebtedness. Both debt service payments as a proportion of current receipts and the external debt to GDP ratio have been falling steadily during the 1990s. India's external debt stock stood at us

$ 126.4 billion at end- March 2006, reflecting an increase of US $ 3.2 billion over the year.

Non-Resident Deposits

In the last sixteen years ending 2005-06, non-resident deposits remained an important and relatively stable source of capital flows. As a proportion of total capital flows, it had strengthened in the four- year period 2000-04 to above 20 per cent. But such deposits became a source of negative flows in 2004-05. There was a resumption of the earlier trend in 2005-06 with the proportion rising to 11.5 per cent.[13] Non-resident Indians are sending more money home. Individual remittances from Indians working overseas have surged 50 per cent at $ 8.6 billion in the first quarter of 2007-08, against $ 5.9 billion in the year ago period, according to the balance of payment data released by the RBI.

Foreign Trade (Export-Import)

India's imports increased by 31.1 per cent in April-August, 2007. Imports grew faster, reflecting in part the ongoing investment boom, and the high international Petroleum price. In 2005-06, imports (in US dollar terms and customs basis) had grown by 33.8 per cent. In the first nine months of the current year, imports grew by 36.3 per cent.

India's exports (in US dollar terms and customs basis) have been growing at a high rate of more than 20 per cent since 2002-03. During 2005-06, with growth of 23.4 per cent India's exports crossed the US $ 100 billion mark. During 2006-07 after a slow start, exports gained momentum to grow by an estimated 36.3 per cent in the first nine months to reach US $ 89.5 billion. Buoyancy of exports was driven by the resurgence in the manufacturing sector, and sustained demand from major trading partners.

Trade in services has been growing faster than merchandise trade, and the share of services in total external trade increased from 25.8 per cent in 2004-05 to 27.4 per cent in 2005-06.

Thus we find that the economic reforms in the Indian economy initiated since July 1991 have led to fiscal consolidation, control of inflation to some extent, increase in foreign exchange reserve, and greater foreign investment, and technology towards

India. This has helped the Indian economy to grow at a faster rate. Presently more than 100 of the 500 fortune companies have a presence in India as compared to 33 in China. The result of all this can be seen in the appreciation of Rupee. An escalating rupee has triggered the U.S. dollar to drop from Rs. 44-45 levels to Rs. 39.[14]

The rupee has not only appreciated against the dollar (12-13 %) but also against the pound, sterling and euro during the last six months. (See Figer 11.5)

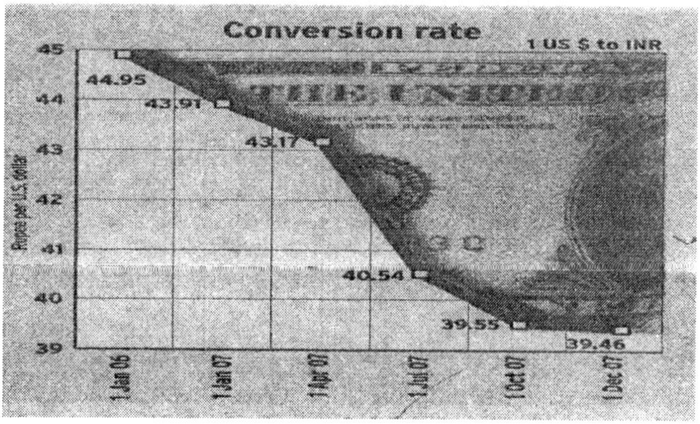

FIGER 11.5

This is the matter of national pride for us , and it shows the gaining strength of our economy day by day. The sensex has also moved up from 13,000 to breach the 20000 mark to hover around its present level, and some mega deals such as Arcelor- Mittal, Tata- Corus and Vodafone- Hutch are finalised in this year 2007. All this gives impression, that, in case of Indian economy, globalization has played the significant role of its supporter. .

Side affects of Globalization

Everything has some positive and negative effects, though globalization has provided many opportunities, yet all the problems are still not solved. There are some areas where the impact of globalization remained negative, and still we have some challenges to fight. We all know that India is an agricultural society. Agriculture employs 60 per cent of the Indian population, yet it contributes only 20.6 per cent to the GDP. (Isaac, 2005),[15] agricultural production fell by 12.6 per cent in 2003, which is one of the sharpest drops in independent India's history. Agriculture growth slowed from 4.69 per cent in 1991 to 2.6 per cent in 1997-1998 and to 1.1 per cent in 2002-2003. According to the advance estimates of GDP for 2006-07, India's growth rate was 9.2 per cent (the fastest growing economy) but at the same time agriculture shows the growth rate of 2.7 per cent and its share in GDP dips to 18.5 per cent only. (Economic Survey of India 2006-07).[16]

This is the poor condition of Indian agriculture; the economic reforms in the agriculture sector in particular came under severe criticism in the late 1990s, when 221 farmers in the south Indian state of Andhra Pradesh committed suicide. (The damage done, 2005).[17] The trend was noticed in several other states. According to a leading journalist and activist, P. Sainath, the number of Indians committing suicide each year rose from around 96,000 in 1997 to roughly 1.14 lakh in 2005. In the same period, the number of farmers taking their own lives each year shot up dramatically, from under 14,000 in 1997 to over 17,000 in 2005. (P. Sainath, 2007).[18] Indian farmers are forced to suicides because of the gradual increase in debt burden on them. This is negative impact of India's liberalising policy on agriculture.

In 2001, when the farm suicides were not yet at their worst, the farm suicide rate (FSR) at 12.9 was much higher than the general suicide rate (GSR) at 10.6 for that year. But the GSR slowed down after that to 10.3 by 2005, even as the total number of suicides went up. It means that the increase in the number of general suicides did not keep pace with the growth in general population. But the FSR seems to have risen more steeply after 2001.[19] By all accounts, while the number of farm suicides kept increasing, the number of farmers has fallen since 2001, with countless thousands abandoning agriculture. In 2005, the Big Four or suicide SEZ states, Maharashtra, Andhra Pradesh, Karnataka, and Madhya Pradesh (including Chhattisgarh) accounted for 43.9 per cent of all suicides and 64 per cent of all farm suicides in the country. Karnataka, and Andhra Pradesh, which are rich and developed states, and the centres of IT revolution in India, have performed well in such areas, and the supporters of India's liberalization policy, and performed several tasks of reforms in industry and government. Then it is really surprising to see, high Farm suicide rate (FSR) in these states. The reason behind all this is a big question. It is quite obvious, that reform in agriculture according to liberalization policy is not favourable for Indian farmers. These reforms have kept Indian farmers into the well of debt burden, and this has become the major reason of increasing farm suicide rate (FSR).

In case of Andhra Pradesh, the then Chief Minister Chandra Babu Naidu envisaged corporate style agriculture Plan in A.P. and implemented World Bank liberalization policies with great enthusiasm, but the result was negative due to high input and less output. For example, many Indian farmers purchase seeds from the state government institutions like AP's APSSDC3. These institutions produced their own Seeds, and were responsible for their quality and price. (The damage done, 2005).[20] After liberalization, India's seed market was opened up to global agribusinesses like Monsanto, Cargill and Syn Genta. For implementing liberalization policy according to the guidelines of the IMF, 14 of the 24 units of the APSSDC's seed processing units were closed down in 2003, with similar closures in other states. This hit farmers doubly hard: in an unregulated market, seed prices shot up, and fake seeds made an appearance in a big way. Seed cost per acre in 1991 was Rs. 70 but in 2005, after the dismantling of APSSDC and other similar organizations, the price jumped to Rs. 1000, a hike of 1428 per cent, with the cost of genetically modified pest resistant seeds like Monsanto's BT cotton costing Rs. 3200 or more per acre, a hike of 3555 per cent (Sainath 2005).[21] The success of this BT cotton is disputed: farmers in A.P. and Maharashtra now claim that yields are far lower than promised by Monsanto. Expecting high yields, farmers invest heavily in such seeds. Also BT cotton and other new seeds guarantee a much lower germination rate of 65 per cent as opposed to a 90 per cent rate of state certified seeds. Hence 35 per cent of the farmer's investment in seed is a waste (Sainath 2004).[22] Output was not commensurate with the heavy investment in the seeds, and farmers were pushed into debt. The abundant availability of spurious seeds is another problem, which leads to crop failures. So the reason of this indebtness is high input and low output, and after liberalization, when, many foreign agro companies were present here it was difficult for farmers to compete with them.

The other adverse effect of liberalization policy on farmers, was the devaluation of the Indian Rupee in 1991 by 25 per cent (an explicit condition of the IMF loan). Indian crops became very cheap and attractive in the global market, and led to an export drive. This situation has encouraged farmers to grow cash crops (export oriented: chilli, cotton, Tobacco) in place of traditional crops (The Damage done 2005).[23] These need far more inputs of pesticide, fertilizer and water than traditional crops. Liberalization policies reduced pesticide subsidy (Condition of the IMF agreement) by two thirds by 2000. Farmers in Maharashtra who spent Rs. 90 an acre now spend between Rs. 1000 and 3000 representing a hike of 1000 per cent to 3333 per cent. Fertilizer prices have increased 300 per cent (Sainath, 2005)[24] Electricity tariffs have also been increased: in Andhra Pradesh tariff was increased 5 times between 1998 to 2003. (Seeds of ruin 2005)[25] Also, the fact that only 39 per cent of India's cultivable land is irrigated makes cultivation of cash crops largely unviable, but export oriented liberalization policies, and seed companies looking for profits continue to push farmers in that direction (ISAAC, 2005).[26]

Liberalization policy favours to withdraw tariffs and duties on imports, which protect, and encourage domestic industry. By 2001, India completely removed restrictions on imports of almost 1500 items including food. (The damage done, 2005).[27] As a result, cheap imports flooded the market, pushing prices of crops like cotton and pepper down. Import tariffs on cotton now stand between 0-10 per cent, encouraging imports into the country. This excess supply of cotton in the market led cotton prices to crash more than 60 per cent since 1995. This resulted in, most of the farmer suicides in Maharshtra in the cotton belt till 2003. (Hardikar, 2006).[28]

Branco Milanovic, a World Bank economist describes that liberalisation helps developing countries to achieve growth, according to him, it will increase productivity and reduce inefficiency, which will lead to economic growth, and in a few generations, if not less, the poor will become rich, illiteracy will disappear and poor countries will catch up with the rich (The damage done, 2005).[29] But here Mr. Milanovic forgets to mention that rich countries which now preach liberalization, protected their 'infant industries' at the time they began to industrialize, till they were strong enough to compete at global level. The U.S. government, for example, had a protectionist trade policy in the late nineteenth century to help the US companies to become competitive in the world. A German economist Friedrich list says, the adoption of these values of liberalization assumes that all countries are at the same starting place. Which is clearly not the case. We can see the huge disparity among developed and developing counties. Their starting place was not the same. In fact, it is this very reason that has brought about the crisis that Indian agriculture is facing today. Most of the Indian farmers were already in a position of minimum security. With no education system, credit facilities, access to alternative employment, or efficient technology. Their only support was government subsidy, and regulation. But after liberalization, situation has changed. These policies dismantled their only support structure, and the result was that they were fighting for their survival.

Actually globalization encourages the well positioned, to use tools of economics and politics to exploit market opportunities, boost technical productivity, and maximize short-term material interests. But in case of India the gap between one who is well positioned and one who is not, is very big. For example, Indian big businessman like Ambanis, Tatas, are enjoying the opportunities, they are going abroad for accumulation and profits. They are also involved in mega business deals. Indian Engineers, Doctors and MBAs are also going abroad for better jobs. Many of our young graduates are seeking jobs through outsourcing. We have already discussed all such things in the positive aspect of globalization. But on the other side we have 28.6 per cent people of the total population, who are living below poverty line (World Development Report 2007).[30] Unemployment and underemployment are chronic problems in India, with the rate of unemployment being close to 10 per cent in 2004. Primary education in rural areas is mismanaged. Still we have not achieved the target of 100 per cent literacy. We have only 65 per cent literate people. In this condition there is no possibility for many of our people to be the part of globalization.

It is really difficult to arrive at precise assessment of the impact of Globalization on income inequalities but it is clear that even after nearly one decade of advent of Globalization in India a vast gulf exists- between the different income earners. Planning commission Deputy chairman Montek Singh Ahluwalia admits that inequality in the Indian economic and social system have increased overtime.[31] As per world Development Report, 1999, top 20 per cent of the population accounted for 39.3 per cent of the total income, while share of the bottom 20 per cent was only 9.2 per cent. In the same way the inter-state variations in the growth pattern shows, that two states with high per capita income in 1980-91 viz. Punjab and Haryana lost momentum in the nineties, while Maharashtra and Gujarat overshot them indicating that during the Globalization era the Green Revolution lost stream, while industry-based growth of Maharastra and Gujarat was gaining momentum. (Economic Survey of India 2002-03).[32] The real situation is that in 2003, inter-state, intra-state and inter-regional disparities have got accentuated during the decade of economic reforms; Orissa and Bihar "Continue to be the two poorest states with poverty ratios of 47 and 43 per cent respectively." This situation was running continuously till 2007. So these are the biggest threats posed by globalization.

According to the United Nations Development Report 2007 (UNDP) India's ranking is 128, falling down 2 points from last year to 126. It means other nations did much better than us, and hence we went down to rank 128 this year. Each year since 1990, the Human Development Report (HDR) of the UNDP publishes the Human Development Index (HDI). This index "looks beyond GDP to a broader definition of well being". The HDI seeks to capture "three dimensions of human development; a long and healthy life (measured by life expectancy at birth). Being educated (measured by adult literacy and enrolment in primary, secondary and tertiary education). And third: GDP per capita (measured in the U.S. dollars of purchasing power parity). There are several countries, which have performed well than us. Even nations, that are far below us in the HDI rankings, and which have nothing like our growth numbers, dollar billionaire, have done much better than us on many counts. El Salvador, which saw a bloody civil war for over a decade from the 1980s, ranks 25 places ahead of us at 103. Bolivia, often called South America's poorest nation, is 11 steps above us at 117. Guatemala, nearly half of whose citizens are poor indigenous people, saw the longest civil war in Central America, ranks 10 places above us at 118. In Africa, Botswana-

ranked below us in the 2006 HDI at 131-climbed four places above us at 124 this time. In Asia, countries like Vietnam-victim of the bloodiest conflict since world war II- rose further in the charts, to rank 105 this year (2007). Sri Lanka is also way ahead of us at 99. (P. Sainath 2007).[33] Some of these nations rank up to 30 slots above others and we fall within 30 nations below us. Not one of them has had our 9 per cent growth. Neither they have been touted an emerging economic superpower, nor even as a software superpower. Not even as a blossoming nuclear power. Together, they probably do not have as many billionaires as India does. In short, even nations much poorer than us in Asia, Africa and Latin America have done a lot better than us. All this is happening in the era of globalization. Indian rose in the dollar billionaire rankings from rank 8 in 2006 to number 4 in the Forbes list this year (2007),[34] but we slipped from 126 to 128 in human development. Our top 10 billionaires are doing fine. "Their collective wealth has soared 27 per cent since July this years (2007). They had got "richer by $ 65.3 billion" in just three months since July. That is by more than Rs. 119 Crore an hour are not far from Rs. 2 Crore every minute. Mukesh Ambani alone " increased his wealth by roughly Rs. 40 lakh every single minute." Most of our billionaires seem to be from Mumbai, also home to a quarter of India's 100,000 millionaires. Mumbai is the capital of Maharashtra, perhaps our richest state on many counts. But has seen close to 32,000 farmers commiting suicide since 1995, also a state where rural poverty has gone up even in official reckoning.[35]

Meanwhile, the UNHDR records, that almost a third of India's children, or 30 per cent, are below average weight at birth. Amongst children under the age of five, 47 per cent in India are underweight. We are home to the largest number of malnourished children in the world.[36] So these are the realities, and we cannot ignore it. Crisis of Agriculture and the disparity in the nation are the biggest problems. Few of us are gaining the benefits of globalization and going to become richer, and the many of us are fighting for our survival, and these conditions are not favourable for them. They are forced to commit suicide. If we want to have a healthy society, we should develop harmonious relation in the society. For this, there should be equal distribution of wealth, and it is possible only when the process of globalization should be managed and for this, we have to control and remove the weakness of our system and should work at grass root level.

- The first weakness lies in its underdeveloped character which is proved by the limited resource base of the Indian state. We have always collected less revenue from its required value.[37] If 50 million out of a population of one billion are in the tax net of the central government of India, its serious fiscal weakness is quite clear. If Income Tax, Excise, Custom and corporate taxes are not yielding enough fiscal resources for the Indian state, it has direct implications for the state, and the national economy.
- The second structural weakness of Indian economy is 'demand constraint' because it has not been able to deepen and broaden its market for production and consumption. Basically India is an agrarian country, and if the economic health of rural society is not sound, 'demand constraint' will remain a specific feature of India, which will put a brake over its total economy.
- Third, the decade of 1990s has witnessed neglect of rural India because gross capital formation in agriculture and Allied sector has declined interestingly in a few years of the 1990s and it is the private investment which has outstripped the public investment in rural capital formation. Now we should move towards second green revolution.
- Fourth, lack of infrastructure is another problem. To enhance business activities, it is quite necessary to develop sound infrastructure in the nation.
- Fifth, corruption at every level, is one of the biggest problems. Many policies, schemes that government launches for the welfare of people are actually not reaching them. Former Prime Minister Rajiv Gandhi said that only 15 paise reach to the people while 85 paise becomes the part of corruption. So this is very much sad situation.

Summing up

Though it is clear that Indian economy is facing grave challenges in some sectors and has shown negative outcomes, yet it is one face of the coin. The other side we can see how globalization has helped our economy to grow, we should not forget that we had spent our fifty years with socialist ideology and faced severe economic crisis in 1991, this situation has forced us to join economic reforms and to be the part of globalization. It is true that it had many arms and some of them were benign and some others harmful. We will have to be careful towards its harmful arms. Globalization had several facets and the country should not blame the process for all the evils faced by it. Globalization might have its sins but for India it did a lot of good to improve our economy.

In this global age it is also not possible to live alone. Prime Minister Manmohan Singh advocated greater interaction with the world and warned that "if our economy is not equipped to absorb, assimilate, and to adopt this technical change which is taking place, all over the world, I think we will be marginalised. Many developing economies are already being marginalized in the new global economic system that has emerged." So it is necessary to create an environment in which each and every part of Indian society could get the benefit of globalization and liberalization.

Reference

1. Singh, Yogendra, *Modernization of Indian Tradition,* New Delhi: Thompson Press (India) Ltd., 1973.
2. *Economic Survey of India,* 2006-07.
3. International Research Journal of Finance and Economics Issue 5, 2006.
4. Economy At a Glance, Dec., 2007. Vol. I, Issue 5, Delhi.
5. *Economic Survey of India,* 2006-07.
6. UNCTAD'S World Investment Report 2007.
7. Ibid.
8. Ibid.
9. 'TISCO eyes Rs. 25,000 Crore Sales,' *The Business Standard,* New Delhi, November 1/2 2002, p. 1.
10. Tata Sign MOU to Buy Daweoo Unit,' *The Hindustan Times,* New Delhi, November 6, 2003.
11. Sabarinath M. Abhinaba Das,' - On Take over spree abroad: *The Economic Times,* New Delhi, November. 27, 2003, p. 10.
12. Going Global: India Multinationals Abroad, *The Indian Express,* New Delhi, November 25, 2003, p. 10.
13. *Economic Survey of India,* 2006-07.

14. *The Hindu,* 24, December, 2007.
15. Issac, R. 2005. *The Globalization Gap*; Pearson Education Inc. New Jersey.
16. *Economic Survey of India* 2006-07.
17. The Damage Done : Aid, Death and Dogma', May 2005, Christian Aid.
18. P. Sainath, Farm Suicides rising, *The Hindu,* 12 Nov. 2007.
19. Ibid.
20. The Damage Done : Aid, Death and Dogma', May 2005, Christian Aid.
21. Sainath, P., 'Spice of Life Carries Whiff of Death', *The Hindu,* Feb.13, 2005.
22. Sainath, P., 'Seeds of Suicide', *The Hindu*, July 20, 2004.
23. The Damage Done 2005, op. cit.
24. Sainath P., op. cit., 2005.
25. 'Seeds of ruin', *The Indian Express*, July 3, 2005.
26. Issac, op. cit., 2005.
27. The Damage Done, op. cit., 2005.
28. Hardikar J., 'The Rising Import of Suicides', India Together, viewed, June 10, 2006.
29. The Damage Done, op. cit., 2005.
30. World Development Report, 2007.
31. These remarks from Ahuluwalia, While Releasing the Survey Findings of NCAER, Max New York Life, Study on 'How India Earns, Spends and Saves' on Thursday, Feb. 07, 2008.
32. Economic Survey 2002-03, p. 13, Privatization of National Assets in on the March in the 1990s.
33. Sainath, P., "India, 2007 : High Growth low Development " *The Hindu,* 24 Dec. 2007.
34. *The Times of India,* 8 October, 2007.
35. *The Hindu*, 24 Dec. 2007
36. Ibid.
37. *The Economic Times,* New Delhi, October 10, 2003, p. 3.

12. ISLAM IN AN ERA OF GLOBALIZATION

Mohammad Shahid

Introduction

Much has been written both in favour of and against Islam. The Orientalists have definitely given an academic boost to the study of Islam with their agenda of deriding this religion. What has been the source of attack by the orientalists against Islam has in fact, been thwarted by the orthodox religious scholars of Islam. The defiling methodology adopted by scholars in the West has no doubt some exceptions like that of Thomas Arnold—'The preaching of Islam' and Will Durant—The Age of Faith, H.A.R. Gibb—wither Islam? and Arnold J. Toynbee—Civilisation on Trial. The irony is that many persons who speak about Islam, do it on flimsy knowledge of Islam and even they do not try to go deeper in the understanding of Islam. Most of the scholars try to put Islam as the religion founded by Muhammad (pbuh) in the year 610 of the Christian Era (AC).[1] There is no such things as 'Mohammadanism' or 'Mohammadans'. In fact, some of the authorities mentioned above have tried to present Islam as 'Mohammadanism'.

Islam literally means 'peace through submission to God'. 'Muslim' literally means ' anyone or anything that submits itself to the Will of God'. Islam is not a cult. It is a complete way of life- moral, spiritual, social, political, economic and intellectual etc. This, then, is the main reason for the failure of western project of secularization of Islam.

In the Quran it is made clear that from most ancient times the word Islam has been used by all divine messengers and their followers as the name for their religion—

> Allah has ordained for you that religion which He has already commanded to Nuh (Noah), Ibrahim (Abrahman), Musa (Moses) and Isa (Jesus).[2]

Therefore, Muslims believe in and acknowledge all the prophets of old from Adam to Jesus. Muslims believe that they brought the message of peace and submission (Islam) to different nations and communities at different times.[3] The two religions viz Judaism and Christianity which emanated from the land of Palestine were Islam of their time. Islam is therefore, not a new religion founded by Muhammad (peace be upon him). Islam is the last edition of divine message revealed to Muhammad (pbuh). The Holy Quaran was not authored by Muhammad. It was revealed by God to Muhammad and written in physical form by Muhammad's companions. Muslims neither worship Muhammad nor pray through him. Muslims also believe that Quran is the final revelation of God. The original version has never been changed or tampered with An actual seventh century Quran complete and intact is on display in Topkapi museum in Istanbul. If all Qurans in the world today were burned and destroyed, the original Arabic would still remain.[4] This is because three million Muslims (called Hafiz, p. 1. Huffaz, or 'preservers') have memorized the text letter for letter from beginning to end- every word and syllable throughout the world.[5]

Tenets of Islam

Islam in its simplicity is based on five pillars- (1) that there is no god but Allah and that Muhammad is His Messenger, (2) five times daily prayers, (3) payment of zakah, (4) fasting in the month of Ramdan and (5) Hajj i.e. pilgrimage to the holy Ka'baha at Makkah by those who are able. In its complex formation indeed all the five pillars are a kind of revolution/ transformation carried by religio-social movements. Take for example the first pillar that is Shahadah (there is no god but Allah...) is a revolution against a wordly authority which has usurped the fundamental prerogative of humanity. The second pillar Salah (five times daily prayer) is a strong check against inaction on the part of the faithful, readying him constantly watchful of his relation with God and fellow human beings. Salah is not only a gathering of people for a common prayer but also for personal immediate contacts, and as such, it is in direct opposition to negative individualism and separation. Life segregates people; mosques bring them together again and mixes them. It is an everyday school of harmony, equality, community and good will through social solidarity. Zakah as the third pillar reflects the strong sense of belongingness with the community thereby sharing the sorrows, miseries and disadvantages of its parts by disbursing a small portion of wealth (which is sufficient) with the sense of pleasing God. Zakah reflects the principle according to which the higher part of the society is obliged to financially help the poorer part. The very institution of Zakah in its practicality is going to reduce/ remove the chances of conflicts between the rich and poor. Fasting during the lunar month of Ramdan as well brings unity of the whole community of believers (Ummah) and it also stands for coming close to the feelings of hunger and thirst (a tool of purifying the body and the soul) and thereby nourishing sympathy with the poor and wretched of the earth. During Ramdan, all Muslims are required to abstain from food, drink and other pleasures between dawn and sunset as an act of mortification and self denial designed to promote righteousness. Then what about Hajj? Is it a religious rite, an international trade fare, a political gathering, an international forum for exchanging the views and perceptions towards the differing conditions of the faithful, or all in one? It is clearly a religious rite but definitely a great qualizer between different races, ethnic and linguistic groups plus presenting the idea of unity and equality of man as all the male pilgrims are in simple untailored clothes reminding them the hereafter life which is central theme of the religion of Islam.[6]

Spread of Islam

Islam, as the last edition of divine religion reappearing from the rugged hills of Arabia some 1400 years ago spread within short period of human history to different parts of the old world. Missionary zeal, military conquests, high notion of culture and civilization, large scale trade and commerce, Islamic education, the high spirit of tolerance and reconciliation, strong sense of communitarian life based on the doctrine of fraternity and human equality were some of the strong reasons for the spread of Islam. Belief in Muhammad as the messenger of God also implies believing him as the last and final prophet. As no more prophet is to come, therefore, this realization has put the responsibility of preaching the religion of Islam to humanity on the shoulders of all the Muslims.[7] In this sense many nationalities shared the task of spreading Islam: Arabs, Berbers, Persians, Moors, Kurds, Turks, Negroes, Indians, e.g. "Arabs helped the spread of Islam over Western Asia, North Africa, Central Asia, Sind and Spain; Turks helpd the spread of Islam in Southern Russia, India, Asia Minor, the Balkans; Negro leadrship helped the spread of Islam in Africa, particularly in the Niger Basin; multi national missionary endeavour largely helped its spread in Indonesia and China". Imperialism and colonialism in the wake of European renaissance and industrial revolution although tried to halt the pace of spread of Islam, but it miserasbly failed. In fact, colonial administration in different parts of the world proved as blessing in disguise for the spread of Islam to newer people and places. It looks a puzzle to explain the factors for the spread of Islam on a large scale in the eastern part of Indian sub-continent after the collapse of Mughal power during the British colonial administration. Islam won converts by traders and local administration officials employed by the colonial powers in different countries of Africa. It is amazing that the rate of growth of Islam is higher during the period of its political decline than during the days of its political glory.[8] The countries of Islam were all under subjugation by the Christians, except for a few like- Persia, Afghanistan and Turkey who were only nominally independent. There were no riches to flaunt and no petro-dollars to bribe with, It seems that Islam is the fastest growing religion in the world. The overall increase of all the sects and denominations of Christianity was a staggering 138 per cent with the incredible increase of Islam by 235 per cent in the same period of time of half a century (1934-1984). 'History makes it clear however, that the legend of fanatical Muslims sweeping through the world and forcing Islam at the point of sword upon conquered races is one of the most fantastically absurd myths that historians have ever repeated."[9]

If one looks at the world map, it easily will become clear to him that at each epoch of history Islam has been able to gain more territory. What is astonishing is the fact that even in the event of a political or military defeat by the powers who are known Islamic, Islam never has been a loser. The bright example is the conversion of the less civilized, Mongols who embraced Islam half a century after they had devastated Baghdad in the middle of the thirteenth century, the then center of Islamic caliphate and thereby they became the very defenders and propagators of the faith which they raised to destroy. Further, when the Tartar armies were devastating the land of Islam, Islam was penetrating peacefully to the Southeast Asian archipelago.

The Muslims of central Asia faced persecution and oppression over a long period first at the hands of the Czars and then under the Soviet regime. In the 17th century, Czar alexi Mikhailovich band coversion to Islam and prescribed severe punishment for those who embraced Islam. The Tatar Muslims of Poland were bitterly persecuted by the Czarist regime. Kazakhastan was occupied by Russia in 1730. Kazakhastan has a rich soil and vast fodder lands which led to migration and settlement of large numbers of Russians. By 1914 almost half of the population of Kazakhastan was Russian. Thousands of kazakhs were massacred on the orders of Stalin, leading to a massive decimation of Kazakh population. Stalin tried to eradicate the presence of Islam in the former Soviet Union by closing down mosques, madrasas and Sufi hospices, by proscribing the observance of religious rituals. The establishment of Soviet Union in the wake of great October Revolution (1917), gradually incorporated neighbouring Muslim states of Central Asia under the red iron curtain abolishing religious freedom under heavy state control. The new Czars (CPSU) tried to disrupt the demographic concentration of Muslims in those republics by compulsorily ordering the large numbers to migrate to the cold regions of Siberia to work in oil installations. At the same time, people of Russian origin were settled at cities and towns of Central Asian republics to outnumber the Muslim presence. But government failed to take out the spirit of Islam from the hearts of Muslims which was evident immediately after the collapse of Soviet Union. Furthermore, the government's policy of forcible eviction of Muslims from their native places to Siberia helped the spread and establishment of Islam in that place. Today one can find Muslims practising their faith in every city of Siberia. The collapse of Soviet Union also helped in broadening the Islamic concept of brotherhood. The then Turkish government initiated cultural exchanges to such republics by offering scholarships to the students of newly independent Muslim Republics and sending Imams and sermonizers (Turkish = Imam Hatib) to them.

The modern day diaspora and its colonial counterpart in the shape of indentured labourers has facilitated the spread of Islam to newer lands. One and half century ago, Muslims presence was hardly noticed in Great Britain, France, Germany, Australia, New Zealand, Canada, North America and countries of Latin America but today one can find a sizeable number of Muslims in all such countries. The conflict situation in the Muslim world and neo-imperialist interference has further caused the spread of Islam to hitherto unknown areas. For example, the Somalian civil war resulted in the flow of refugees to different parts of the world resulting in carrying the rituals, practices and message of Islam to the countries of refuge. The Bosnian conflict paved the way for the victims to travel to Canada and USA. Military coup in Fiji against the Indians resulted in their getting settled in affluent developed world's cities. The Palestinian diaspora, on account of Israel's inhuman actions leading to suppression and subjugation of Palestinians is flourishing in the countries of Latin America.[10] They are not only refugees, traders, small, vendors but also practitioners and preachers of Islam. Further, Islam also won many eminent personalities of its fold. Leopold Weiss, an Austrian by birth of Jewish family, embraced Islam in 1926-27 and became Muhammad Asad. He spent his greater time in the Orient. His classic 'Road to Mecca' (1954) became the best-seller. He was indeed, the twentieth- century's most influential European Muslim. Similarly Marmaduke Pickthal, better known for his translation of the Holy Quran in English, was born in Christian family and later, after deep study, embraced Islam and spent number of years in the service of the erstwhile Nizam of Hyderabad. He is famous for his eight lecture series at Madras in 1926. The scholarly lecturers are compiled in the 'Cultural Side of Islam'. T.B. Irving, professor of Arabic and Spanish at the University of Tennessee in Knoxville, U.S.A., a widely travelled scholar to different Islamic countries embraced Islam. His book '**ISLAM RESURGENT**: The Islamic World Today' published in 1979 is an important contribution to the study and analysis of Islam as a faith and civilization. It is essential reading for any one who would like to know more about the complexity of the Islamic world, its problems and difficulties encountered while trying to live in a world that appears, and often is , hostile to its ideas and hopes. Wilfried Hofmann, a German diplomat had served many years at Morocco and other Arab countries, lastly embraced Islam by inserting Murad in his name. However, this is not an exclusive list of new converts to Islam. Internet is also playing substantive role in spreading the knowledge of Islam to the curious seekers.

Islam and Scientific Temper

Then it is clear from the above statements that there are manifold reasons for the spread of Islam. Quaran calls everyone to reflect, to think and to look at the signs of the creator in the universe. It enhances and boosts the scientific temper. The great achievements during the Muslim rule in Spain and in the eastern world in the field of algebra, astronomy, architecture, medicine, mathematics, optics, surgery, geology, geography and so on have been well documented by historians of eminence which shows that Islam never has been enemy to civilization.[11] In fact, we can say that Islam was harbinger of progress and civilization. The spirit of accommodation was more than evident in the flowering of a rich Islamic scientific culture during the period of the Caliphates. Until the rise of the modern science, no other civilization engaged as many scientists, produced as many scientific books, or provided as varied and sustained support for scientific activity as Islam. Islamic science inherited all the earlier pre-Islamic, Indian, Greek and Iranian scientific traditions and fused them into one new whole. Baghdad was at the centre of this scientific activity. Here the Abbasid Caliphs Harun al-Rashid and his son Al Mamun patronized scientific activity of higher calibre. At the time of caliph Mansur (754-775) a good number of Indian physicians, philosophers and mathematicians had migrated to Baghdad. The Muslim rule in Sindh (712 onwards) facilitated this cultural and scientific exchange. This started the tradition of translating books of scientific knowledge from Sanskirit to Arabic language. A worth mentioning fact here is that most of these centres of learning under the Muslim rulers had non-Muslim scholars and translators. They were given due recognition of their merits. Baghdad, Damascus,

Shiraz and Isfahan (Iran) emerged as centres of scientific enquiry. Scientists from Muslim Spain-Andalusia and Cordoba travelled to these centres of training. This narrative of Islamic expansion reveals that Islam carries a rich intellectual legacy of tolerance of other cultures and a spirit of open mindedness to learn and adopt the good points of other civilizations.

Terrorism and Islam

Terrorism in any form does not have the sanction of Islamic ethics. The Holy Quran has repeatedly warned Muslims to live a pious and peaceful life and eschew violence. Even in few wars, which were fought during the life of the Prophet, Muslims mostly remained defensive. The wars were mainly against the tribes of Mecca and were in retaliation. According to the reports preserved in the annals of history, only 250 pagans lost their lives within a period of 10 years of the war which they waged against the believers during the time of the Prophet. The general amnesty provided to the Meccans in the 8th year after hijrah when they were under total control of Muhammmad and his companions does not have any parallel in human history. The Muslim losses were much less. Those who blame Muslims as militant, tend to forget their own history. They fought two world wars and wiped out about 7.5 million lives in the First World Ward and 22.5 million in the Second World War. The Korean and Vietnam wars, and wars in Afghanistan and Iraq did cost millions of lives. Islam, as usual, is being demonized today by its enemies. A deliberate campaign is launched across the globe, broadcasting that Islam is a backward religion. It is medieval, militant, fanatical, and terrorist in nature. It is an enemy of democracy etc. The red peril is replaced by the green peril. It will destroy the world order and world civilization. The onslaughts cannot be catalogued even in volumes.

Islam and Modern Western Civilization

A serious debate is needed to bring out the differences between the achievements of Islamic civilization and the darker side of the votaries of modern civilization. For example the absence of racial discrimination and signs and traces of slavery in the world of Islam today contrasts with the west (specially USA) with its strong racial feeling and strict segregation. This shows how Islam succeeded in solving the problem of slavery by complete and all-embracing integration of the society, a task that Christendom and the West have not been able to achieve even to the present day. The trade in slaves on a large and inhuman scale came to international markets through European Christian effort. At first, Europeans imported slaves to Europe, but soon the chief markets for them came to be the Americas. The extent of the trade may be judged from the following figures:

16th Century (from 1530)	900,000 = 13,000 a year
17th Century	2,750,000=27,000 a year
18th Century	7,000,000= 70,000 a year
19th Century	4,000,000= (1,25,000 in 1830)

Islam and Muslim community, mainly because of Islamic doctrine of equality, has provided serfs, slaves and the low caste with many opportunities. In fact, Islamic social theory concerning the equality of mankind with no discrimination of any kind has encouraged the slaves to establish slave dynasties. There have been indeed quite a few ruling dynasties in Muslim history which were established by slaves; e.g. the Mamlook dynasty in Egypt, the Ghaznavi dynasty in the East, and the slave dynasty of India established by Qutb al-Din Aybak. Many slaves became highly respected scholars in the history of Islamic intellectualism.[12]

Similarly in other fields of human progress like Human Rights, Dignity to women, conduct of war and treatment to prisoners, Islamic history stands quite superior to that of other civilizations. The world body could succeed to document the Geneva Convention on Prisoners of war only in 1949 whereas Islam made distinctions between combatants and non-combatants much earlier. Universal declaration on Human Rights, 1948 by the UNO often goes into violation. To the student of the Quran not one word in the preamble or in the objectives of the Charter and not a single article in the text of the 'UDHR' will seem unfamiliar. Under a creed which places man next to God, and brushes aside all distinctions of race, colour and birth and calls upon all mankind to live together as a family of God. The ideology and the Human Rights articles have not been upheld and respected by the big powers who proclaim their rights and responsibilities to protect the weal and small nations. The Glorious Quran has laid greatest emphasis for protecting rights and doing justice as has been lucidly expressed : "O you who believe! Be steadfast witness for Allaha in equity, and let not hatred of any people seduce you that you deal not justly. Deal justly, that is closet to your duty. Observe your duty to Allah. Surely Allah is aware of what you do" (5:8) Equity and justice without any distinction of race, creed or colour are stressed in the Quran. "If you judge, judge in equity, for Allah loves those who judge in equity." (5:45)

Justice in Islam is no secular quality or function, it is enjoined as an act which is equivalent to standing firmly for God, an act which honestly performed attracts the love of God. One can contrast the barbarous and inhuman treatment of prisoners in Abu Gharib (Iraq) and Guantanaomo Bay (Cuba) by the soldiers of super power. So far the position of women is concerned, prophet said at time of his passing away from this world that they be treated well. 1400 years ago it banned the killing of girl child and also female foeticide.

Then what role globalization is playing towards Islam. The ethos of globalization has been largely derived from the dominant values of American society. Such as the glorification of freedom and individualism, the compulsive pursuit of material prosperity, and consumerism. The world-wide diffusion of American pop culture is represented by fast food restaurants which are mushrooming across the world by the global popularity of T-Shirts, Sneakers, baggy jeans, baseball caps, and Hollywood films and television soaps, Mc Donald's, an MNC based in Oak Brook, Illinois, has 18400 restaurants in over a hundred counters.

The powerful western media project western products, cultural symbols, and images, such as MTV, Mc Donald, Madonna, Michael Jackson, Britny Speare, Barbie dolls, Coca-Cola, Levi Jeans, Mickey Mouse, as global ones, purportedly aimed at global audiences.

But the paradoxes which globalization has produced, brings its threats to nought. Islam is for all times and climes. Therefore, globalization is a challenge to Islam but is not a threat to it Modern information technology has played an important role in islamic revival and resurgence. Since the 1970's audio cassettes have became an important and highly effective means of communication in the Islamic world. The tradition of Haji has been providing The Muslims across the world, a platform for universal (read global) ideas and principles of equality, and fraternity. Global tourism has also paved the way of Muslim travellers trotting the World-East and West, South and North with Islamic knowledge and Islamic Culture. Further, the negative aspects of human progress as an outcome of globalization are always a kind of strength for the practitioners of Islam. The Family system in Islam against the breaking of families and marriages in western societies, treatment to women, weak and children in Islam and the hard reality of eve teasing, in Western society are cases in points. The following realities require attention:-

(i) There are nevertheless around 827.50 million people in over 50 countries who are malnourished (UNDP 2003, p-54) and at least 40,000 die every day from hunger related causes. The 9/11 attack was responsible for killing of 3000 people. Hindustan Times reported (14-09-2007) that 3000 children die everyday in Africa because of malaria related diseases.

(ii) Around 80 per cent of the 27 million refugees around the planet are women. Two thirds of the 300 million children who have no access to education are girls.

(iii) 70 per cent of World's 1.3 billion poor-those living on less than one dollar per day are women.

(iv) 83 per cent of part time workers in European are women.

(v) In Europe women are the heads of household in nine out of the ten single parent families.

(vi) Over 200,000 women die every year as a result of back street abortion.

(vii) Exporting women is big business. Recruitment agencies banks and airlines profit from it. So do the exporting states in the form of remittances for examples an estimated & 3 billion per year to Philipines.

Islam in India

Certainly there are myths and false ideas regarding Islams and Muslims. In India too myths and misconceptions are abound. We need to understand Islam from its original sources. Bride burning is anti Islamic, antihuman phenomenons. So is wife beating and domestic violence, state and society in India require being more egalitarian. Bigamy, divorce, increase in population are social phenomena as not linked to any specific group. Sometimes the biased view of national and international media weaves our own thought pattern but a critical analysis is called for before arriving at any judgment. The Development of Nuclear Bomb by Pakistan was projected as Islamic Bomb. Al-Qaida, very much a creation of CIA during the Anti-Soviet war in Afghanistan is projected by the same media as the mainstream Islam out to destroy the fruits of civilization. India's National Security Advisor M.K. Narayanan's testimony that no Indian Muslim is linked to Al Quaida, The story of sleeper cells, terror networks, mosques and Madrasas a terrorist teams are projected in Mas Media with regular intervals.

Conclusion

It is clear from the above that history of relations between Muslim and Western Societies and Hindu-Muslim relations is not primarily one of conflict. Despite periods of war, Islam, Christianity, Judaism and Hinduism have all benefited from each other through trade and intellectual exchanges.

It is again a paradox that west has waged a war against terrorists but the same enemy has been able without hindrance to use the light arms and weapons manufactured in West. West, further, needs trust in the mind of global man to readily work for development, peace and ecological balance. It is amazing that USA, the biggest votary of world peace and sustainable development has not signed Kyoto Protocol for global warming.

In today's interconnected world, as global neighbours we all share the responsibility of building a common edifice of respect and promoting a tolerant environment to debate about issues that threaten to divide us. We will be able to achieve progress not by division but by cohesion, by respecting diversity of faith systems and beliefs. We require to sharpen our vision and adopt the holistic approach for the betterment of mankind. Biased and unrealistic approach is nowhere leads us but to peril and destruction.

Notes and References

1. As per the doctrine of Islam Jesus Christ (Isa Alaihisslam) was a

human being born of virgin Mary without a Father as a Sign of Almighty God, not as the Son of God as majority of Christians of today believe. The Muslims therefore prefer to indicate the time by AC (After Christ) instead of AD (*Anno Domini)* in the year of our Lord. This is in consonance with the period of history showing before Christ as BC. Islam is against the divinity of Christ.

2. Quran 42:13 for the beginners it is helpful to know that Quran being the most authentic source of Islam, is the last Divine Revelation upon Muhammad (pbuh). It is divided into 30 parts having 114 chapters (*Surahs*). Each sentence in Quran is known as verse (*Ayet*). So the first number indicates Chapter and the second number after colon indicates the verse no(s). One should also refer 3:67, 10:72, 2:128, 2:132, 2:133, 10:84, 5:111, 5:3 etc.
3. Islam declares itself to be synonymous with natural, primordial religion of Man or Adam who stands for the primordial man. Whole existence is Muslim, so to speak, according to Islam. Adam and the great succession of Prophets had one religion – the religion of Islam. Hindu *rishis* and 'prophets' though unnamed in the Quran can't stand outside the prophetic cycle of Islam as every nation has been blessed by a prophet according to the Quran. Manu, Rama, Krishna-all have been appropriated in Islamic succession of prophets. Islam in that sense is as ancient as Hinduism claims to be. [For more details see Maroof Shah, 'Hinduism and Islam are Comparable', Islam and the Modern Age, vol. xxxvii (2) May 2006, pp 62-78.]
4. The American project for (amended version of) Quran (2005) miserably failed to attract followers in the Middle East.
5. It will be of importance to know that many blind persons in South Asia, Middle East, West Africa and Southeast Asia have also memorized Quran. Modernity has also created space for Muslims to open girls' madrasas in different places where female students also learn Quran by memorizing. It is also amazing that Britain, South Africa, USA, Canada, Fiji, Mauritius, West Indies and Panama are countries where Muslims have opened religious schools (also imparting secular subjects) which produce *Hafiz in bulk* numbers. Now these institutions also export *Hafiz* to different neighbouring countries to fulfill the religious demands of the community. The religious services provided by educational and charity foundations in the traditional Muslim societies are apart from those mentioned above. The *Tarawih* special prayers during the month of Ramdan are also specific measure for literal preservation of Quran.
6. The deeper analysis of the five pillars of Islam is found in almost

all scholarly books on the subject. I am highly indebted to Alija Ali Izetbegovic's *Islam Between East and West,* (1999) American Trust Publications, Indianapolis.

7. You are best of peoples ever raised up for mankind; you enjoin what is right and forbid what is wrong. And you believe in Allah'- Quran 3:110. But read this Quranic obligation with 2:256 there is not compulsion in religion. Verily the Right Path has become distinct from the wrong path'.
8. It would be interesting to go through certain books giving historical account of the spread of Islam. For example A Ezzati, 'An Introduction to the History of the Spread of Islam'. Islamic Publications Bureau, Lagos Nigera, 1979, (ii) Chinedu N Ubah, 'Islam in African History', Kaduna (Nigeria), 2001, (iii) Mohamed Bakari and Saad S. Yahya (eds.) 'Islam in Kenya', Mewa Publications, Nairobi (Kenya) 1995.
9. De Lacy O' Leary, Islam at the Crossroads, London, 1923, p. 8.
10. In fact Arabs from Lebanon are in controlling position of International Trade at the world's second largest free port a Colon on the mouth of Panama Canal in Panama.
11. See for details Watt, W Montgomery : *Islamic Spain* (Edinburgh, **1965**), The Influence of Islam on Medieval Europe (Edinburgh, 1972) and *The Majesty that was Islam* (London, 1974). Loyd Graham in his book entitled *'Deception and Mythos of the Bible'* under the heading *'The Church : Its False Foundation'* says- "yet there were no knowledge and learning everywhere except in Catholic Europe. At a time when even kings could not read or write, a Moorish king had a private library of six hundred thousand books. At a time when 99 per cent of the Christian people were wholly illiterate, the Moorish city of Cordova had eight hundred public schools' and 'there was not a village within the limits of empire where the blessings of education could not be enjoined by the children of the most indigent peasant", and 'it was difficult to encounter even a Moorish peasant who could not read and write'. Also see SP Scott, *'The History of the Moorish Empire in Europe'.* The book complied by Abbas Mahmoud Al Hadi, *'The Arabs's Impact on European Civilization,'* Cairo n.d. is also one of interest. The following books reflect on the present position of Muslims in the Western world.

    (i) Yvonne Yazbeck Haddad (ed.) *Muslims in the West : From Sojourners to the Citizens*, Oxford University Press, Oxford 2002, (ii) Jamal Malik (ed.) Muslims *in Eruope : From the Margin to the Centre,* LIT Verlag, Munster, 2004.

12. For more details see A Ezzati, *An Introduction to the history of the*

Spread of Islam, Lagos Nigeria, 1979.

13. For the impact of globalization, I have consulted various issues of American Journal of Islamic Social Sciences and John Baylis-*The Globalization of World Politics,* Oxford University. Press, New Delhi 2004.

13. NAM TODAY

K.K. Misra

The cold war politics of contention, confrontation, and competition is gradually giving way to dialogue, co-operation and re-construction. The world environment has improved as a result of the initiatives taken by the superpowers especially by Gorbachov who in his relentless pursuit of peace created history. The main parameters of his philosophy or that of international relations should be based on co-creativity and co-development. Cold war which because visible soon after the end of the second world war determined the behaviours of the east and west for decades. The situation has now changed with the end of cold war, and the ushering in of a period of New Detente. The last nail in the coffin of the cold war was inserted with the demolition of the Berlin Wall and the ultimate Unification of the two Germanis. As a result the most visible reminder of the cold war, and hostility between differing ideologies, was done away with. Another positive step was the termination of the warsa pact (Military Alliance) in March 1991. This positive action underlined that New Detente is not going to remain a mere theoretical assertion but would be action oriented process to make the world a better, and peaceful place. Another proof of reduced hostility between the two superpowers is the co-operation between the two sides against IRAQ in the recent gulf war. This is incontrast with past Practice when the superpowers invariably took opposite sides in any regional conflict. If this event is any indication the coming years will witness the super powers joining hands on a number of issues in which the world public opinion is solidly behind them.

In view of these changes an argument has been advanced in

certain quarters that since the NAM has all along worked against blocks and block Politics which were responsible for developing cold –war, and since the cold war has ended the movement has lost its rationale.

This view betrays an understanding of.

(1) The motives of the NAM, (2) and the new Detente.
(1) It is true that some of the parameters of Non-alignment developed during the cold- war period, but it would be wrong to think that cold war was its sole reference point. Historically speaking, Seeds of Non-alignment were sown before the mid forties when the cold war came into vogue.

(2) The process of New Detente initiated as a result of bold steps taken by Gorbachov has brought about a qualitative change in the global strategic scenario, but New Detente is fraught with certain shortcomings which require an increasing role for the NAM.

(i) The New Detente with all its positive implications is a fragile, and constrained process. In spite of INF treaty and the prospects of eliminating a part of the strategic, and conventional weapons, the international security situation will remain unstable, and threatened by the ongoing arms race, and the weapons still remaining in the arsenal of major military powers. Also the doctrine of Nuclear Deterrence holds sway. Some countries possess chemical weapons also. The NAM has obligation to persist with the objectives of achieving nuclear weapons free world.

(ii) One of the main concerns of the NAM over the years has been elimination of economic imperialism, to secure economic growth, and development. In this task very limited success has been achieved. Hence NAM has to work relentlessly in this area. This is an area of concern irrespective of whether cold war or detente is prevailing.

(iii) International relations are still characterized by the use of wars, intervention, and application of coercive measures. The east –west conflict has become less acute though it has not totally disappeared altogether. All this envisages an increasing role for the NAM.

(iv) NAM has so far failed to make a positive contribution in resolving regional conflicts , except lending its support to the efforts of the U.N. while the role of the UN in this field has to be strengthened. NAM should evolve mechanisms whereby such Conflicts are moderated, and resolved through negotiated means.

(v) The UN secretary General feels that the New Detente is still too fresh, and fragile to warrant any categorical prediction of its future course. Secondly it is common knowledge that first detente between the two super –powers in the early seventies (70s) evaporated by the end of that decade. This Detente may also prove to be a temporary phase to be replaced by cold war again. It seems that the phases of cold war, and Detente are likely to alternate periodically because of the functioning of sovereign state system, Cold war and Detente are hence transient – factors in international relations. On the other hand, policy, and movement of non-alignment are enduring factors. The transient factors of the cold war and Detente do not affect the continuing validity and relevance of the enduring factor of the NAM.

(vi) New Detente is in fact, supportive of the policy of Non-alignment. It will release the pressure on NAM to conform to the cold war stance of the aligned so that the non-aligned can breathe, more freely than during the cold war years. As a result of the New Detente NAM will cease to be an issue of conflict between the two super powers, but this situation will pose an additional responsibility on the movement. The reduction of tension, and the development of consensus on important issues between the super powers is likely to oblige them to run the world in their mutual interests. NAM, then has the duty to continue fighting against the hegemonism either single handed, or jointly.

(vii) Many of the important objectives of NAM are of a long term nature, such as establishing NIEO and democratization of international system, and its functioning. Surely NAM will have to struggle for a long term before such demands are achieved. This is to assert the relevance of NAM in the foreseeable future.

Therefore, recent developments in international relations though welcome, in no way diminish the relevance of the NAM, in fact they provide greater opportunity to the NAM for working more vigorously .

While concluding, that NAM still has an important relevance for the present day world, It should be admitted that the emphasis of NAM should shift from traditional disarmament issues to more challenging present day issues . This is very much needed if NAM is to be made a more meaningful movement in the long run:

(i) Time has come to treat economic and ecological issues as integrated ones of global development, and the environmental pollution on the global scale is affecting the developed and developing countries alike.
The non-aligned, who are for one world, will have to stress increasingly this common threat faced by all nations , a threat against which no single nation, however, wealthy and powerful can protect itself. Only common global action can ensure human survival. Apart from this problems of drug trafficking, terrorism, religious fundamentalism, are cutting across the boundaries of the developing and the developed world. Multilateral internationalism, co-operative effort is required to deal with these issues. These facts, if highlighted, and addressed to the industrialized nations are likely to have greater impact than the earlier pleas of NAM for general disarmament, the NIEO, and the north- south dialogue.

(ii) The NAM should look for allies among the industrialised nations who are likely to share the objectives of promoting the concept of one world, ensuring the future habitability of the planet, democratizing the international decision making and subscribing to a co- operative economic order.

(iii) If these goals are to be achieved then NAM will have to regenerate itself, and discontinue its routine triennial exercises of updating a draft document within a somewhat rigid framework. The main focus of nations and mankind has to shift to (1) economic (2) developmental (3) ecological factors.

Non alignment should start addressing itself to this transition.

14. PROBLEMS OF SECULARIZATION OF INDIAN POLITY AND NATIONAL INTEGRATION

Subhash Shukla

Introduction

For centuries the principal characteristics of Indian civilization have been its great size, its multi ethnic character, its diverse languages and religions, its myriad sub-cultures and social divisions, its infamous internecine conflicts which have frequently been the cause of its undoing; in a word it can be summed up as its diversity. United by the historical forces of Indian nationalism directed against British colonialism, this problem re-appeared with the departure of the British and was succinctly phrased by Jawaharlal Nehru thus: How shall we promote the unity of India and yet preserve the rich diversity of our inheritance?

To be sure, many of these problems of secularization of the polity and national integration have been accentuated in the very process of the institutionalization of a political centre and the emergence of the concomitant structures of coalition-making, political succession, and ideological consensus. As development proceeded it gave rise to new patterns of participation and bargaining, and as these were diffused outwards from the political centre they engendered a new consciousness of diversities and distinctive identities which became the rallying points of new demands and cleavages. While the challenges now become more pragmatic and less ideological - occasional secessionist demands notwithstanding - they put the capabilities of the elite to the more crucial test of political development; the continuous allocation of political resources and support structures to the resolution of pressing issues as the nation moves from one threshold of 'unity in diversity' to another.

Caste

To come to the specifics of this 'politicization of diversities', caste has frequently been identified as an impediment to both national integration and secularism. However, unless our concept of integration and secularism amounts to a quashing of all other identities, this view appears to be misplaced. Caste does have a 'secular' dimension in as much as patterns of alignment and realignment among the various strata, and a continuous striving for social mobility have always been prominent features of the caste system. What has really changed is the context, following the rise of the nation-state and political democracy, and their organizational concomitants. Moreover, caste is also an integration structure of a specific type, namely, one that is more intense in its small group orientation and particularistic loyalties, and where wider loyalties operate only when they are structured through the prevailing differentiations. Here again, the competitive style of democratic politics, has involved not only distributive and conflictual aspects but also aspects of group action and cohesion. Differentiation has all along been an essential ingredient in the Indian approach to integration, and it has now become an important variable in the development of democratic politics. In general, the process of politics has tended to attenuate caste conflicts by rendering them as sub-constituents of larger political and coalitional identifications.

Nonetheless, instances of caste violence remain and it is the duty of the state machinery to contain them. Conversely, in the metropolitan or industrialized centres caste has an increasingly diminished importance as the rallying point of political forces. A word is also called for with regard to the scheduled castes in particular. Here social reform movements dating back to those initiated by Gandhi, legislative and administrative measures such as abolition of untouchability and reservations, and political mobilization through party channels have served to bring them into the national mainstream. However, the emergence of elite enclaves and corresponding alienation in the remaining strata remain problems and political assertions have often resulted in violence. Besides, policies of reservation have invited similar calls from the so-called 'backward castes'. Evidently, this cementing of smaller group identities has its limits as a factor working for national integration.

Tribes

More acute, perhaps, is the problem of integrating the **tribal** regions of the country. The tribal perspective is well expressed by P. Moaso Sung, a Naga intellectual who wrote that India was declared to be a secular state but there were visible signs of the nation becoming a monolithic society where the majority might define the limits of national society and where the majority were often confused with the national society. Apart from age old alienation from the mainstream of Hindu Society where they were accorded a low status, a 'secondary tribalization' seems to be underway in the modern world. There is a growing self-consciousness accompanied by a growing alienation from the technologically sophisticated intruder which reinforces the minority complex.

It is also important that separatist identities in India have been more potent in the unassimilated tribal periphery in the north-east region of the country. Here too, the processes of political competition and governmental penetration are opening up the possibility of greater assimilation through politicization. In addition the granting of statehood to Nagaland, Meghalaya, Tripura and Manipur coupled with military pressure on hard core insurgents has helped. However, integrative tendencies are still at an early stage and the situation calls for considerable ingenuity in the development of new patterns of federal association. Besides, the Chhota Nagpur area in Bihar, the tribal enclave in Madhya Pradesh, and the movements of autonomy in the tribal regions of south Gujarat and Orissa still remain unaccomodated in any substantial degree.

As political participation grows and education and economic development produce new differentiations, the demands of tribals on the political system are likely to grow. Some of these issues are accentuated by the fact that many of these tribal enclaves are on the border with China and Bangladesh and there have been attempts at either training' some of the discontented elements in guerilla activities or providing sanctuaries' to them. The challenge to policy makers for the region is thus both national and international. The Home Ministry has been handling these issues imaginatively but these do not seem to be any easy way out of this composite challenge of domestic political mobilization and international intervention.

Divisions of Religious Community

Although the divisions of religious community have been less obtrusive since independence than before, they have hardly been eliminated. To be sure, following independence separate electoral rolls were dropped; the Muslim league died a natural death except in the south and the constitution pledged freedom of religion and secularism. Integration of a political kind did take place through Congress and other parties. Yet, recurring communal riots involving Hindus and Muslims in numerous quarters of the country and on numerous occasions testify to a situation of continuing communal consciousness in which the Hindus' distrust and the Muslims' sullen and despairing isolation feed eagerly upon each other. Here is another issue for which only long term secular development will provide the ultimate answer but which does call for short term policies of vigilance and accommodation, not only on the part of the government but also on the part of political parties and organized groups in educational and cultural fields. The prospect of electoral reprisal is inhibiting the various parties from getting too closely associated with such events, but local temptations for making political capital out of such unfortunate events coupled with the demands of local party supporters often defeat such directives from above. Incidents like communal riots are often sporadic but they continue to pose as threats to the overall image of the country as a secular, democratic polity.

The Indian Christian community, previously irrelevant in politics, has become prominent in Kerala affairs, its aspiration having been accommodated with the Kerala Congress. The case of the Sikhs in Punjab, however, has been ambivalent. While the process of democratic politics has, on the one hand, rendered them sub-constituents of larger political and coalitional identifications, a measure of frustration has always marked Sikh politics. Former rulers of the Punjab and even in British days prominent in the life of the state, the Sikhs, following independence, were fearful of losing influence. Talk of a Sikhistan was heard by the British Cabinet Mission of 1946, and was followed by the post independent struggle for a 'Punjabi Suba'. The creation of the state of Punjab restored normalcy though problems with the neighbouring state of Haryana remained. In the 1980's fresh agitations led by the Akali Dal broke ground demanding implementation of the Anandpur Sahib Resolution while in the background there, lurked the secessionist demand for Khalistan.

Language

The linguistic configuration of India is in many respects unique. The Linguistic Survey of India published in 1927 spoke of 179 languages and 544 dialects (and in all 1,652 'mother tongues'). While the 1961 census recorded speakers of 1,018 different languages, of these the constitution recognized no fewer than 14 national languages along with Hindi and English, but enjoined upon the Union government to so encourage the development of Hindi as to assimilate simple and commonly understood words, forms and styles from all the Indian languages and thereby serve as a medium of expression for all the elements of the composite culture of India. It also laid down that the change over from English to Hindi should be gradual so as to avoid the possibility of any harm or wrong accruing to the legitimate interests of any section of the people or the larger interests of the country as a whole (Art. 351). The constitution further guaranteed the right of every minority having a distinct language, script or culture of its own "to conserve the same" and prohibited the state from discriminating against educational institutions on the basis of languages and culture while giving them grants (Art. 29 and 30). Moreover, the President has been empowered "if he is satisfied that a substantial proportion of the state desires the use of any language spoken by them to be recognized by that state, (to) direct that such language shall also be officially recognized throughout that state or any part thereof for such purposes as he may specify, (Art. 347) such accommodation notwithstanding, language conflicts have not abated in independent India. As the regional elites gained self-confidence pressures mounted, and culminated in a mammoth political and administrative re-organization of the states. There is little doubt that the re-organization, once accomplished, led to considerable political consolidation, ease of communication between the government and the people, and greater integration of the political community. But the role of regional linguistic autonomy in the crystallization of administrative and political relationships and the ordering of regional identities towards a "federal consensus" constituted only one part of the language problem. As equally important part was the question of the all-India medium of communication.

Here, the symbolic legacies of the national movement made English unacceptable as the nation's lingua franca inspite of the fact that the Indian elite was well conversant with it. The only other candidate was Hindi but the independence movement had not been able to spread the use of Hindi in non -Hindi areas on an adequate scale and neither the government nor the various 'Hindi Prachar Samitis' had managed to do much in the 15 years moratorium on the issue provided by the Constitution. When the end of the moratorium drew near, regional identities had been sufficiently articulated, the poverty of Hindi in comparison with more richly endowed languages like Bengali, Tamil, Telugu, and Marathi had become glaring, the 'Hindi purists' had alienated other language groups, and the fact that Hindi was no more than one among several regional languages - even if more numerous had been emphasized in the consciousness of the non-Hindi elites.

Nonetheless, the Official Language Commission and the Committee of Members of Parliament on the same issue recommended, along with a few notes of dissent, that Hindi should progressively replace English as the Official language possibly with effective changeover in 1965. This provoked agitation in the non-Hindi areas which compelled Nehru to "pledge" that English would remain for an indefinite period as "an associate language". This led to a shift in emphasis in official statements, as in the resolution of the Congress Party at its Guwahati session in 1958, in the Presidential order of 1960, in resolution of the National Integration Conference of 1961, and in the official languages Act of 1963 which restrained the agitation against Hindi.

The crisis continued to simmer and rose again with the passing away of Nehru and the issue of routine administrative circulars on the' switchover' to Hindi. It exploded in 1965 with the unprecedented art of self-immolation by two DMK leaders in Madras and violent outbreaks in the same state. Cumulative and massive pressure resulted in hectic negotiations which yielded a "three language formula" Every state was to have freedom to transact its own business in the state language, which was also to be a medium of instruction in the state universities, English was to continue as the language of interstate communications (if these were written in Hindi they would have to be accompanied by an official English translation) : non-Hindi states were to correspond with the centre in English: English was to continue as the official language at the centre, including the Parliament: official examinations were to be conducted in English, Hindi and all the regional languages; and there was to be a phased programme for the development of Hindi. Although no sanction was satisfied with this compromise formula, it became the bases for a slow process of consensus.

On the whole, both the crises of the fifties leading to states, reorganization and the crisis of the early sixties leading to the **three language** formula helped crystallize the main issues by an open confrontation between opposing groups, and ultimately led a way out of what at one time, appeared like a situation in which any decision would jeopardize the country's unity. The nation survived both crisis and, from all evidence, perhaps with a greater capability to handle fresh outbreaks of linguistic subnationalism. The situation today is not very different than it always was in India: a special language for the elite (English), a lay language spoken fairly widely in the land but with many regional variations (Hindi), and regional standard languages dominating and bringing together the more numerous sub-regional and local dialects. The main difference now is that the regional standards are becoming important all state vehicles and the gap between these standards and the local dialects is fast narrowing... except in the case of developed sub regional languages as in the case of Nepali in West Bengal or Maithili in North Bihar. Building upon this process of local integration are the emerging national languages - English and Hindi, while the latter has been spreading rather fast in non-Hindi areas. Through education, trade and the mass media (in particular films); English has also had success and currently dominates the national press, the publishing trade and higher educational institutions. This situation is likely to remain unchanged for along time to come.

Regionalism

Related to the language issue is the phenomenon of **regionalism** and the accompanying threat of 'secession' from the union or from one of its constituent states. Some such as Selig S. Harrison have speculated that the country faces the "dangerous" alternatives of either balkanization or authoritarian rule as the movement for regional autonomy gains ground.! There have indeed been such movements in the past as well as in the present. Based partly on historical mythology and partly on caste, ethnic and regional hostility, these developed a powerful intellectual movement for autonomy in the Dravidian south, mainly in the old Madras state. In 1914 the militant Tamils set up the Dravida Kazhagam (D.K.) which called upon the Dravidian peoples of South India "to guard against a transfer of power from the British to the Aryans." It asked for a separate south Indian state, Dravidasthan, and for a complete separation from the Indian Union.

By 1954, however when political power shifted from the Brahmins to a distinctly indigenous "Tamilized" and non-Brahmin leadership under Kamaraj Nadar, the DK threw in its support to the Congress ministry. This led to the formation of a splinter group, The Dravida Munnetra Kazhagam (DMK) which pledged itself to carry on the movement for Dravidasthan. But both the increasing Tamilian character of the Congress and the growth of the DMK as a political party chastened the militant posture of the DMK and led it to seek power through the ballot box. The constitutional Amendment seeking to prevent the fissiparous, secessionist tendency in the country engendered by regional and linguistic loyalties also contributed to the same.

This led to another splinter group led by E.V.K. Sampath who sought to carry on the torch of Tamil separatism. Upon this followed a characteristic process of factionalism and coalition making from which CN. Annadurai emerged victorious. Under Annadurai the party grew and came to power in 1967 State elections. Since 1967, the DMK in power was subject to the same kind of factional pressures as was the Congress party. This secular transformation of primordial sentiment, as Robert L. Hardgrave

Jr. put it, led to a process of regional articulation that, as elsewhere in the country, contributed to the polyarchal nature of the functioning political process.[2] Here it is important to recognize that both the assertion of a regional identity and its assimilation into a larger national identity have been essentially political coalitional processes. Similar developments have already been noted with regard to Punjab and the tribal North Eastern States.

Mention may also be made of the problem of **linguistic minorities** within the states, as also of religious minorities on an average about 18 per cent of a state population has as its mother tongue a language other than the official state language (varying from 5 per cent in Kerala to 35 per cent in erstwhile Mysore) .The problem has not caused much trouble except in areas where the 'outsiders' occupy strategic, administrative or industrial positions and are perceived as 'exploiters' as in the case of Gujaratis and South Indians in Maharashtra, Bengalis in Assam and Orissa, and Marwaris in West Bengal. Militant movements of the 'sons of the soil' against these "outsiders" have emerged as witnessed in the Shiva Sena, the Lachit Sena and the attacks on Kannadas in Goa. Unless the government demonstrably evolves a policy of firm suppression of such excesses, pockets of fascist tendency are likely to develop in the country, fanning middle class frustrations, distorting the instruments of democracy, and turning the natural competition between "majority" and "minority" into irreconcilable opposites. In the long run, of course only a secular consciousness and secular politics - capable of accepting coalitions - can provide a durable solution.

An issue area to which no great thought had been given, earlier in official circles, concerned the general incidence of size and optimality in the territorial design of the country. Large and consequently less manageable states tend to create disparities and consequent fissiparous tendencies. Many of these states have been split into administratively more efficient and politically more homogenous units. The Centre, too, would find it easier to deal with smaller and more numerous but politically more homogenous states.

Conclusion

To conclude, we can say that there seems to be no easy

approach to the development of a manifest and categorical national identity', regardless of the common cultural idiom. Perhaps, a country as vast and pluralistic as India can be effectively united only through a participant and accommodative model of politics.

References

1. See Selig S. Harrison, *India: The Most Dangerous Decades,* 1960.
2. Robert L. Hardgrave Jr., 'The DMK and the Politics of Tamil Nationalism,' *Pacific Affairs,* XXXVII, No. 4, Winter 1964-65.

15. BUREAUCRACY AND LIBERALISATION:
CHANGING ROLE OF ADMINISTRATION

Arvind Kumar Singh

Globalization is a fact of twenty-first century, which cannot be overlooked. It has changed the traditional economic thinking and developed the new ways of integrating economies. It is also bringing about significant changes in the nature of state, government, administration, value system and the people as a community. This is putting pressures on public administration to respond to the widely fluctuating shifts. This entire setup has also changed the role of bureaucracy in the administration.

British Period

Bureaucracy reflects the philosophy of the state and government at any particular moment. The bureaucracy, particularly the higher civil service, in India, handed over by the Britishers to the independent India was the creature of British colonial power and its main responsibilities were to maintain law and order and collect revenue. It is the complimentary part of executive branch of government and responsible for implementing the policies which are decided by their political master. In British period bureaucracy was used as tools for the fulfilment of the British Interest. We all know that East India Company had come to India for business and had nothing to do with India's people and their welfare. They therefore, recruited such civil servants who could make the company profitable anyhow. They had to work only in favour of company rather than the people. Their main function was to ensure the control of the government over the nation and also to exploit the natural resources for the benefit of the mother country i.e. the United Kingdom.

After Independence

After attaining freedom we had no option but to accept British system of governance with minor reorganization and readjustment. This was the time when actual moulding of the bureaucracy started. After Independence India adopted socialist Philosophy and centralized planning and in this entire scenario, bureaucracy got a preferential boost and treatment because it was the real mechanism of government to implement and execute its policies. During the period between fifties and eighties, bureaucracy became *omnipotent omnipresent*, and even *omniscient.* With the rising concept of welfare state the importance of bureaucracy grew to a large extent with the assumption of new functions and responsibilities. Now it was also involved in a large variety of developmental activities, called development administration, and implementing thousands of projects throughout the nation. Due to this the role of Bureaucracy has increased. Bureaucrats came to think that they were omniscient and nobody should challenge their authority and decisions. Due to the role of congress party for a long time, dangerous element of politicization came into existence and thus, started the process of political interference in the internal working of the bureaucracy and, consequently, the beauraucracy also started losing its political impartiality. The concept of neutrality and committed bureaucracy totally changed. During emergency period (1975-77), the entire bureaucratic, machine became a pliable tool in the hands of unscrupulous political set up.

Due to the adoption of the ideal of a welfare state, there was rapid multiplication of the function of the state, which assigned unfamiliar duties to the bureaucracy. Regulations, controls licenses and permits were introduced which increased the new opportunities for corruption and bureaucracy found a congenial climate for its nourishment under the Permit-License Raj.

Era of Globalization

At the end of the four decades of centralized planning and a highly regulated economy, India has now decided to enter towards market economy system. A new chapter has evolved in the Indian Administrative history with the adoption of New Economic Policy in 1991. This process of economic liberalization was initially started during the Janta Dal regime, and it gathered momentum during the successive governments of Indira Gandhi, Rajiv Gandhi, and V.P. Singh. However the P.V. Narsimha Rao government gave a big push to the idea of restructuring the Indian economy. This changed economic process which was known by various names, i.e. New economic reforms, liberalization, Privatization, etc. The new approach has focused on stabilizing the economy; reforming the financial sector, public enterprises and the investment, trade and tax regimes; and giving the private sector a much greater role in India's development. Actually globalization is ushering in new societal expectations, changing value systems, altering the nature of state and governing systems. This is putting pressures on public administration to respond to the widely fluctuating shifts. The information technology revolution has transformed the tasks of administration. This process of economic liberalization and globalization in its basic conceptual formulation seeks reduced intervention of government in the economic sector and seeking a reduced role of bureaucracy in the process of development.

Globalization has affected public administration due to impact of pressures generated on it by global institutions, information technology and increasing concern for efficiency and productivity. Under the new phase of liberalization there is a drastic need for re-vamping the Indian bureaucracy. The new rules must become citizen-friendly and in tune with the constitution and the new policy. Right to information and citizen charter act are the good example for this. Now the time has started to re-inventing government that is entrepreneurial government or good governance, means A government must be *catalytic, community owned, competitive, mission driven, Result oriented, customer driven, enterprising Decentralised and market oriented.* This has given a new concept of *"New public management"*, having 3 aims *efficiency, economy* and *effectiveness.* It educates a basic change in the role of state in society and economy. It emphasises on the vital role of the 'market' as against the 'state' as the key regulator of the society, and economy. Thus the new public management suggest a series of shifts of emphasis in the way in which the public sector should be organized and managed to meet the new challenges of liberalization, globalization and privatization. The role of bureaucracy also must change, according to the role of state.

In the new era of liberalization India is opening itself to the world and mixing itself with the world economy. A large number of bureaucrats are getting global exposure and would need knowledge of economics, international trade, and other specialist fields. Bureaucracy has to be re-structured in such a way that government machinery not only becomes effective but is also empowered to practice new methods of management.

Another area of re-inventing bureaucracy under liberalization is an urgent need for transforming the attitudes of the bureaucrats. They have to be more accountable and responsible towards the interest of citizens. They should not behave like rulers or having thinking of Separate Identity and elite class mentality, but to think that they are service providers and the friend of common people. So there is a need for ethical reforms and a self imposed code of conduct for bureaucrats in the critical phase of liberalization.

Changing Role of the State

Traditionally, many countries embarked on the concept of welfare state - a political system with high degree of responsibility for the welfare of the population. But globalization has brought tremendous change in role of state. A powerful new paradigm of determining the scope and limits of government action that was dominant in Western democracies held the view that government should:

— Do less
— Reduce or relinquish their previous overburdening responsibilities.
— Privatize public services or their delivery wherever practicable and
— Reform their own operations in accordance with the market concepts of competition and efficiency.

The market theory argues that the government is less efficient than markets over providing services to individuals. In other words, this indicate the general trend towards 'state minimalism' and market friendliness' (allowing the market more free play). So the changes are also required in the mindset of bureaucrats. While the role of state intervention in development is not denied, it is argued that such intervention must be 'market friendly'.

Globalization, no doubt impacts heavily on the 'state' its policies, institutions, and personnel. The "Public sphere" and the space for citizen involvement have been shrinking and the corporate state is making its presence. Now the biggest challenge for administration is to recast the role of the state. There is a need for evolving a new regulatory state with an expanded agenda. It is also necessary to develop social consciousness and strengthen non-state actors like civil societies, which provides a single civic identity, which is distinct, and belonging to various groups of citizens, acts as mediating link between the state and the markets. Changes are also required in the bureaucratic ethics because ethics acts as a metaphor for increasing concern for democratic values and public interests.

INDEX